CABLE AND X-FORCE

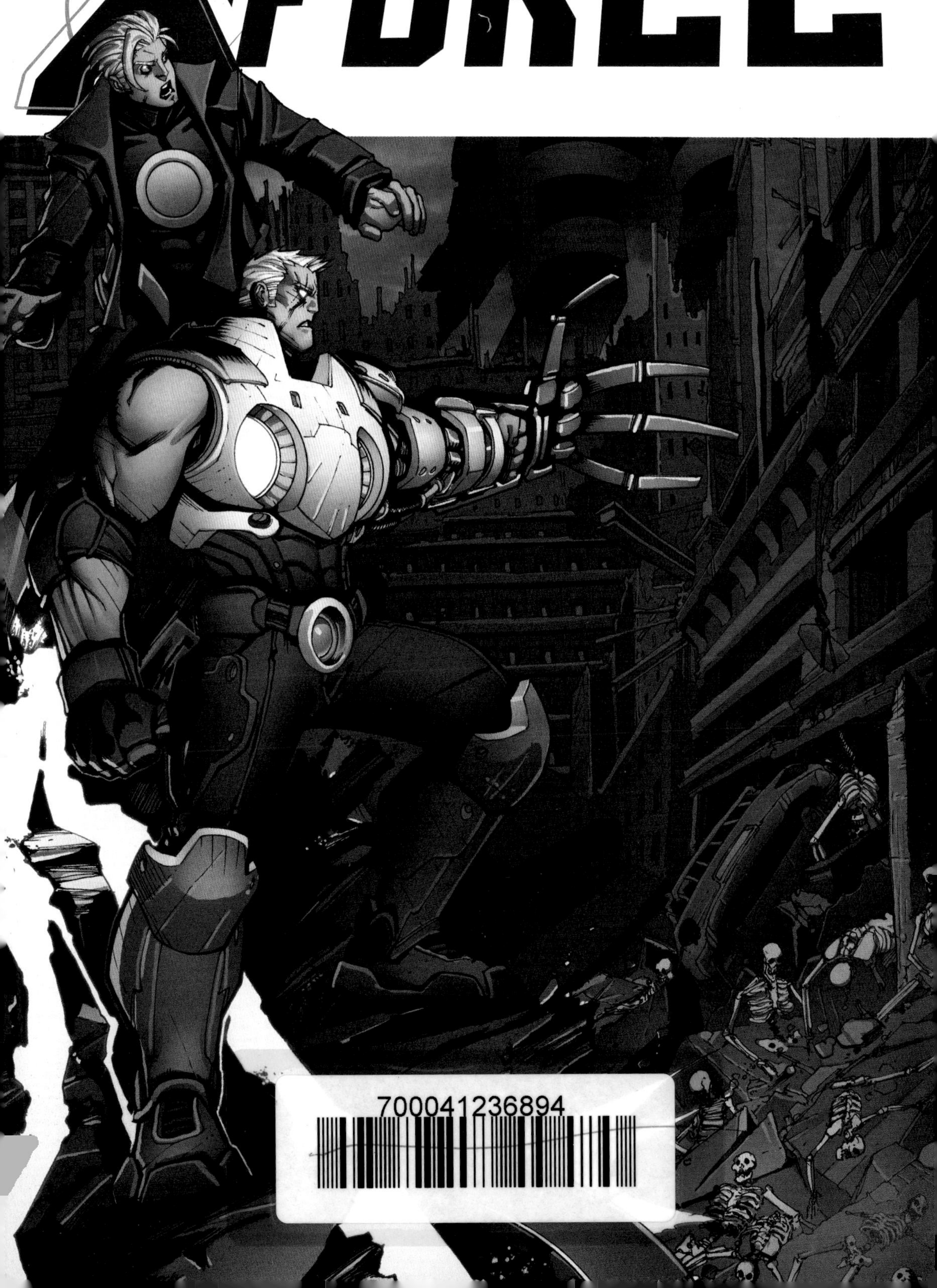

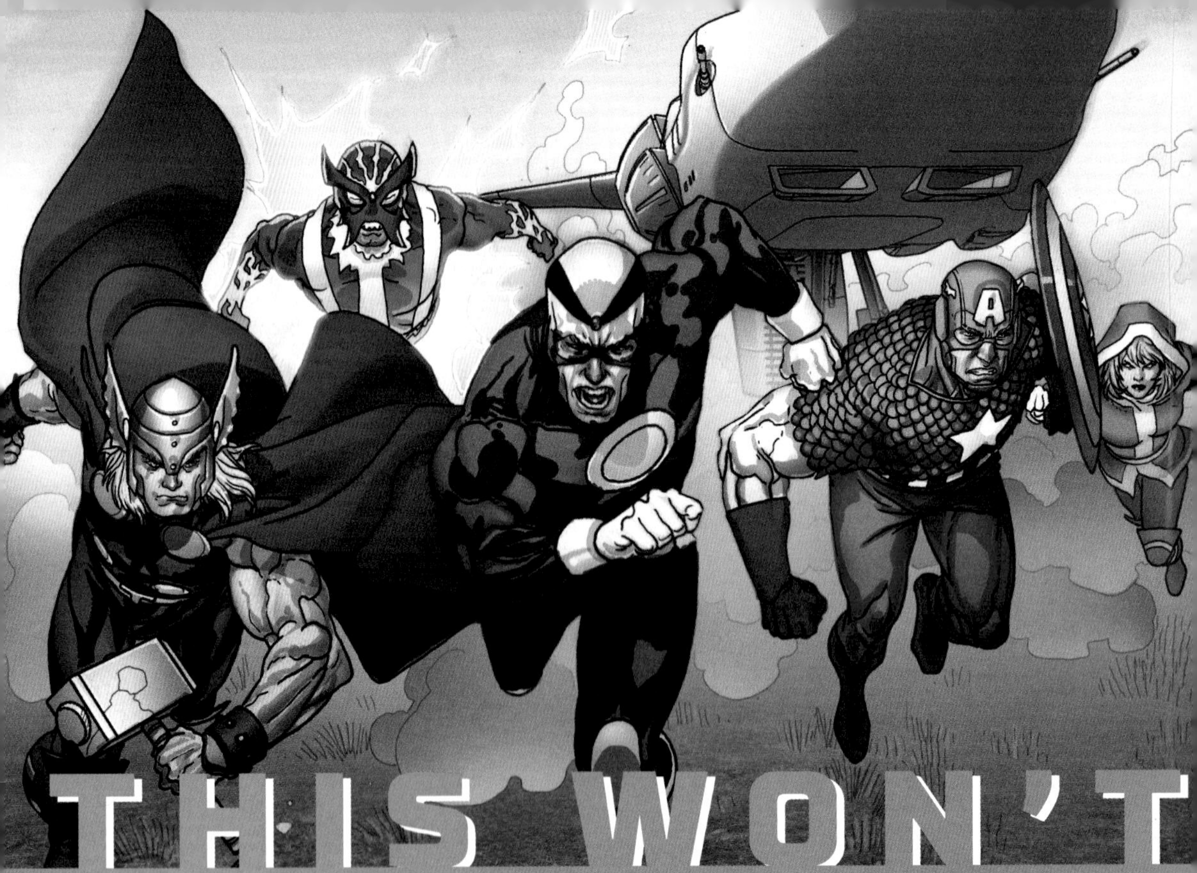

THIS WON'T END WELL

WRITER
DENNIS HOPELESS
WITH CULLEN BUNN **(SCRIPT, #12-13)**

ARTIST
SALVADOR LARROCA
WITH GERARDO SANDOVAL **(#13)**

COLOR ARTIST
FRANK D'ARMATA

LETTERER
VC'S JOE SABINO

COVER ART
SALVADOR LARROCA
& FRANK D'ARMATA

ASSISTANT EDITORS
JENNIFER M. SMITH
& XANDER JAROWEY

EDITOR
DANIEL KETCHUM

GROUP EDITOR
NICK LOWE

COLLECTION EDITOR: **CORY LEVINE** • ASSISTANT EDITORS: **ALEX STARBUCK & NELSON RIBEIRO**
EDITORS, SPECIAL PROJECTS: **JENNIFER GRÜNWALD & MARK D. BEAZLEY**
SENIOR EDITOR, SPECIAL PROJECTS: **JEFF YOUNGQUIST**
SVP OF PRINT & DIGITAL PUBLISHING SALES: **DAVID GABRIEL** • BOOK DESIGN: **JEFF POWELL**

EDITOR IN CHIEF: **AXEL ALONSO** • CHIEF CREATIVE OFFICER: **JOE QUESADA**
PUBLISHER: **DAN BUCKLEY** • EXECUTIVE PRODUCER: **ALAN FINE**

CABLE AND X-FORCE VOL. 3: THIS WON'T END WELL. Contains material originally published in magazine form as CABLE AND X-FORCE #10-14. First printing 2014. ISBN# 978-0-7851-8882-7. Published by MARVEL WORLDWIDE, INC., a subsidiary of MARVEL ENTERTAINMENT, LLC. OFFICE OF PUBLICATION: 135 West 50th Street, New York, NY 10020. **Printed in the U.S.A.** ALAN FINE, EVP - Office of the President, Marvel Worldwide, Inc. and EVP & CMO Marvel Characters B.V.; DAN BUCKLEY, Publisher & President - Print, Animation & Digital Divisions; JOE QUESADA, Chief Creative Officer; TOM BREVOORT, SVP of Publishing; DAVID BOGART, SVP of Operations & Procurement, Publishing; C.B. CEBULSKI, SVP of Creator & Content Development; DAVID GABRIEL, SVP of Print & Digital Publishing Sales; JIM O'KEEFE, VP of Operations & Logistics; DAN CARR, Executive Director of Publishing Technology; SUSAN CRESPI, Editorial Operations Manager; ALEX MORALES, Publishing Operations Manager; STAN LEE, Chairman Emeritus. For information regarding advertising in Marvel Comics or on Marvel.com, please contact Niza Disla, Director of Marvel Partnerships, at ndisla@marvel.com. For Marvel subscription inquiries, please call 800-217-9158. **Manufactured between 12/6/2013 and 1/13/2014 by QUAD/GRAPHICS, VERSAILLES, KY, USA.**

10 9 8 7 6 5 4 3 2 1

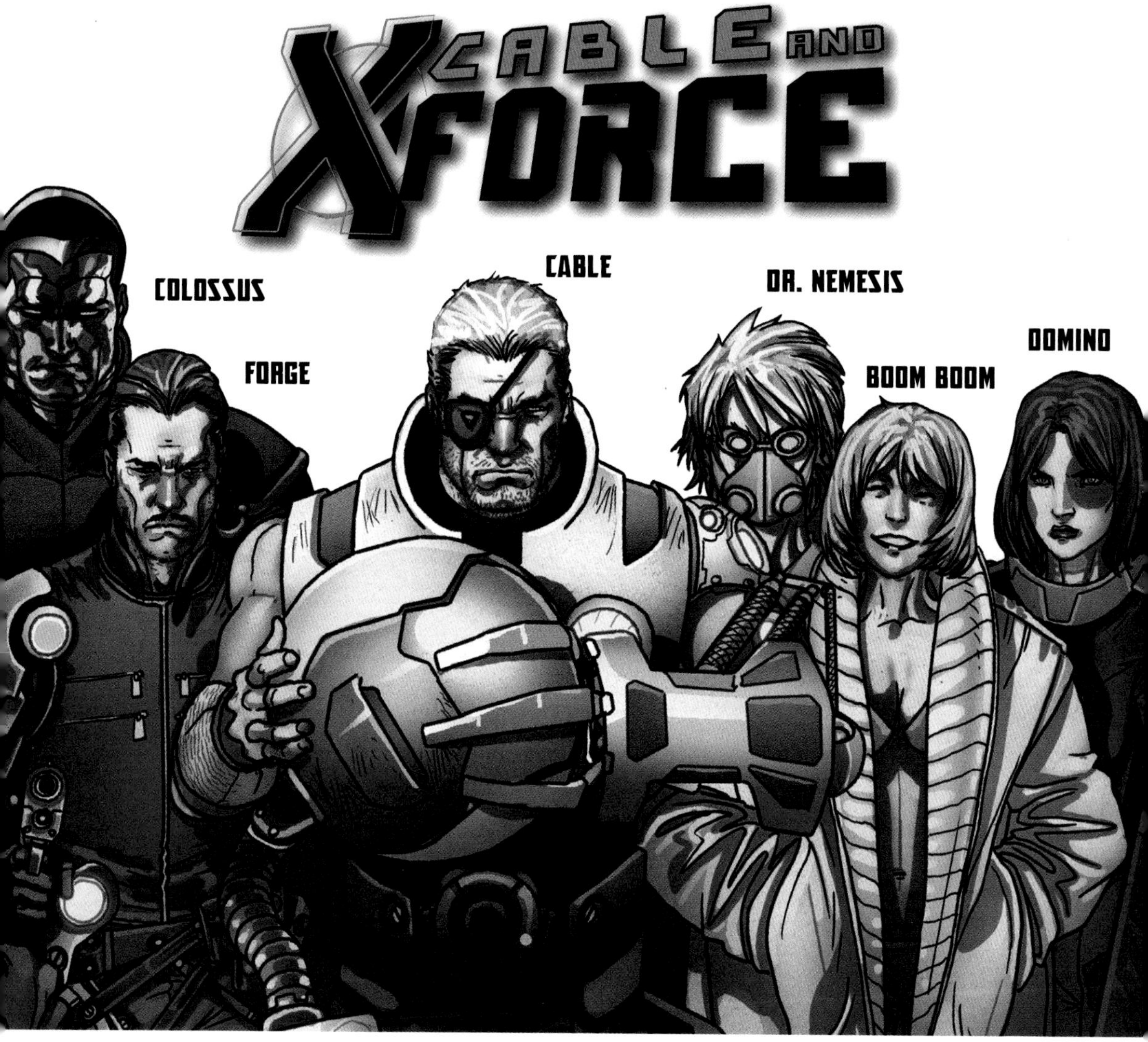
CABLE AND X-FORCE
COLOSSUS
FORGE
CABLE
DR. NEMESIS
BOOM BOOM
DOMINO

PREVIOUSLY...

Time-traveling X-Man Cable has been having terrible visions of the future, accompanied by debilitating headaches. While he copes with his condition, Cable has assembled a new X-Force to prevent those visions from coming true. Unfortunately, from the outside, their violent actions appear criminal and inexplicable, and the team has landed on the most wanted list of the Uncanny Avengers, the team led by Cable's uncle, Havok.

Meanwhile, Cable's daughter, Hope, is determined to help her father at any cost. After escaping from her own encounter with the Uncanny Avengers, she's set off on a secret mission of her own...

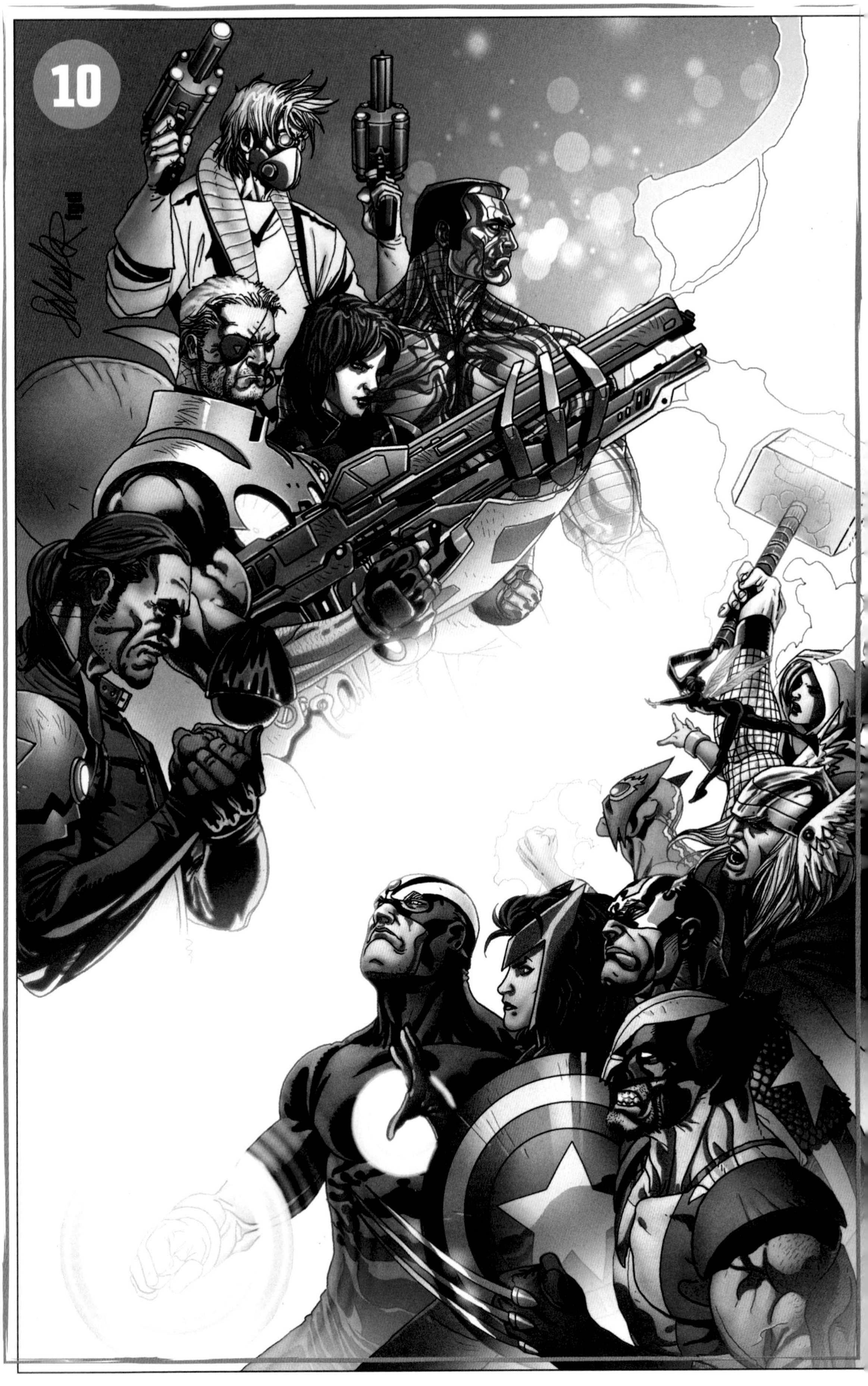
10

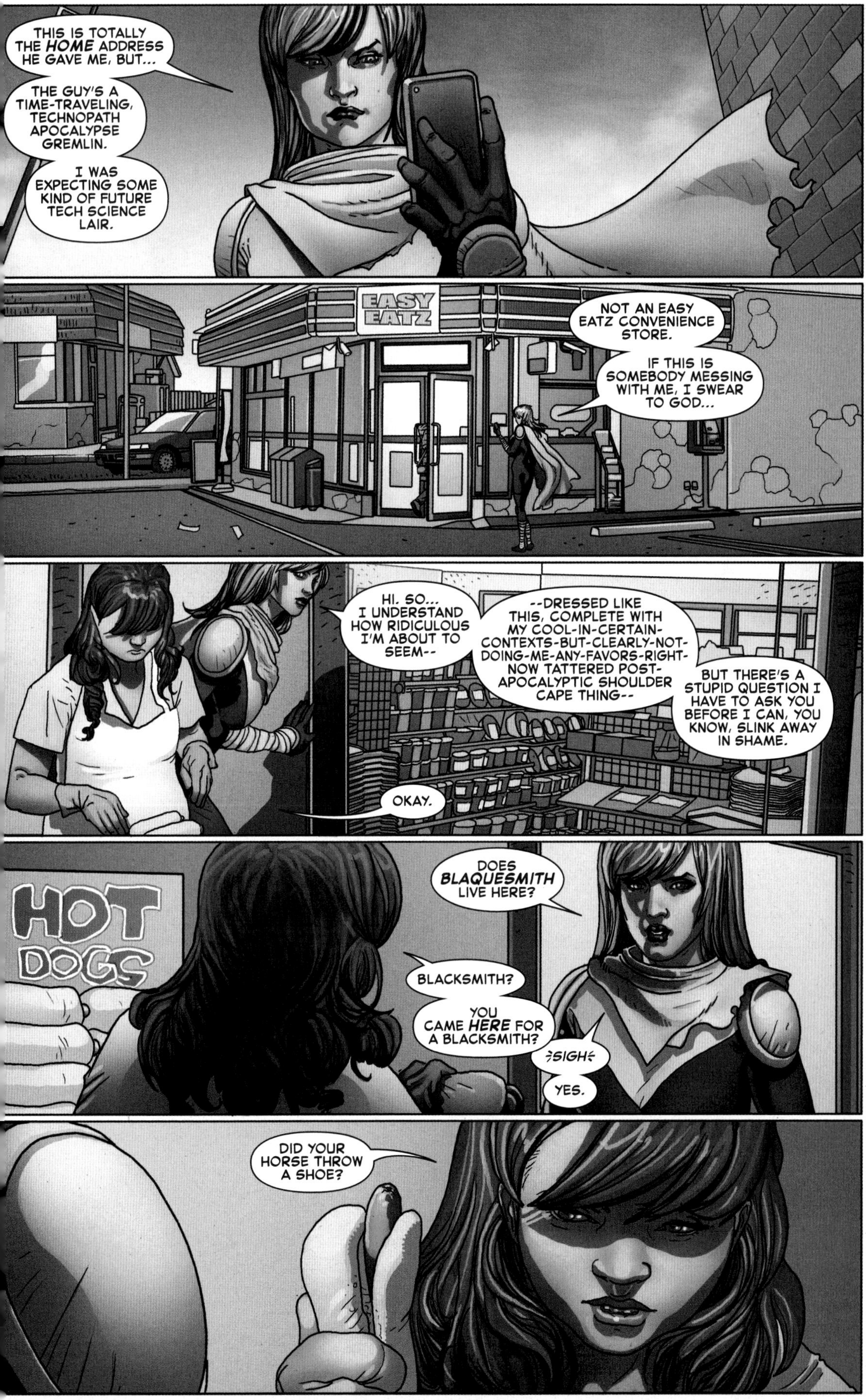
THIS IS TOTALLY THE HOME ADDRESS HE GAVE ME, BUT...
THE GUY'S A TIME-TRAVELING, TECHNOPATH APOCALYPSE GREMLIN.
I WAS EXPECTING SOME KIND OF FUTURE TECH SCIENCE LAIR.
EASY EATZ
NOT AN EASY EATZ CONVENIENCE STORE.
IF THIS IS SOMEBODY MESSING WITH ME, I SWEAR TO GOD...
HI. SO... I UNDERSTAND HOW RIDICULOUS I'M ABOUT TO SEEM--
--DRESSED LIKE THIS, COMPLETE WITH MY COOL-IN-CERTAIN-CONTEXTS-BUT-CLEARLY-NOT-DOING-ME-ANY-FAVORS-RIGHT-NOW TATTERED POST-APOCALYPTIC SHOULDER CAPE THING--
BUT THERE'S A STUPID QUESTION I HAVE TO ASK YOU BEFORE I CAN, YOU KNOW, SLINK AWAY IN SHAME.
OKAY.
HOT DOGS
DOES BLAQUESMITH LIVE HERE?
BLACKSMITH?
YOU CAME HERE FOR A BLACKSMITH?
SIGH
YES.
DID YOUR HORSE THROW A SHOE?

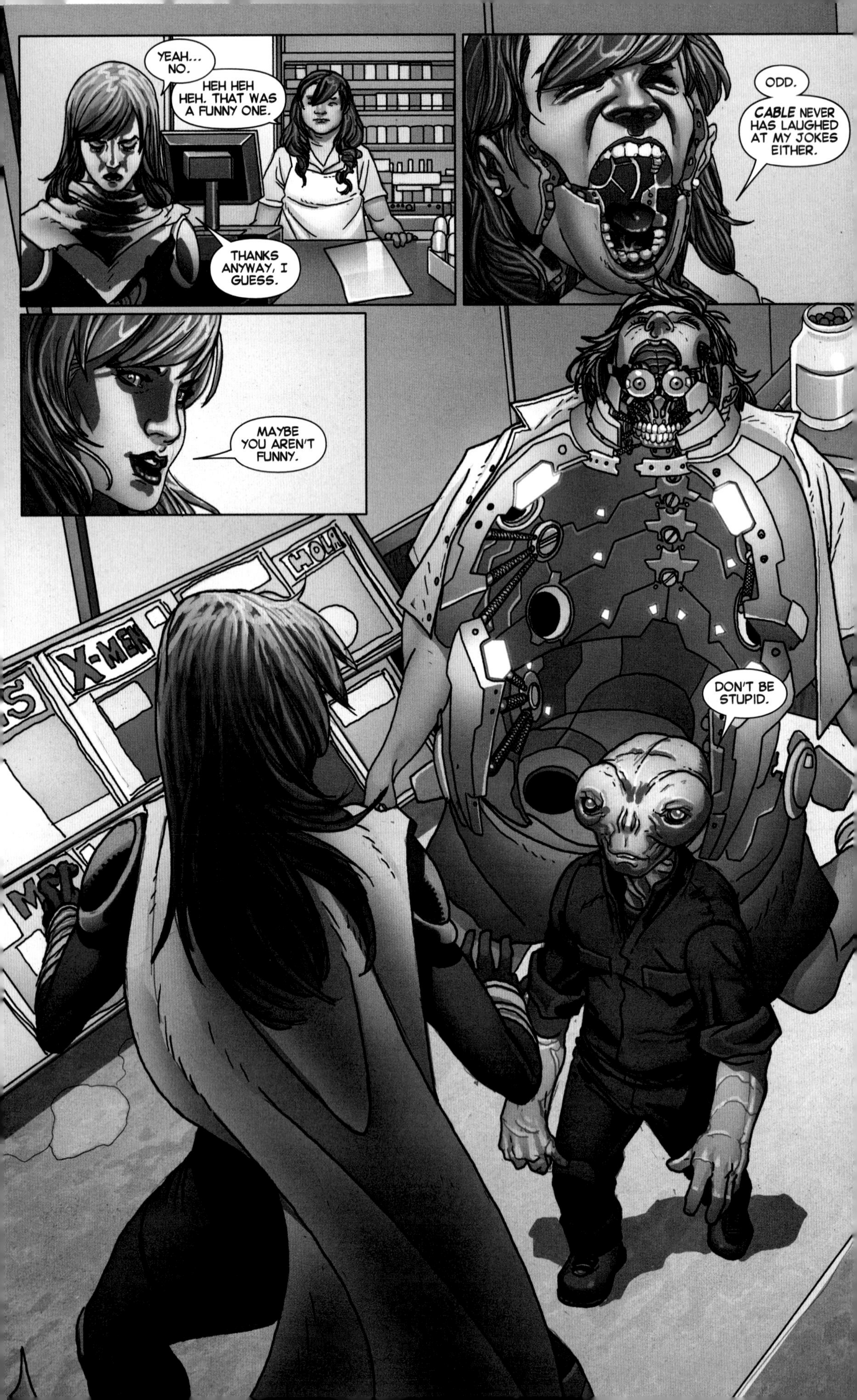
YEAH... NO.
HEH HEH HEH. THAT WAS A FUNNY ONE.
THANKS ANYWAY, I GUESS.
ODD.
CABLE NEVER HAS LAUGHED AT MY JOKES EITHER.
MAYBE YOU AREN'T FUNNY.
X-MEN
DON'T BE STUPID.

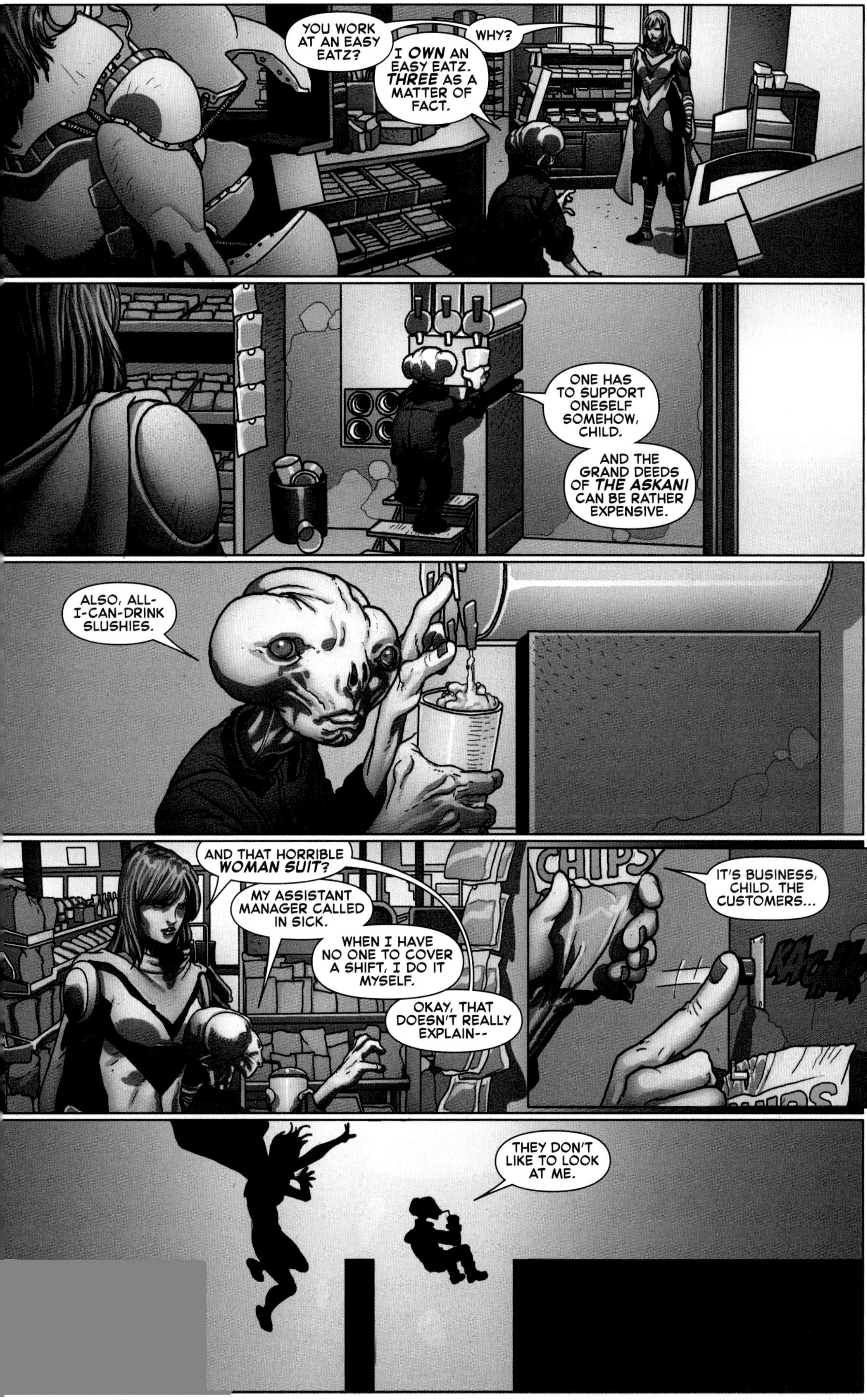
YOU WORK AT AN EASY EATZ?
WHY?
I *OWN* AN EASY EATZ. *THREE* AS A MATTER OF FACT.
ONE HAS TO SUPPORT ONESELF SOMEHOW, CHILD.
AND THE GRAND DEEDS OF *THE ASKANI* CAN BE RATHER EXPENSIVE.
ALSO, ALL-I-CAN-DRINK SLUSHIES.
AND THAT HORRIBLE *WOMAN SUIT*?
MY ASSISTANT MANAGER CALLED IN SICK.
WHEN I HAVE NO ONE TO COVER A SHIFT, I DO IT MYSELF.
OKAY, THAT DOESN'T REALLY EXPLAIN--
CHIPS
IT'S BUSINESS, CHILD. THE CUSTOMERS...
THEY DON'T LIKE TO LOOK AT ME.

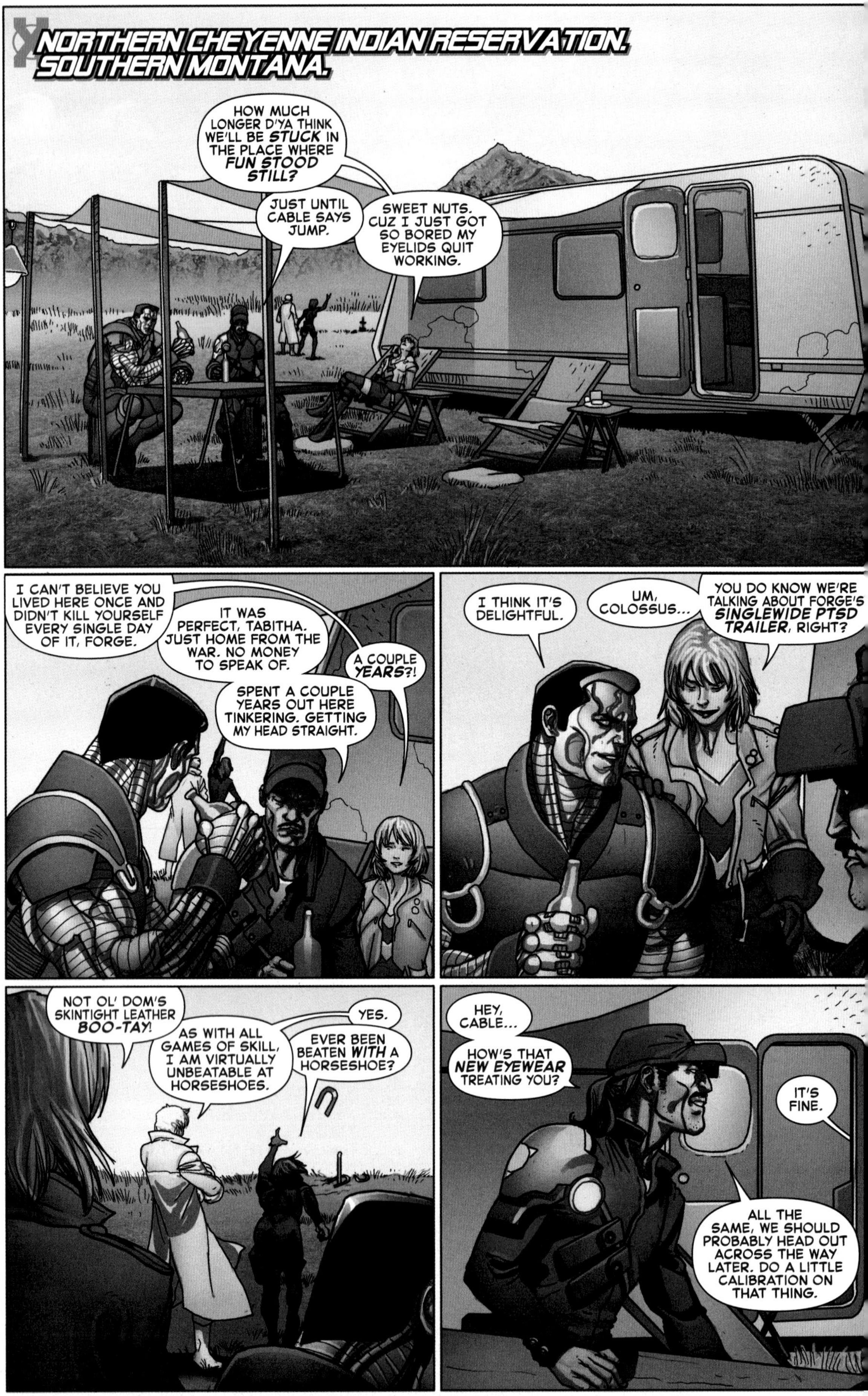
NORTHERN CHEYENNE INDIAN RESERVATION. SOUTHERN MONTANA.
HOW MUCH LONGER D'YA THINK WE'LL BE STUCK IN THE PLACE WHERE FUN STOOD STILL?
JUST UNTIL CABLE SAYS JUMP.
SWEET NUTS. CUZ I JUST GOT SO BORED MY EYELIDS QUIT WORKING.
I CAN'T BELIEVE YOU LIVED HERE ONCE AND DIDN'T KILL YOURSELF EVERY SINGLE DAY OF IT, FORGE.
IT WAS PERFECT, TABITHA. JUST HOME FROM THE WAR. NO MONEY TO SPEAK OF.
A COUPLE YEARS?!
SPENT A COUPLE YEARS OUT HERE TINKERING. GETTING MY HEAD STRAIGHT.
I THINK IT'S DELIGHTFUL.
UM, COLOSSUS...
YOU DO KNOW WE'RE TALKING ABOUT FORGE'S SINGLEWIDE PTSD TRAILER, RIGHT?
NOT OL' DOM'S SKINTIGHT LEATHER BOO-TAY!
AS WITH ALL GAMES OF SKILL, I AM VIRTUALLY UNBEATABLE AT HORSESHOES.
YES.
EVER BEEN BEATEN WITH A HORSESHOE?
HEY, CABLE...
HOW'S THAT NEW EYEWEAR TREATING YOU?
IT'S FINE.
ALL THE SAME, WE SHOULD PROBABLY HEAD OUT ACROSS THE WAY LATER. DO A LITTLE CALIBRATION ON THAT THING.

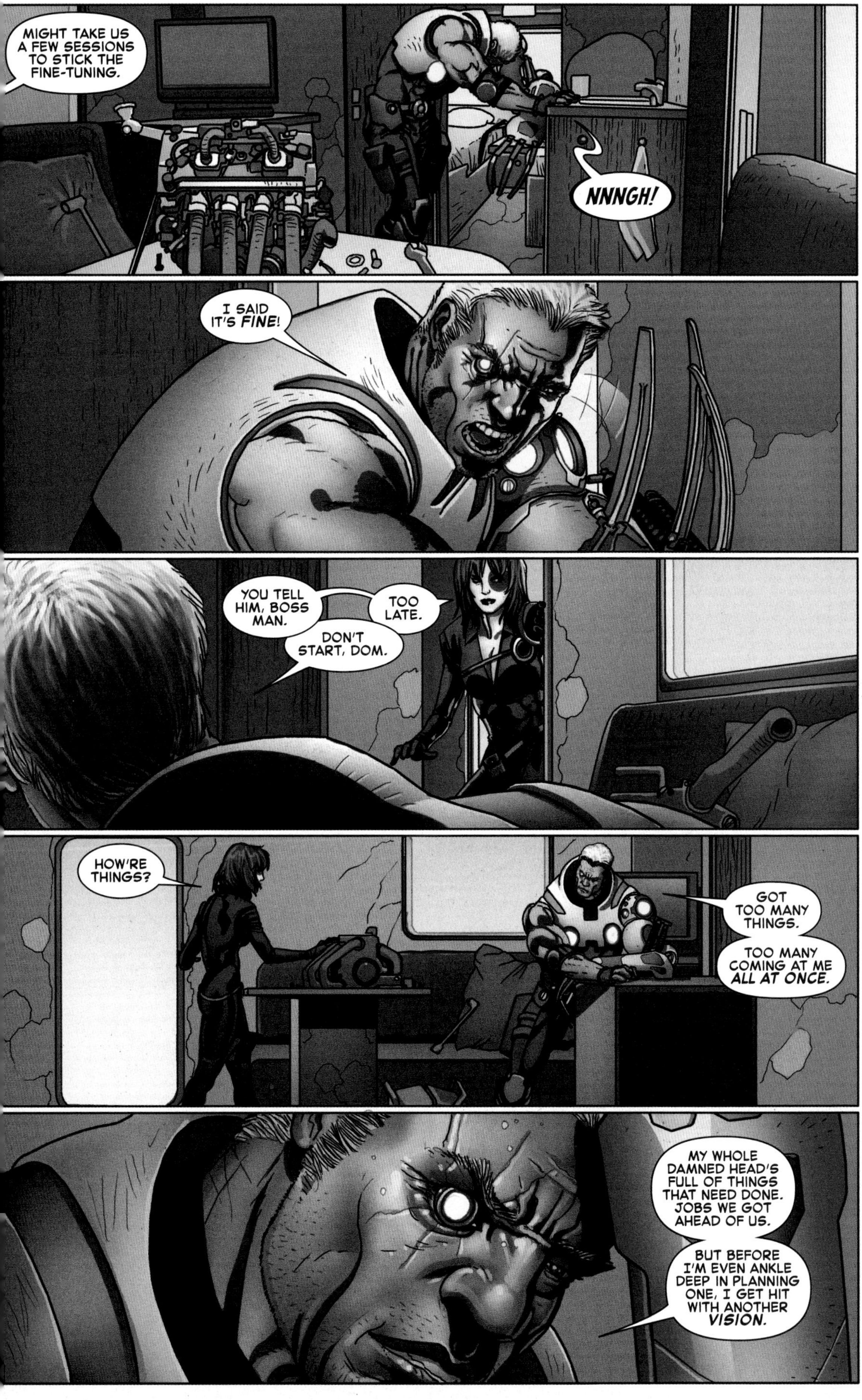
MIGHT TAKE US A FEW SESSIONS TO STICK THE FINE-TUNING.
NNNGH!
I SAID IT'S FINE!
YOU TELL HIM, BOSS MAN.
TOO LATE.
DON'T START, DOM.
HOW'RE THINGS?
GOT TOO MANY THINGS.
TOO MANY COMING AT ME ALL AT ONCE.
MY WHOLE DAMNED HEAD'S FULL OF THINGS THAT NEED DONE. JOBS WE GOT AHEAD OF US.
BUT BEFORE I'M EVEN ANKLE DEEP IN PLANNING ONE, I GET HIT WITH ANOTHER VISION.

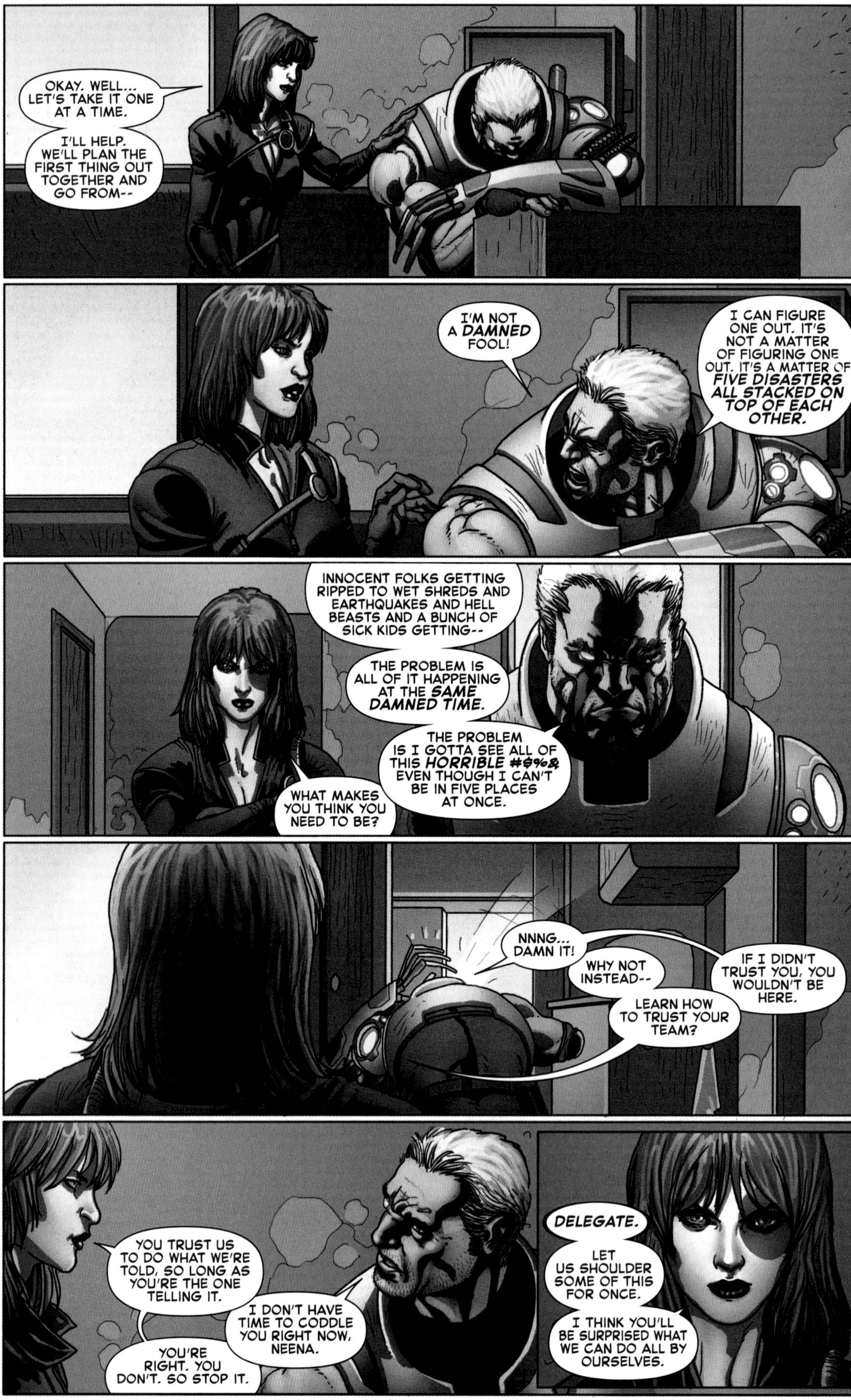
OKAY. WELL... LET'S TAKE IT ONE AT A TIME.
I'LL HELP. WE'LL PLAN THE FIRST THING OUT TOGETHER AND GO FROM--
I'M NOT A DAMNED FOOL!
I CAN FIGURE ONE OUT. IT'S NOT A MATTER OF FIGURING ONE OUT. IT'S A MATTER OF FIVE DISASTERS ALL STACKED ON TOP OF EACH OTHER.
INNOCENT FOLKS GETTING RIPPED TO WET SHREDS AND EARTHQUAKES AND HELL BEASTS AND A BUNCH OF SICK KIDS GETTING--
THE PROBLEM IS ALL OF IT HAPPENING AT THE SAME DAMNED TIME.
THE PROBLEM IS I GOTTA SEE ALL OF THIS HORRIBLE #$%& EVEN THOUGH I CAN'T BE IN FIVE PLACES AT ONCE.
WHAT MAKES YOU THINK YOU NEED TO BE?
NNNG... DAMN IT!
WHY NOT INSTEAD--
LEARN HOW TO TRUST YOUR TEAM?
IF I DIDN'T TRUST YOU, YOU WOULDN'T BE HERE.
YOU TRUST US TO DO WHAT WE'RE TOLD, SO LONG AS YOU'RE THE ONE TELLING IT.
I DON'T HAVE TIME TO CODDLE YOU RIGHT NOW, NEENA.
YOU'RE RIGHT. YOU DON'T. SO STOP IT.
DELEGATE.
LET US SHOULDER SOME OF THIS FOR ONCE.
I THINK YOU'LL BE SURPRISED WHAT WE CAN DO ALL BY OURSELVES.

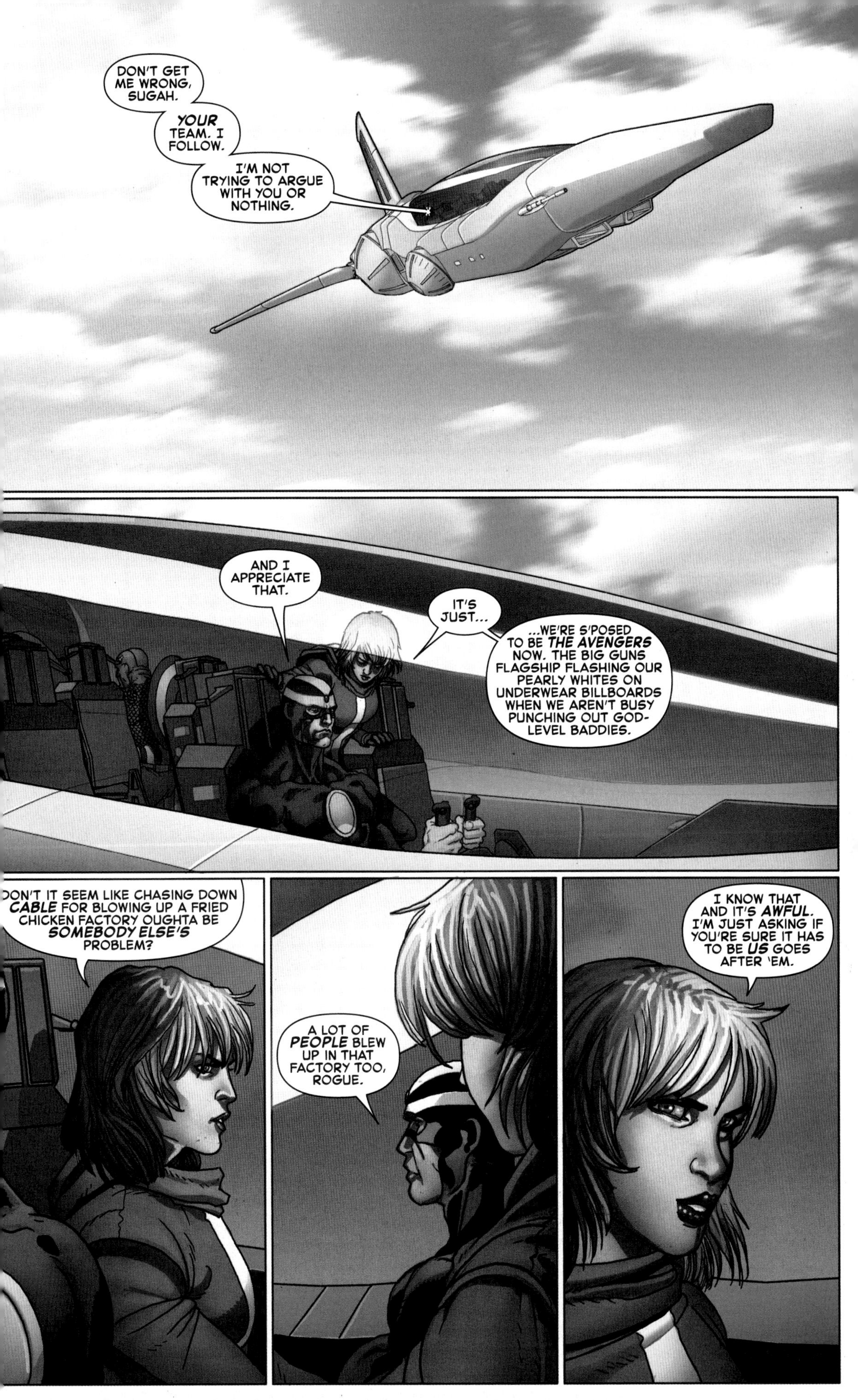
DON'T GET ME WRONG, SUGAH.
YOUR TEAM. I FOLLOW.
I'M NOT TRYING TO ARGUE WITH YOU OR NOTHING.
AND I APPRECIATE THAT.
IT'S JUST...
...WE'RE S'POSED TO BE *THE AVENGERS* NOW. THE BIG GUNS FLAGSHIP FLASHING OUR PEARLY WHITES ON UNDERWEAR BILLBOARDS WHEN WE AREN'T BUSY PUNCHING OUT GOD-LEVEL BADDIES.
DON'T IT SEEM LIKE CHASING DOWN *CABLE* FOR BLOWING UP A FRIED CHICKEN FACTORY OUGHTA BE *SOMEBODY ELSE'S* PROBLEM?
A LOT OF *PEOPLE* BLEW UP IN THAT FACTORY TOO, ROGUE.
I KNOW THAT AND IT'S *AWFUL*. I'M JUST ASKING IF YOU'RE SURE IT HAS TO BE *US* GOES AFTER 'EM.

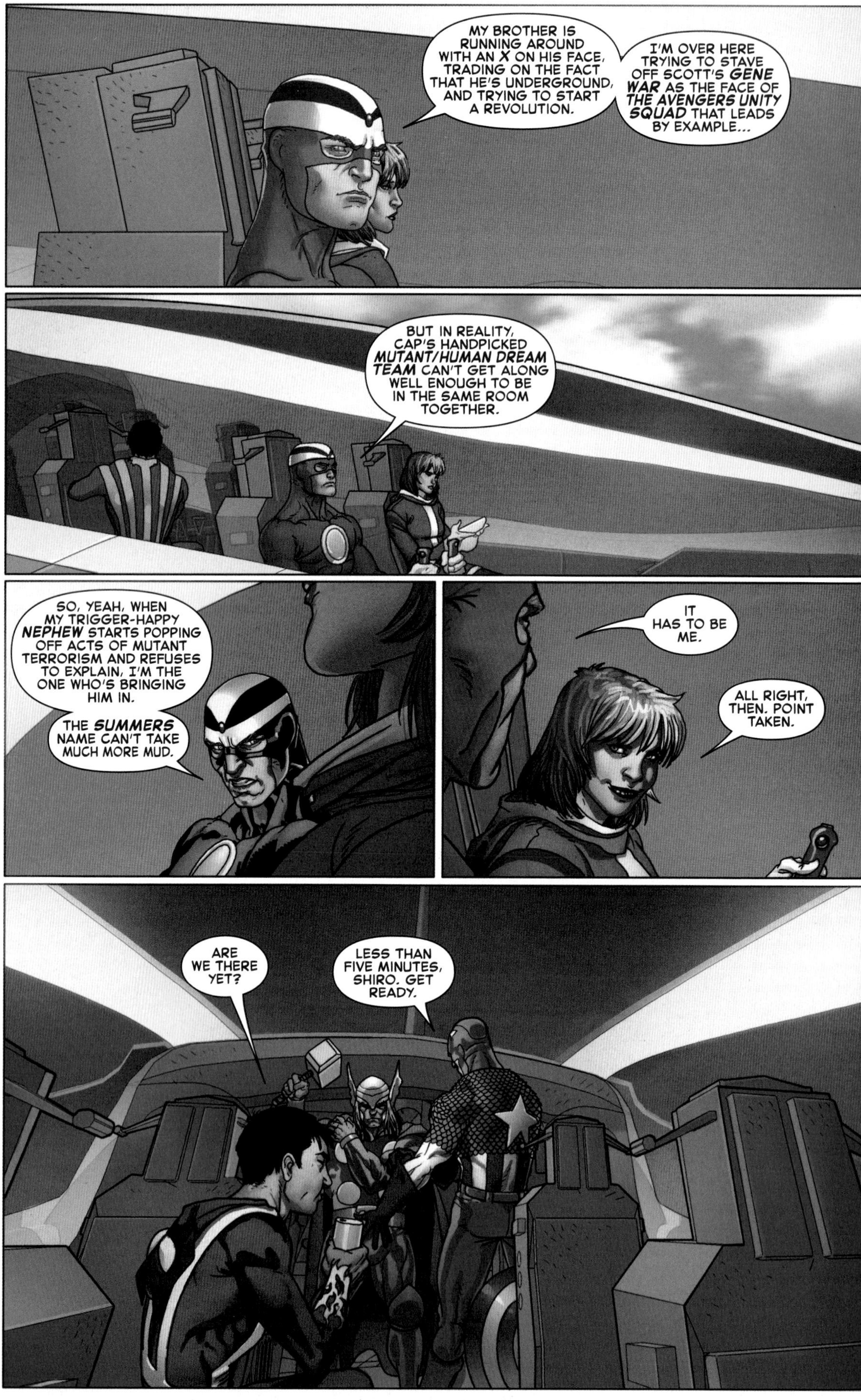
MY BROTHER IS RUNNING AROUND WITH AN X ON HIS FACE, TRADING ON THE FACT THAT HE'S UNDERGROUND, AND TRYING TO START A REVOLUTION.
I'M OVER HERE TRYING TO STAVE OFF SCOTT'S GENE WAR AS THE FACE OF THE AVENGERS UNITY SQUAD THAT LEADS BY EXAMPLE...
BUT IN REALITY, CAP'S HANDPICKED MUTANT/HUMAN DREAM TEAM CAN'T GET ALONG WELL ENOUGH TO BE IN THE SAME ROOM TOGETHER.
SO, YEAH, WHEN MY TRIGGER-HAPPY NEPHEW STARTS POPPING OFF ACTS OF MUTANT TERRORISM AND REFUSES TO EXPLAIN, I'M THE ONE WHO'S BRINGING HIM IN.
THE SUMMERS NAME CAN'T TAKE MUCH MORE MUD.
IT HAS TO BE ME.
ALL RIGHT, THEN. POINT TAKEN.
ARE WE THERE YET?
LESS THAN FIVE MINUTES, SHIRO. GET READY.

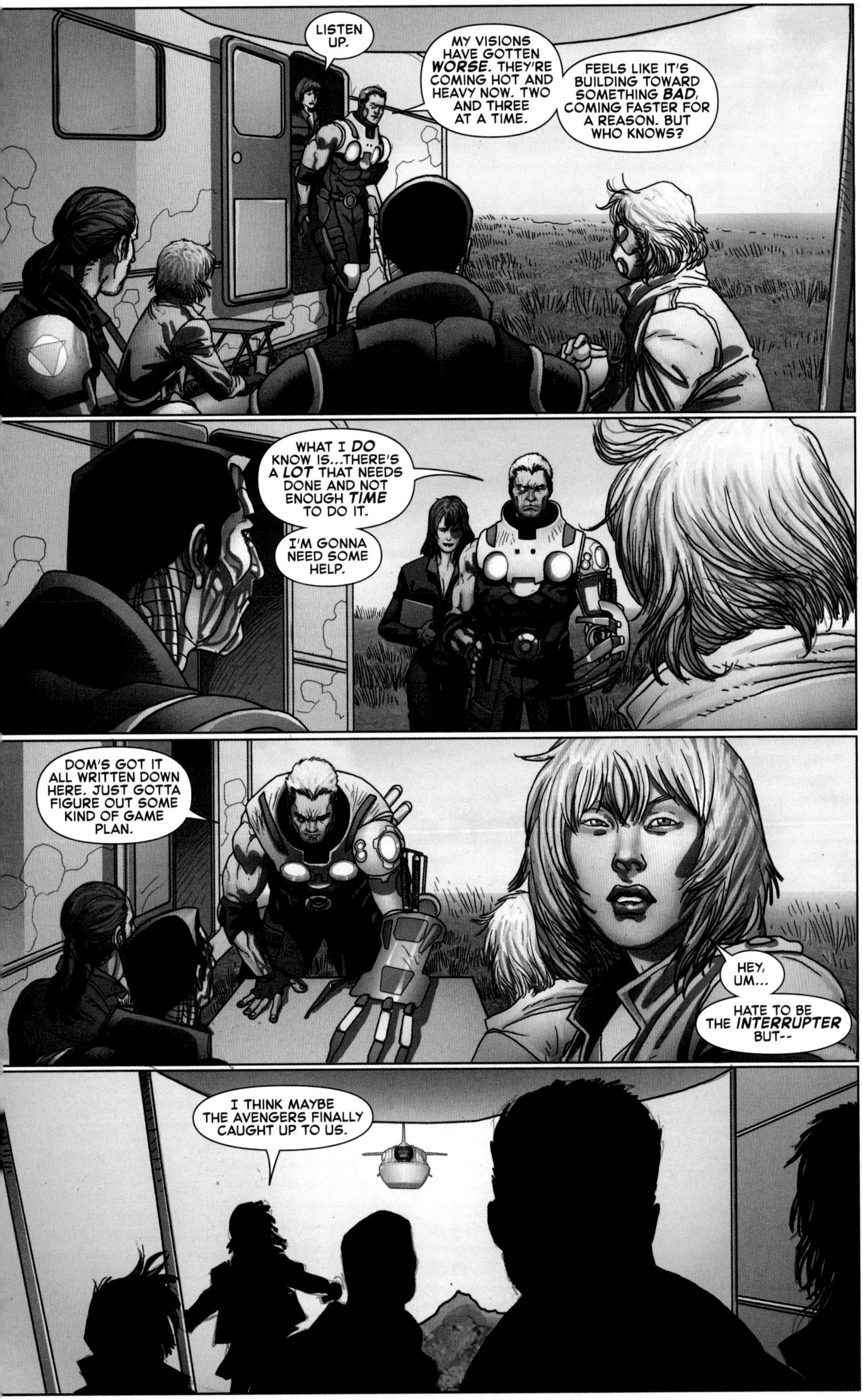
LISTEN UP.
MY VISIONS HAVE GOTTEN WORSE. THEY'RE COMING HOT AND HEAVY NOW. TWO AND THREE AT A TIME.
FEELS LIKE IT'S BUILDING TOWARD SOMETHING BAD, COMING FASTER FOR A REASON. BUT WHO KNOWS?
WHAT I DO KNOW IS...THERE'S A LOT THAT NEEDS DONE AND NOT ENOUGH TIME TO DO IT.
I'M GONNA NEED SOME HELP.
DOM'S GOT IT ALL WRITTEN DOWN HERE. JUST GOTTA FIGURE OUT SOME KIND OF GAME PLAN.
HEY, UM...
HATE TO BE THE INTERRUPTER BUT--
I THINK MAYBE THE AVENGERS FINALLY CAUGHT UP TO US.

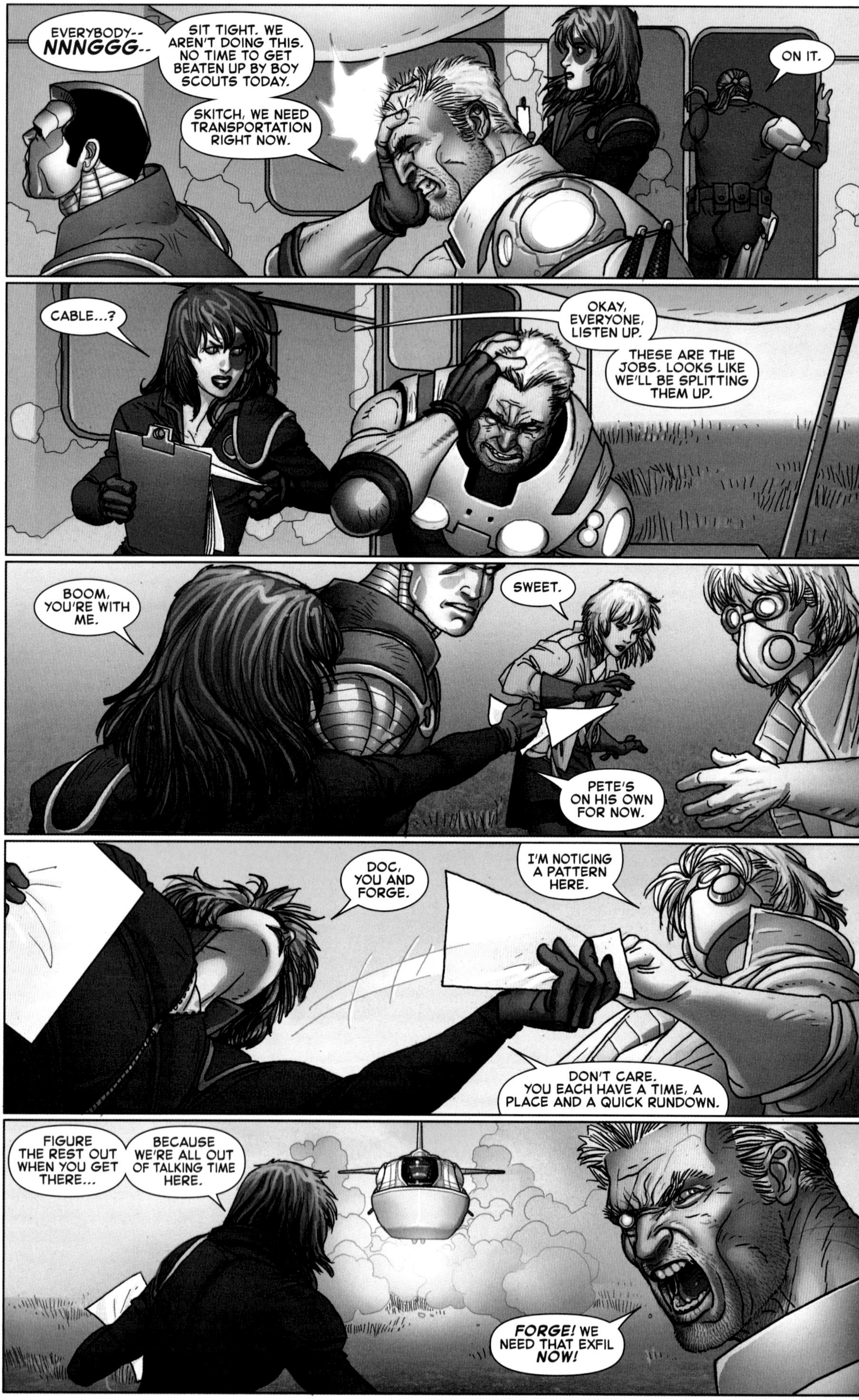

EVERYBODY-- NNNGGG--
SIT TIGHT. WE AREN'T DOING THIS. NO TIME TO GET BEATEN UP BY BOY SCOUTS TODAY.
SKITCH, WE NEED TRANSPORTATION RIGHT NOW.
ON IT.
CABLE...?
OKAY, EVERYONE, LISTEN UP.
THESE ARE THE JOBS. LOOKS LIKE WE'LL BE SPLITTING THEM UP.
BOOM, YOU'RE WITH ME.
SWEET.
PETE'S ON HIS OWN FOR NOW.
DOC, YOU AND FORGE.
I'M NOTICING A PATTERN HERE.
DON'T CARE. YOU EACH HAVE A TIME, A PLACE AND A QUICK RUNDOWN.
FIGURE THE REST OUT WHEN YOU GET THERE...
BECAUSE WE'RE ALL OUT OF TALKING TIME HERE.
FORGE! WE NEED THAT EXFIL NOW!

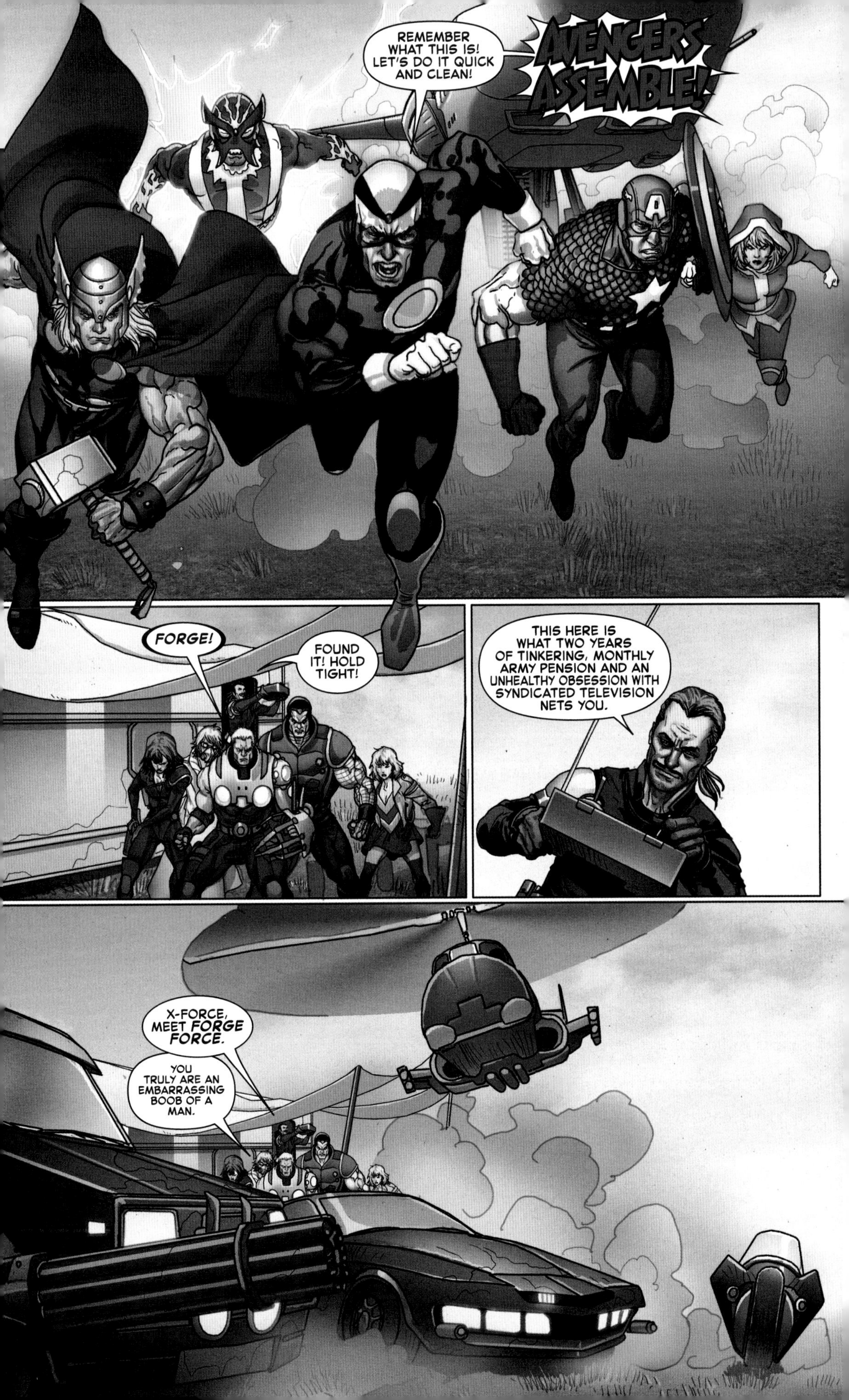
REMEMBER WHAT THIS IS! LET'S DO IT QUICK AND CLEAN!
AVENGERS ASSEMBLE!
FORGE!
FOUND IT! HOLD TIGHT!
THIS HERE IS WHAT TWO YEARS OF TINKERING, MONTHLY ARMY PENSION AND AN UNHEALTHY OBSESSION WITH SYNDICATED TELEVISION NETS YOU.
X-FORCE, MEET FORGE FORCE.
YOU TRULY ARE AN EMBARRASSING BOOB OF A MAN.

AVENGERS, LOOK SHARP!

THAT WON'T BUY US MUCH TIME...

GRAB A VEHICLE AND GET MOVING!

CABLE?

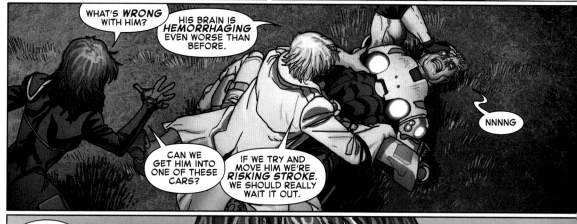

WHAT'S *WRONG* WITH HIM?

HIS BRAIN IS *HEMORRHAGING* EVEN WORSE THAN BEFORE.

NNNNG

CAN WE GET HIM INTO ONE OF THESE CARS?

IF WE TRY AND MOVE HIM WE'RE *RISKING STROKE*. WE SHOULD REALLY WAIT IT OUT.

FINE. *NEW* PLAN.

PICK AN AVENGER AND *HIT* THEM WITH SOMETHING.

LET'S BUY CABLE SOME TIME.

SOUNDS LIKE A *TERRIBLE* PLAN.

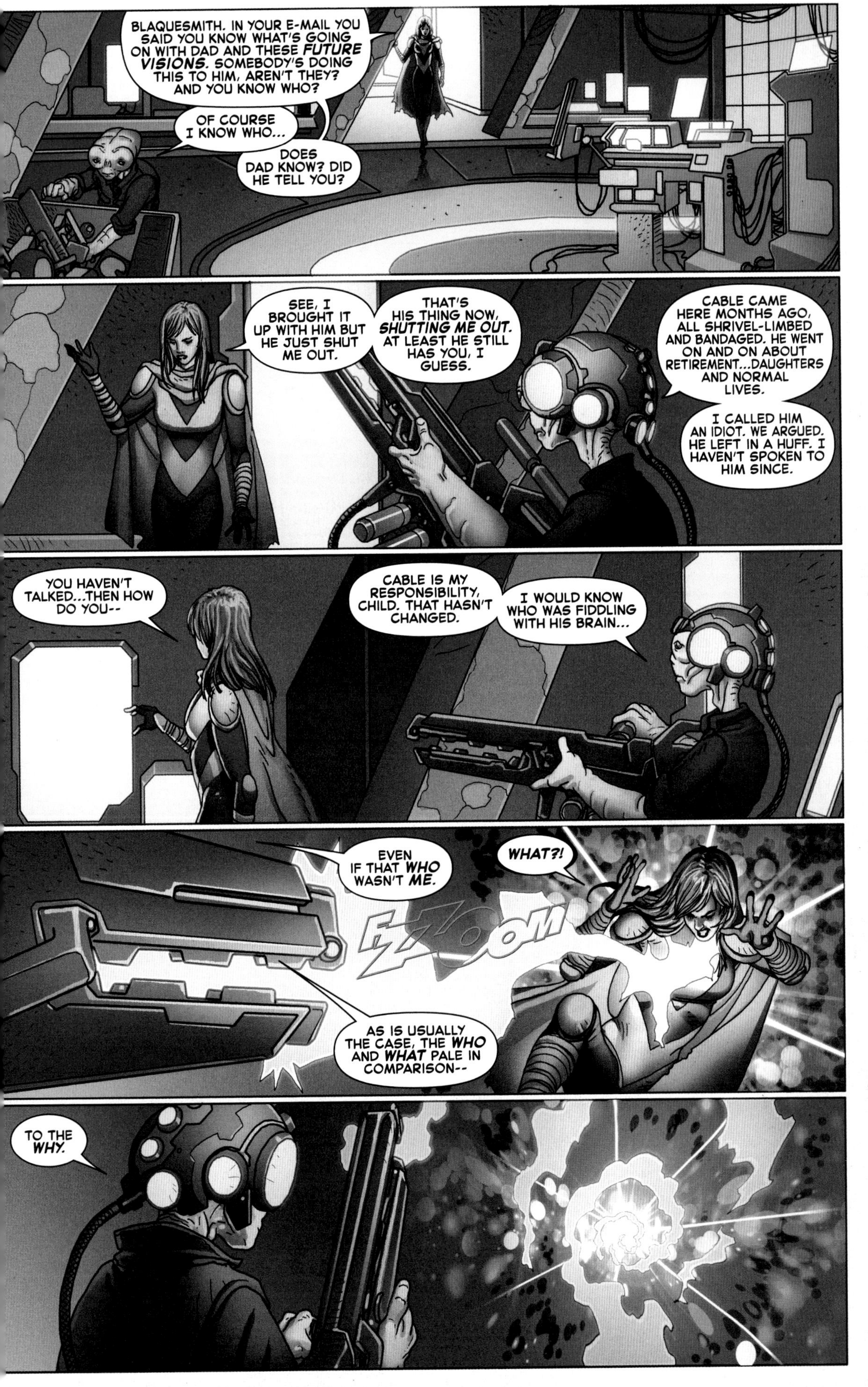
BLAQUESMITH. IN YOUR E-MAIL YOU SAID YOU KNOW WHAT'S GOING ON WITH DAD AND THESE *FUTURE VISIONS.* SOMEBODY'S DOING THIS TO HIM, AREN'T THEY? AND YOU KNOW WHO?
OF COURSE I KNOW WHO...
DOES DAD KNOW? DID HE TELL YOU?
SEE, I BROUGHT IT UP WITH HIM BUT HE JUST SHUT ME OUT.
THAT'S HIS THING NOW, *SHUTTING ME OUT.* AT LEAST HE STILL HAS YOU, I GUESS.
CABLE CAME HERE MONTHS AGO, ALL SHRIVEL-LIMBED AND BANDAGED. HE WENT ON AND ON ABOUT RETIREMENT...DAUGHTERS AND NORMAL LIVES.
I CALLED HIM AN IDIOT. WE ARGUED. HE LEFT IN A HUFF. I HAVEN'T SPOKEN TO HIM SINCE.
YOU HAVEN'T TALKED...THEN HOW DO YOU--
CABLE IS MY RESPONSIBILITY, CHILD. THAT HASN'T CHANGED.
I WOULD KNOW WHO WAS FIDDLING WITH HIS BRAIN...
EVEN IF THAT *WHO* WASN'T *ME.*
WHAT?!
FZZOOM
AS IS USUALLY THE CASE, THE *WHO* AND *WHAT* PALE IN COMPARISON--
TO THE *WHY.*

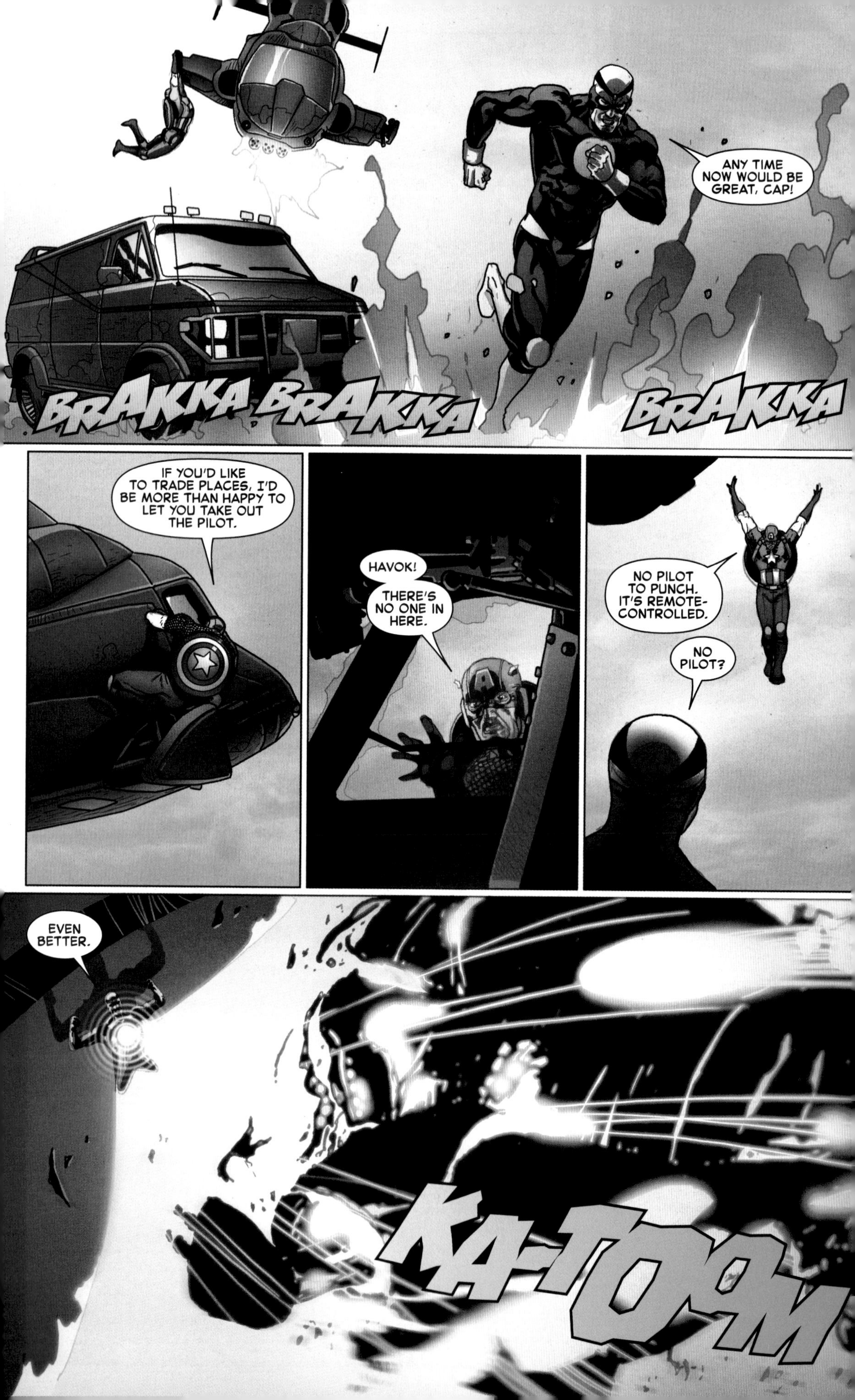
ANY TIME NOW WOULD BE GREAT, CAP!
BRAKKA BRAKKA
BRAKKA
IF YOU'D LIKE TO TRADE PLACES, I'D BE MORE THAN HAPPY TO LET YOU TAKE OUT THE PILOT.
HAVOK!
THERE'S NO ONE IN HERE.
NO PILOT TO PUNCH. IT'S REMOTE-CONTROLLED.
NO PILOT?
EVEN BETTER.
KA-TOOM

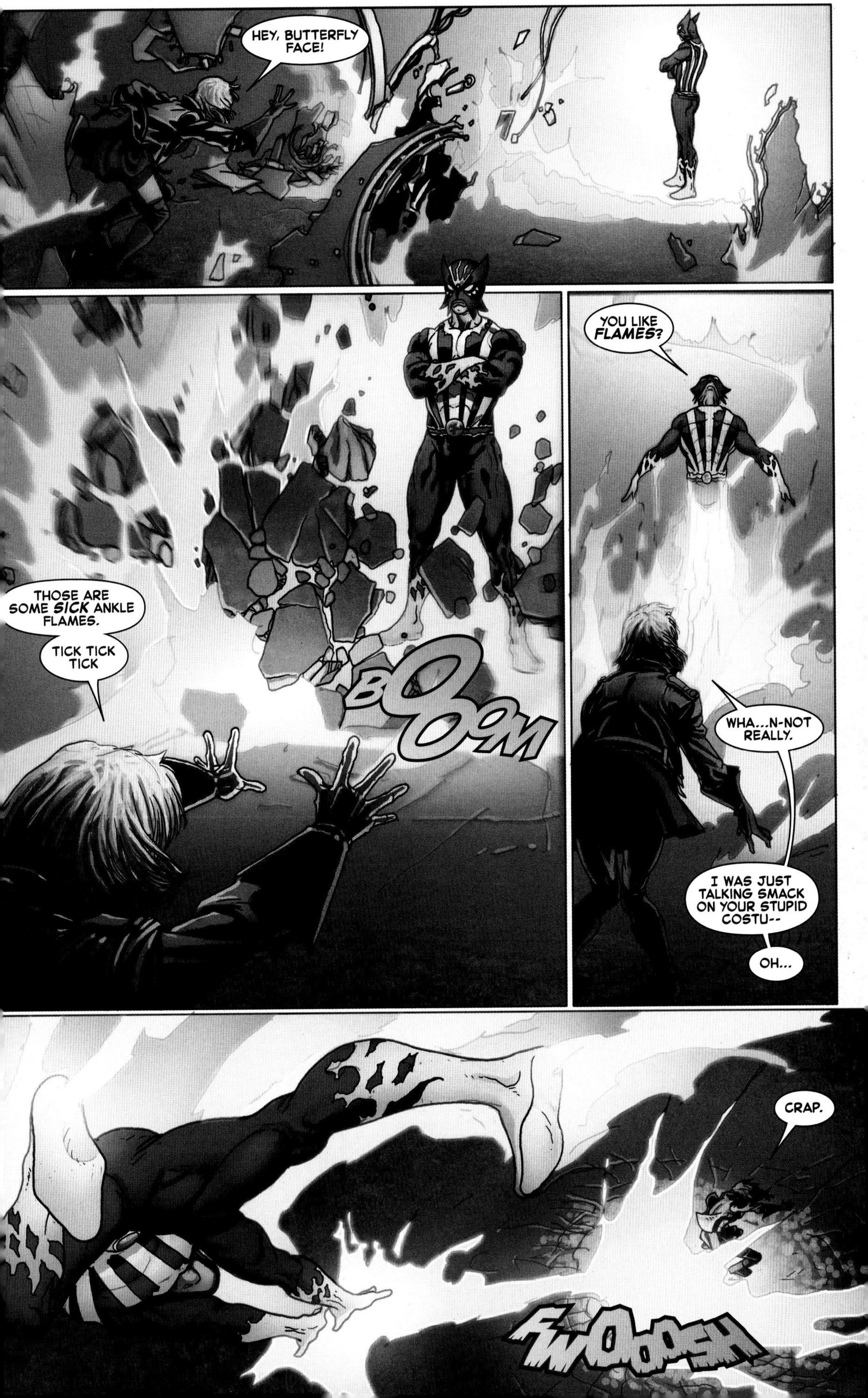
HEY, BUTTERFLY FACE!
BOOOM
THOSE ARE SOME SICK ANKLE FLAMES.
TICK TICK TICK
YOU LIKE FLAMES?
WHA...N-NOT REALLY.
I WAS JUST TALKING SMACK ON YOUR STUPID COSTU--
OH...
CRAP.
FWOOOSH

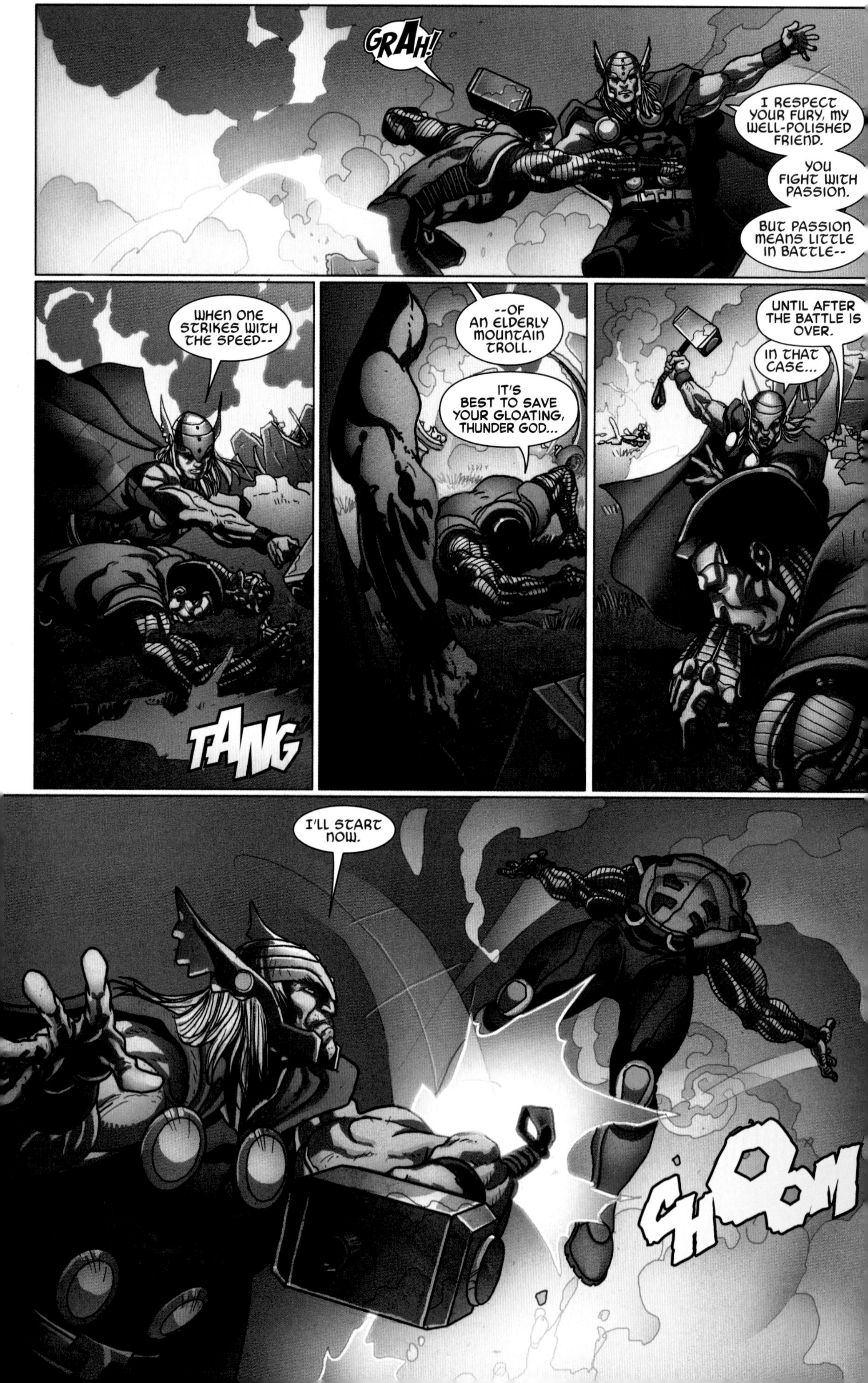
GRAH!
I RESPECT YOUR FURY, MY WELL-POLISHED FRIEND.
YOU FIGHT WITH PASSION.
BUT PASSION MEANS LITTLE IN BATTLE--
WHEN ONE STRIKES WITH THE SPEED--
TANG
--OF AN ELDERLY MOUNTAIN TROLL.
IT'S BEST TO SAVE YOUR GLOATING, THUNDER GOD...
UNTIL AFTER THE BATTLE IS OVER.
IN THAT CASE...
I'LL START NOW.
CHOOM

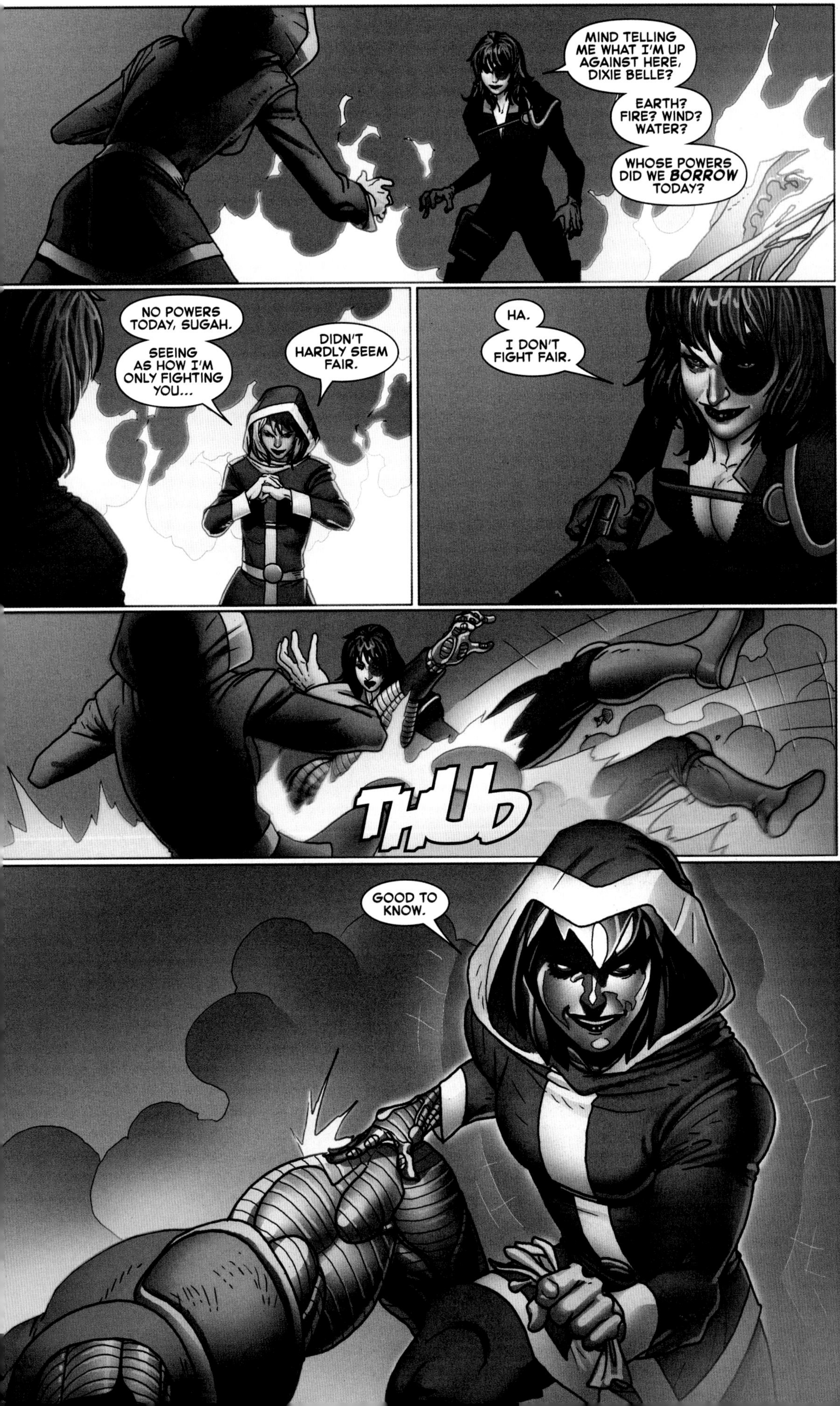

MIND TELLING ME WHAT I'M UP AGAINST HERE, DIXIE BELLE?
EARTH? FIRE? WIND? WATER?
WHOSE POWERS DID WE BORROW TODAY?
NO POWERS TODAY, SUGAH.
SEEING AS HOW I'M ONLY FIGHTING YOU...
DIDN'T HARDLY SEEM FAIR.
HA.
I DON'T FIGHT FAIR.
THUD
GOOD TO KNOW.

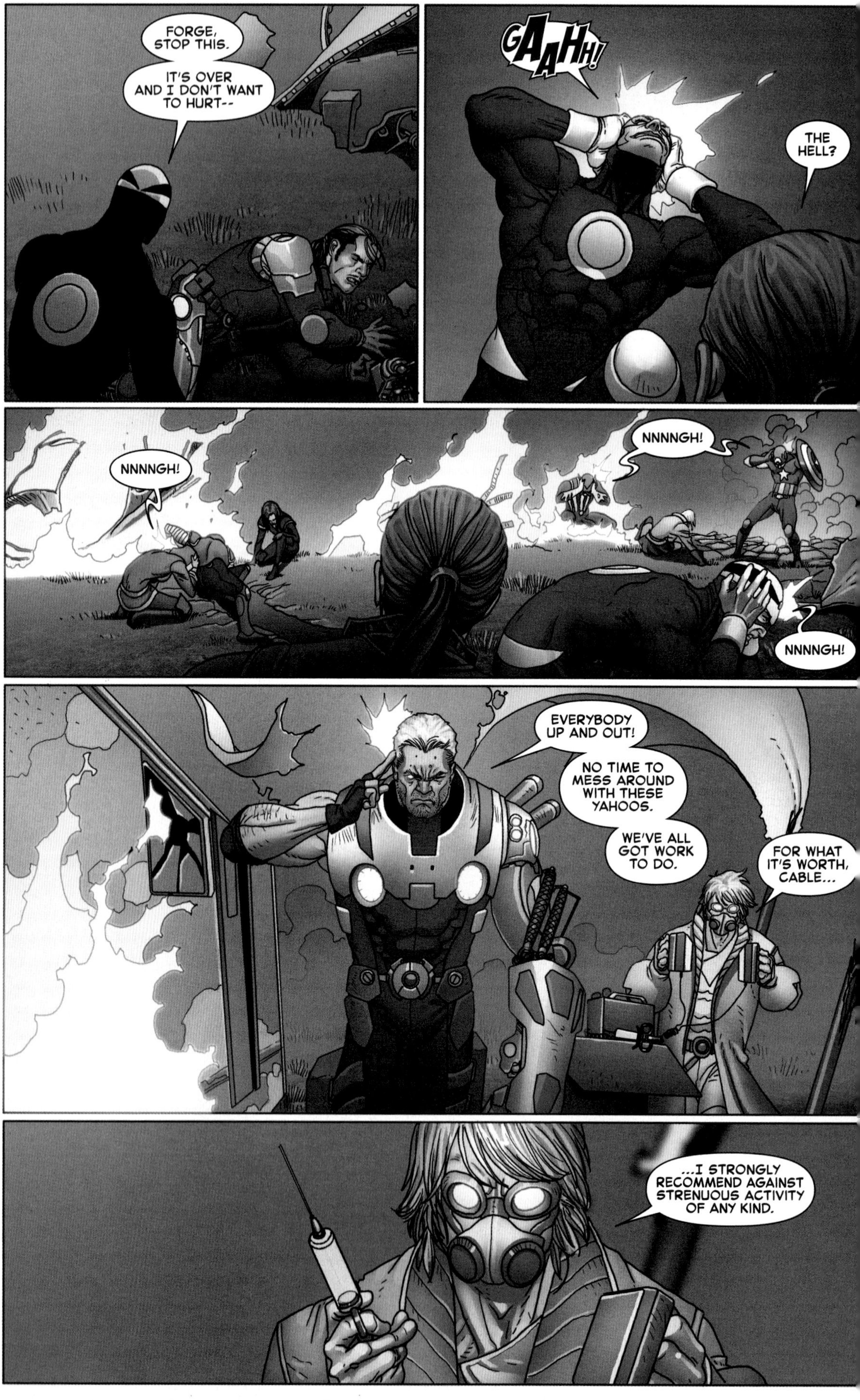
FORGE, STOP THIS.
IT'S OVER AND I DON'T WANT TO HURT--
GAAHH!
THE HELL?
NNNNGH!
NNNNGH!
NNNNGH!
EVERYBODY UP AND OUT!
NO TIME TO MESS AROUND WITH THESE YAHOOS.
WE'VE ALL GOT WORK TO DO.
FOR WHAT IT'S WORTH, CABLE...
...I STRONGLY RECOMMEND AGAINST STRENUOUS ACTIVITY OF ANY KIND.

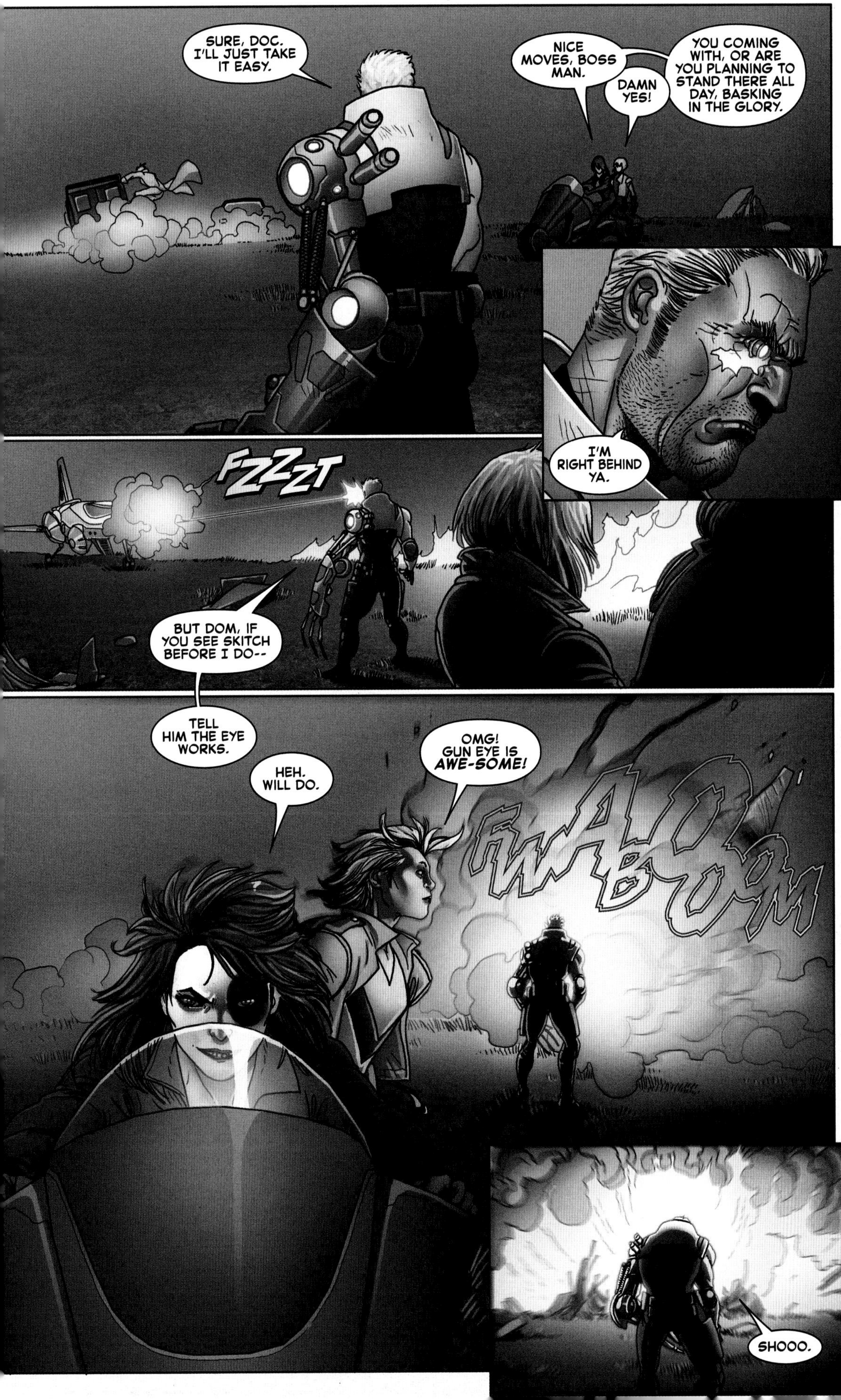
SURE, DOC. I'LL JUST TAKE IT EASY.
NICE MOVES, BOSS MAN.
DAMN YES!
YOU COMING WITH, OR ARE YOU PLANNING TO STAND THERE ALL DAY, BASKING IN THE GLORY.
I'M RIGHT BEHIND YA.
FZZZT
BUT DOM, IF YOU SEE SKITCH BEFORE I DO--
TELL HIM THE EYE WORKS.
HEH. WILL DO.
OMG! GUN EYE IS *AWE-SOME!*
FWABOOM
SHOOO.

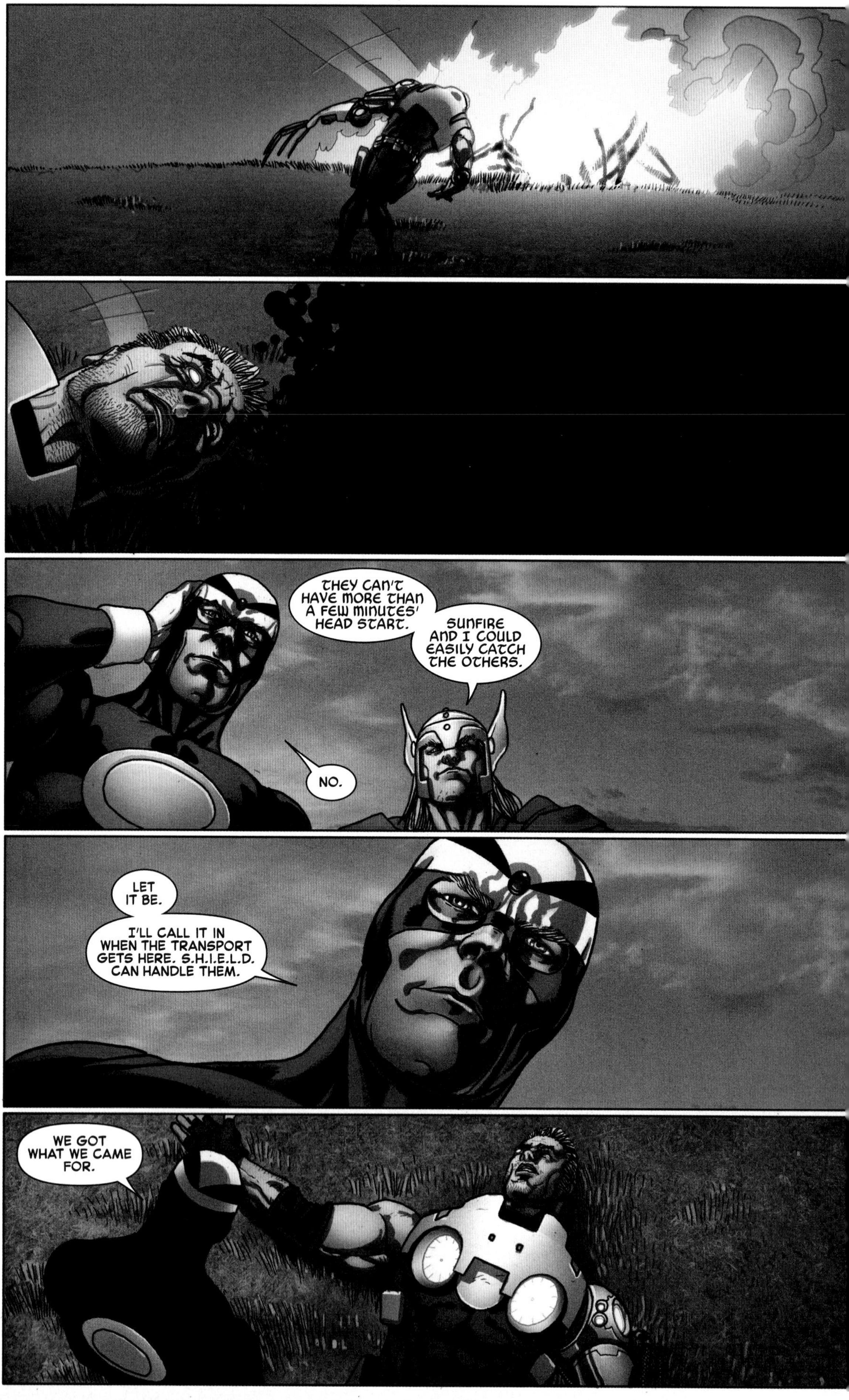
THEY CAN'T HAVE MORE THAN A FEW MINUTES' HEAD START.
SUNFIRE AND I COULD EASILY CATCH THE OTHERS.
NO.
LET IT BE.
I'LL CALL IT IN WHEN THE TRANSPORT GETS HERE. S.H.I.E.L.D. CAN HANDLE THEM.
WE GOT WHAT WE CAME FOR.

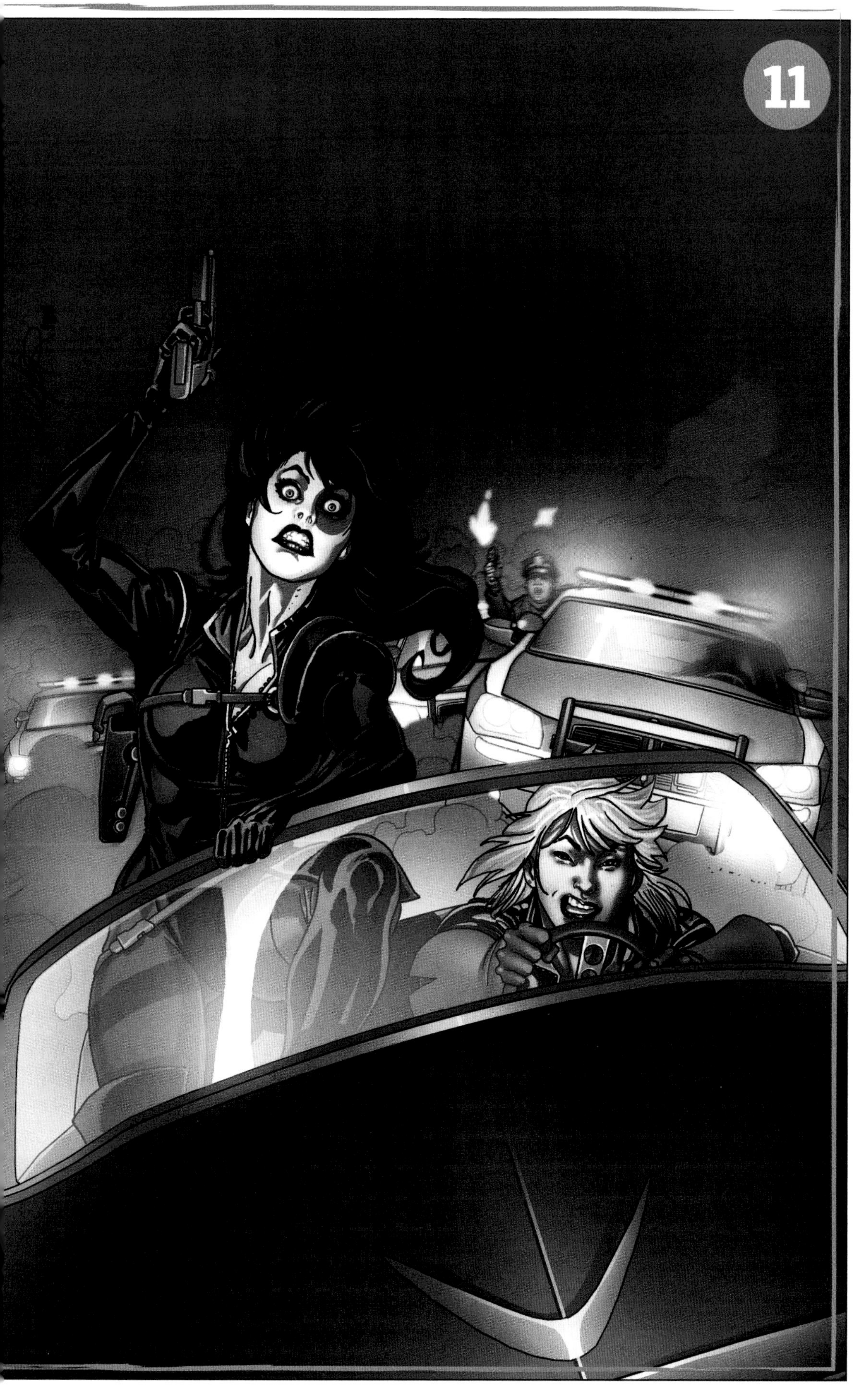
11

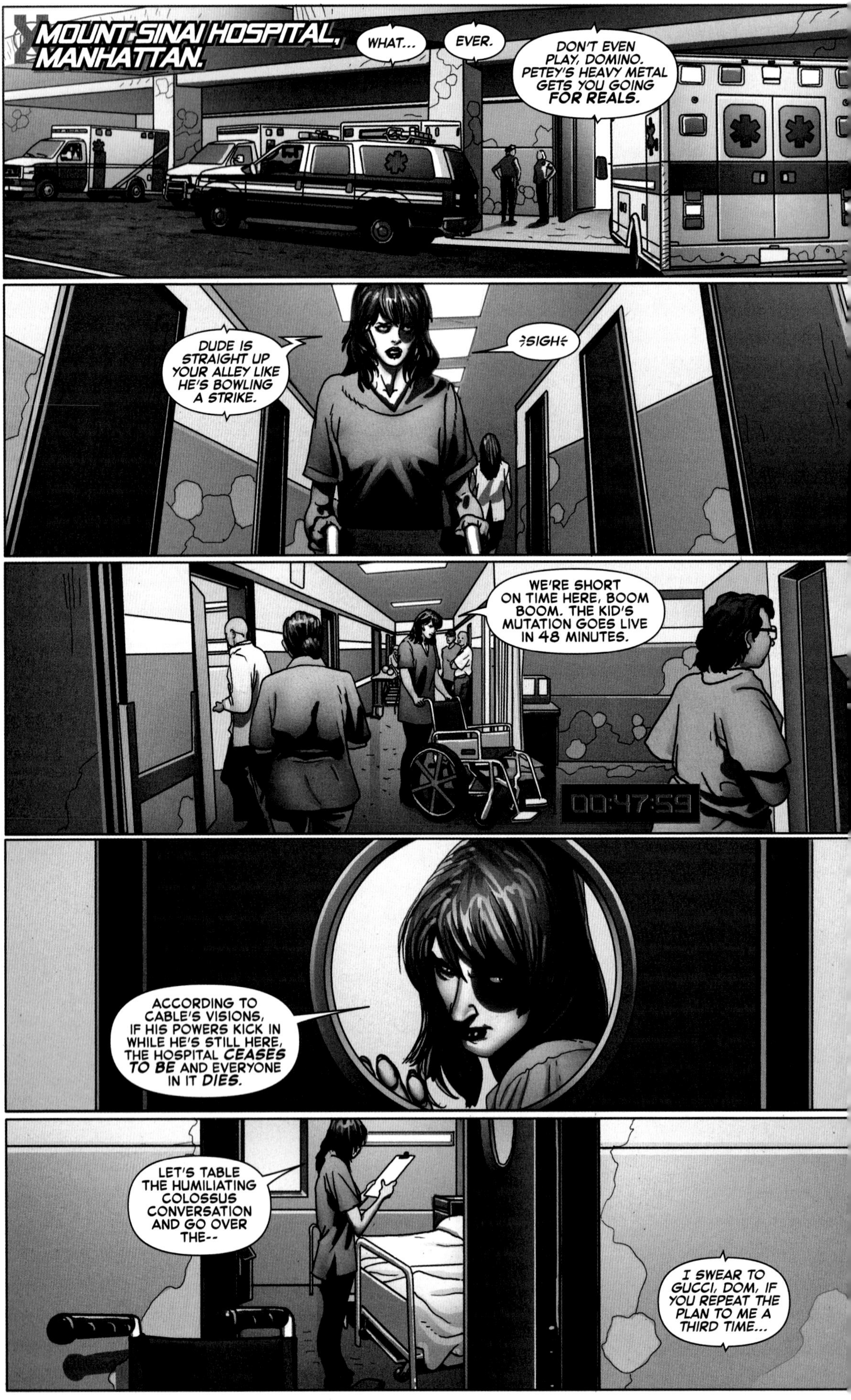
MOUNT SINAI HOSPITAL, MANHATTAN.
WHAT...
EVER.
DON'T EVEN PLAY, DOMINO. PETEY'S HEAVY METAL GETS YOU GOING FOR REALS.
DUDE IS STRAIGHT UP YOUR ALLEY LIKE HE'S BOWLING A STRIKE.
SIGH
WE'RE SHORT ON TIME HERE, BOOM BOOM. THE KID'S MUTATION GOES LIVE IN 48 MINUTES.
00:47:59
ACCORDING TO CABLE'S VISIONS, IF HIS POWERS KICK IN WHILE HE'S STILL HERE, THE HOSPITAL CEASES TO BE AND EVERYONE IN IT DIES.
LET'S TABLE THE HUMILIATING COLOSSUS CONVERSATION AND GO OVER THE--
I SWEAR TO GUCCI, DOM, IF YOU REPEAT THE PLAN TO ME A THIRD TIME...

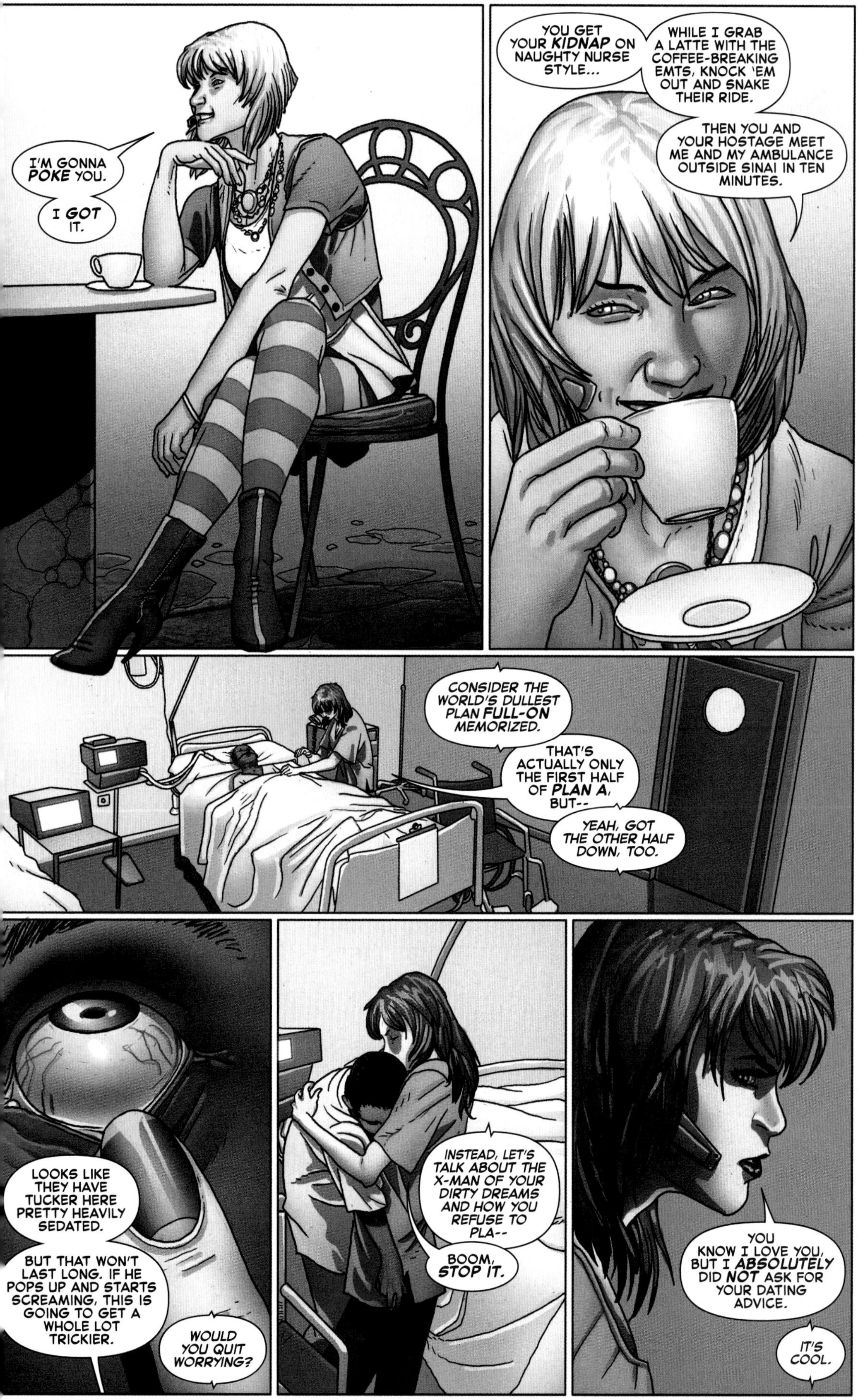
I'M GONNA POKE YOU.
I GOT IT.
YOU GET YOUR KIDNAP ON NAUGHTY NURSE STYLE...
WHILE I GRAB A LATTE WITH THE COFFEE-BREAKING EMTS, KNOCK 'EM OUT AND SNAKE THEIR RIDE.
THEN YOU AND YOUR HOSTAGE MEET ME AND MY AMBULANCE OUTSIDE SINAI IN TEN MINUTES.
CONSIDER THE WORLD'S DULLEST PLAN FULL-ON MEMORIZED.
THAT'S ACTUALLY ONLY THE FIRST HALF OF PLAN A, BUT--
YEAH, GOT THE OTHER HALF DOWN, TOO.
LOOKS LIKE THEY HAVE TUCKER HERE PRETTY HEAVILY SEDATED.
BUT THAT WON'T LAST LONG. IF HE POPS UP AND STARTS SCREAMING, THIS IS GOING TO GET A WHOLE LOT TRICKIER.
WOULD YOU QUIT WORRYING?
INSTEAD, LET'S TALK ABOUT THE X-MAN OF YOUR DIRTY DREAMS AND HOW YOU REFUSE TO PLA--
BOOM, STOP IT.
YOU KNOW I LOVE YOU, BUT I ABSOLUTELY DID NOT ASK FOR YOUR DATING ADVICE.
IT'S COOL.

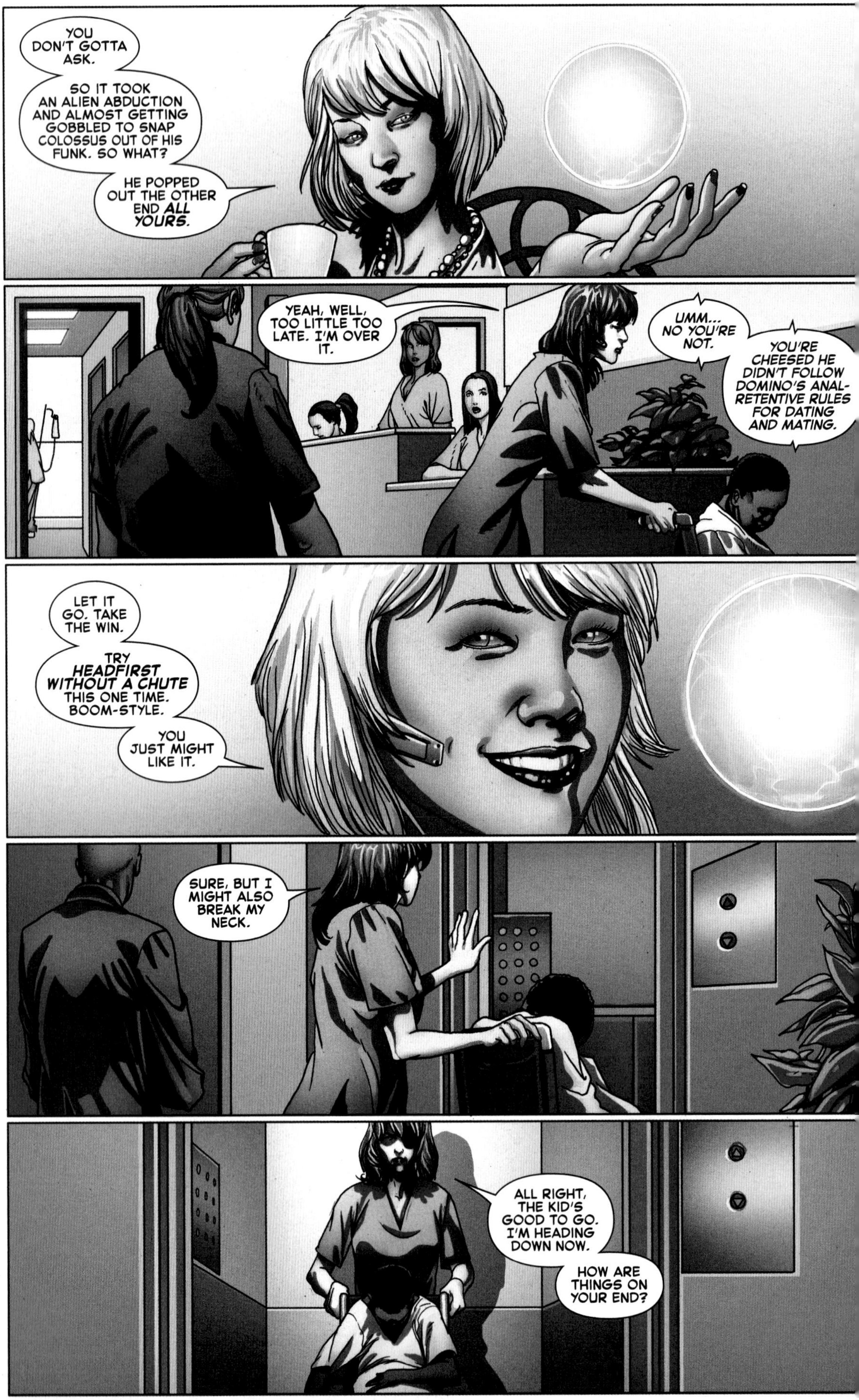
YOU DON'T GOTTA ASK.
SO IT TOOK AN ALIEN ABDUCTION AND ALMOST GETTING GOBBLED TO SNAP COLOSSUS OUT OF HIS FUNK. SO WHAT?
HE POPPED OUT THE OTHER END ALL YOURS.
YEAH, WELL, TOO LITTLE TOO LATE. I'M OVER IT.
UMM... NO YOU'RE NOT.
YOU'RE CHEESED HE DIDN'T FOLLOW DOMINO'S ANAL-RETENTIVE RULES FOR DATING AND MATING.
LET IT GO. TAKE THE WIN.
TRY HEADFIRST WITHOUT A CHUTE THIS ONE TIME. BOOM-STYLE.
YOU JUST MIGHT LIKE IT.
SURE, BUT I MIGHT ALSO BREAK MY NECK.
ALL RIGHT, THE KID'S GOOD TO GO. I'M HEADING DOWN NOW.
HOW ARE THINGS ON YOUR END?

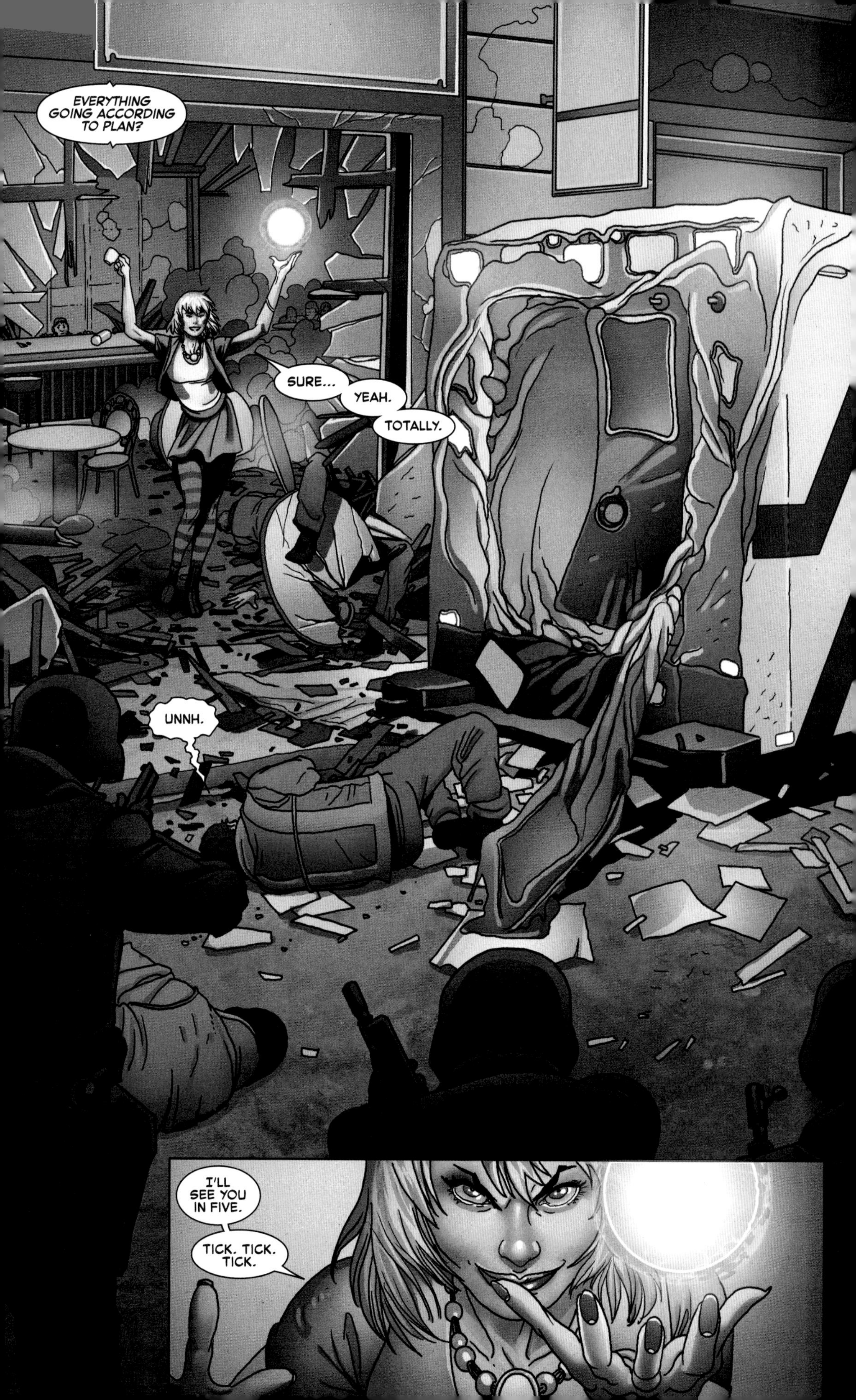
EVERYTHING GOING ACCORDING TO PLAN?
SURE...
YEAH.
TOTALLY.
UNNH.
I'LL SEE YOU IN FIVE.
TICK. TICK. TICK.

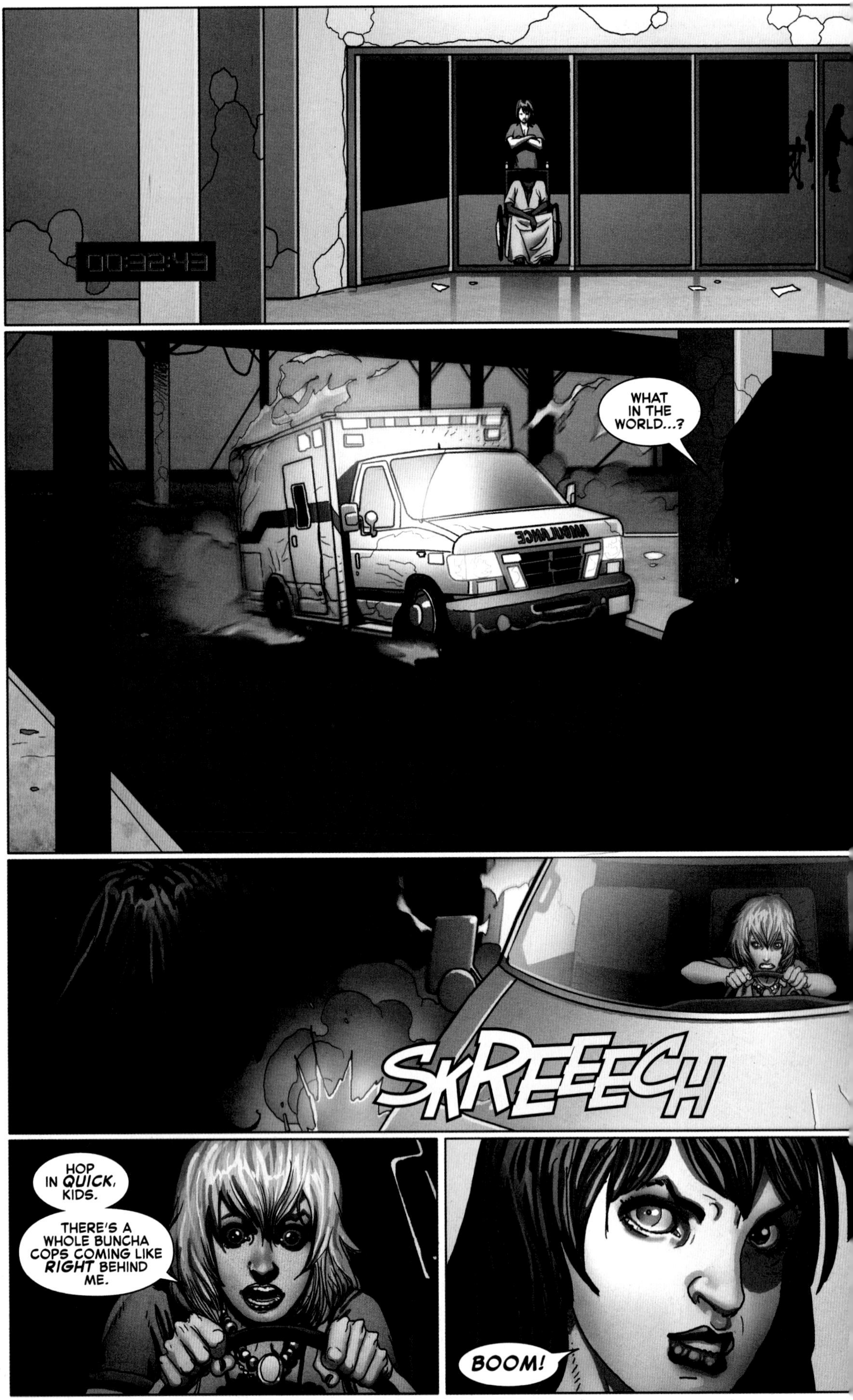

00:22:43
WHAT IN THE WORLD...?
SKREEECH
HOP IN QUICK, KIDS.
THERE'S A WHOLE BUNCHA COPS COMING LIKE RIGHT BEHIND ME.
BOOM!

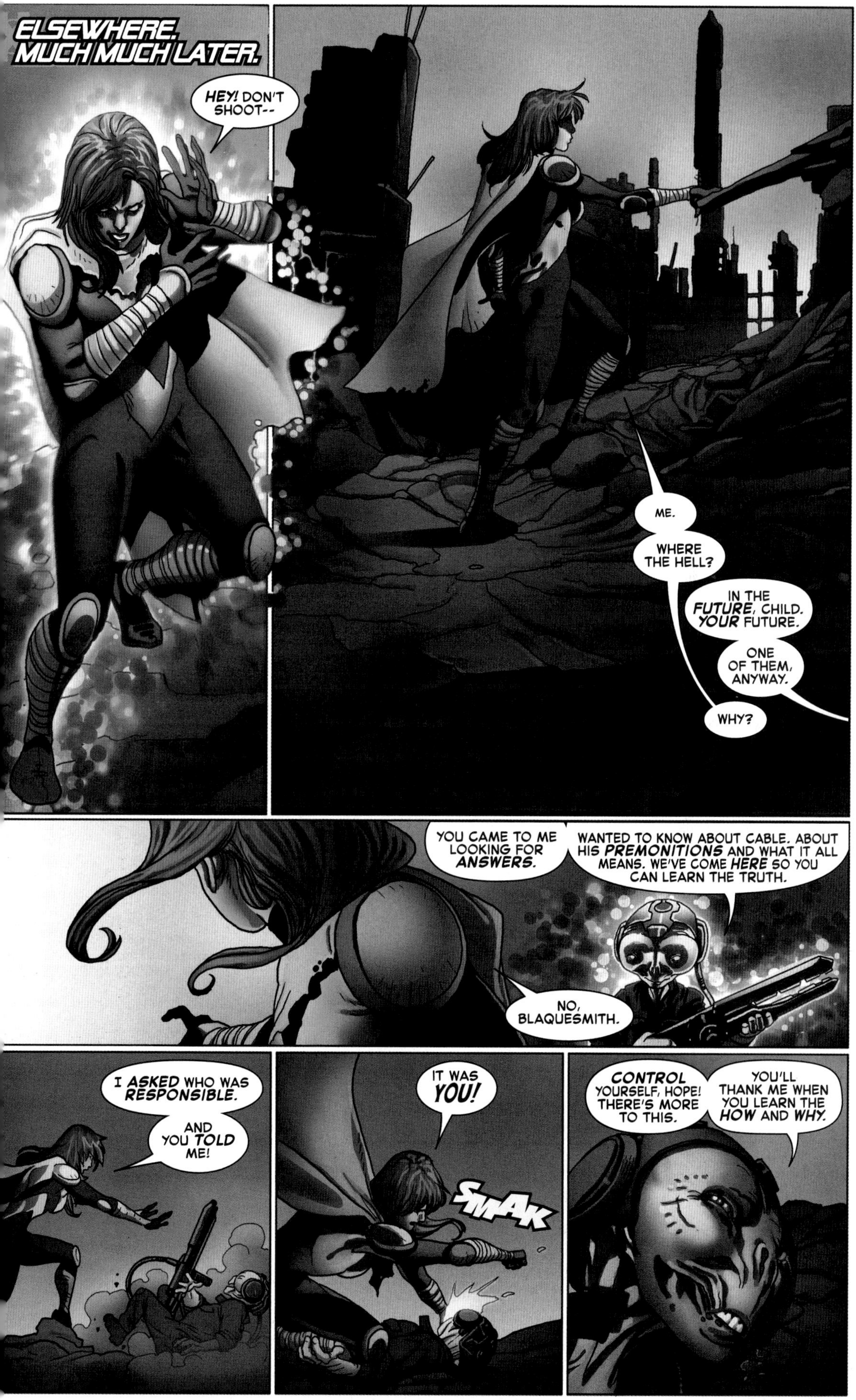

ELSEWHERE. MUCH MUCH LATER.
HEY! DON'T SHOOT--
ME.
WHERE THE HELL?
IN THE FUTURE, CHILD. YOUR FUTURE.
ONE OF THEM, ANYWAY.
WHY?
YOU CAME TO ME LOOKING FOR ANSWERS.
WANTED TO KNOW ABOUT CABLE. ABOUT HIS PREMONITIONS AND WHAT IT ALL MEANS. WE'VE COME HERE SO YOU CAN LEARN THE TRUTH.
NO, BLAQUESMITH.
I ASKED WHO WAS RESPONSIBLE.
AND YOU TOLD ME!
IT WAS YOU!
SMAK
CONTROL YOURSELF, HOPE! THERE'S MORE TO THIS.
YOU'LL THANK ME WHEN YOU LEARN THE HOW AND WHY.

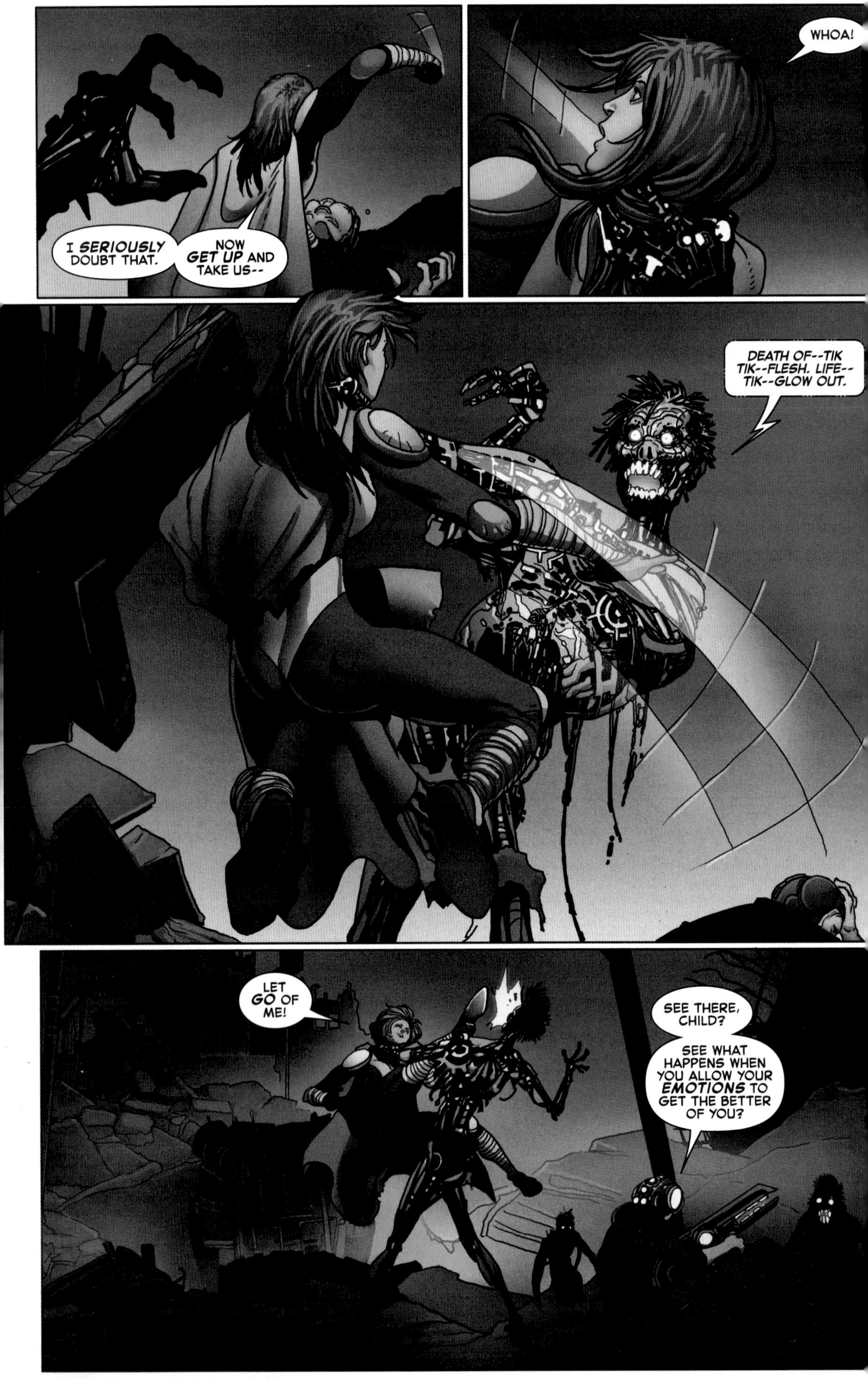
I SERIOUSLY DOUBT THAT.
NOW GET UP AND TAKE US--
WHOA!
DEATH OF--TIK TIK--FLESH. LIFE--TIK--GLOW OUT.
LET GO OF ME!
SEE THERE, CHILD?
SEE WHAT HAPPENS WHEN YOU ALLOW YOUR EMOTIONS TO GET THE BETTER OF YOU?

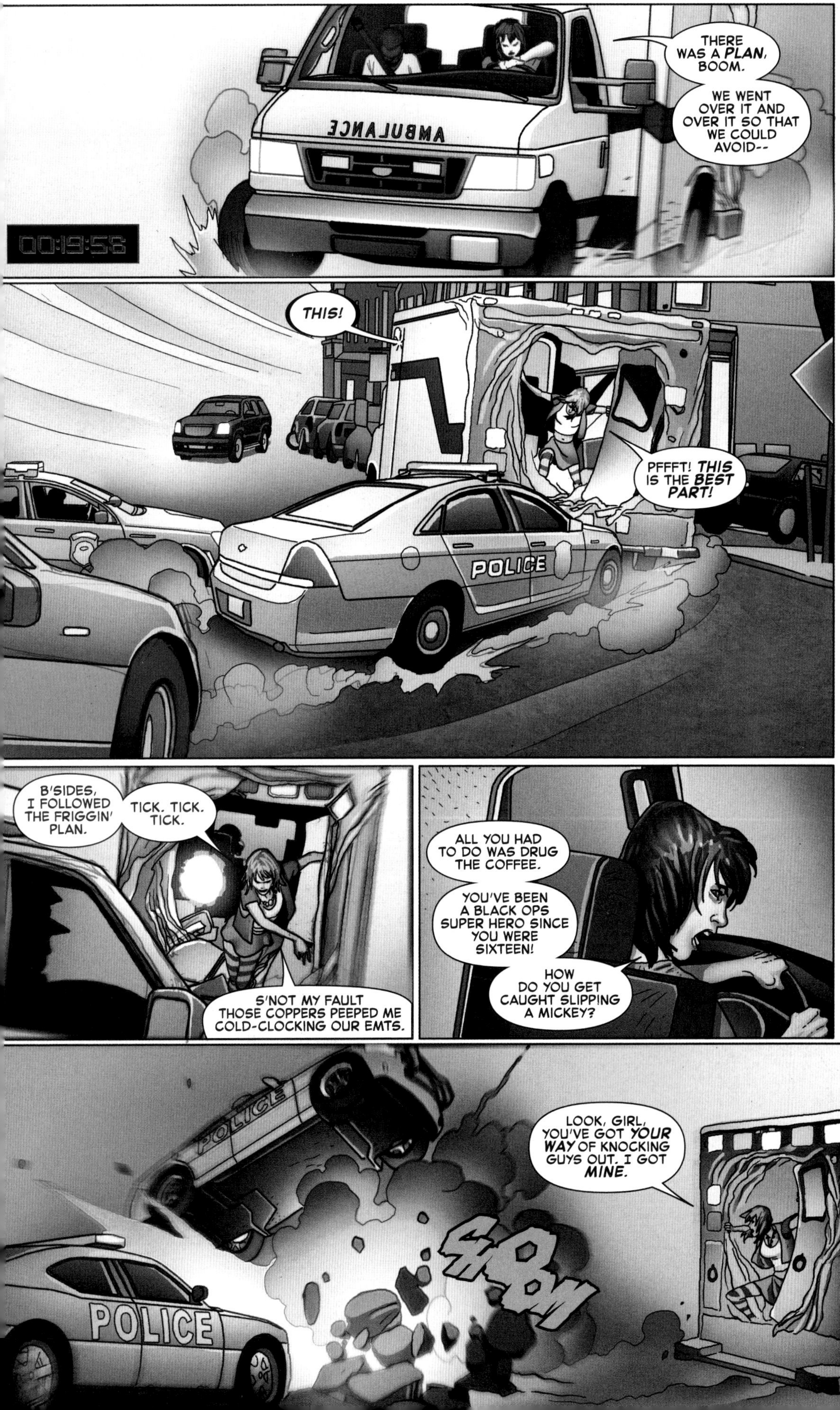

AMBULANCE
00:19:56
THERE WAS A PLAN, BOOM.
WE WENT OVER IT AND OVER IT SO THAT WE COULD AVOID--
THIS!
PFFFT! THIS IS THE BEST PART!
POLICE
B'SIDES, I FOLLOWED THE FRIGGIN' PLAN.
TICK. TICK. TICK.
S'NOT MY FAULT THOSE COPPERS PEEPED ME COLD-CLOCKING OUR EMTS.
ALL YOU HAD TO DO WAS DRUG THE COFFEE.
YOU'VE BEEN A BLACK OPS SUPER HERO SINCE YOU WERE SIXTEEN!
HOW DO YOU GET CAUGHT SLIPPING A MICKEY?
POLICE
LOOK, GIRL, YOU'VE GOT YOUR WAY OF KNOCKING GUYS OUT. I GOT MINE.
POLICE

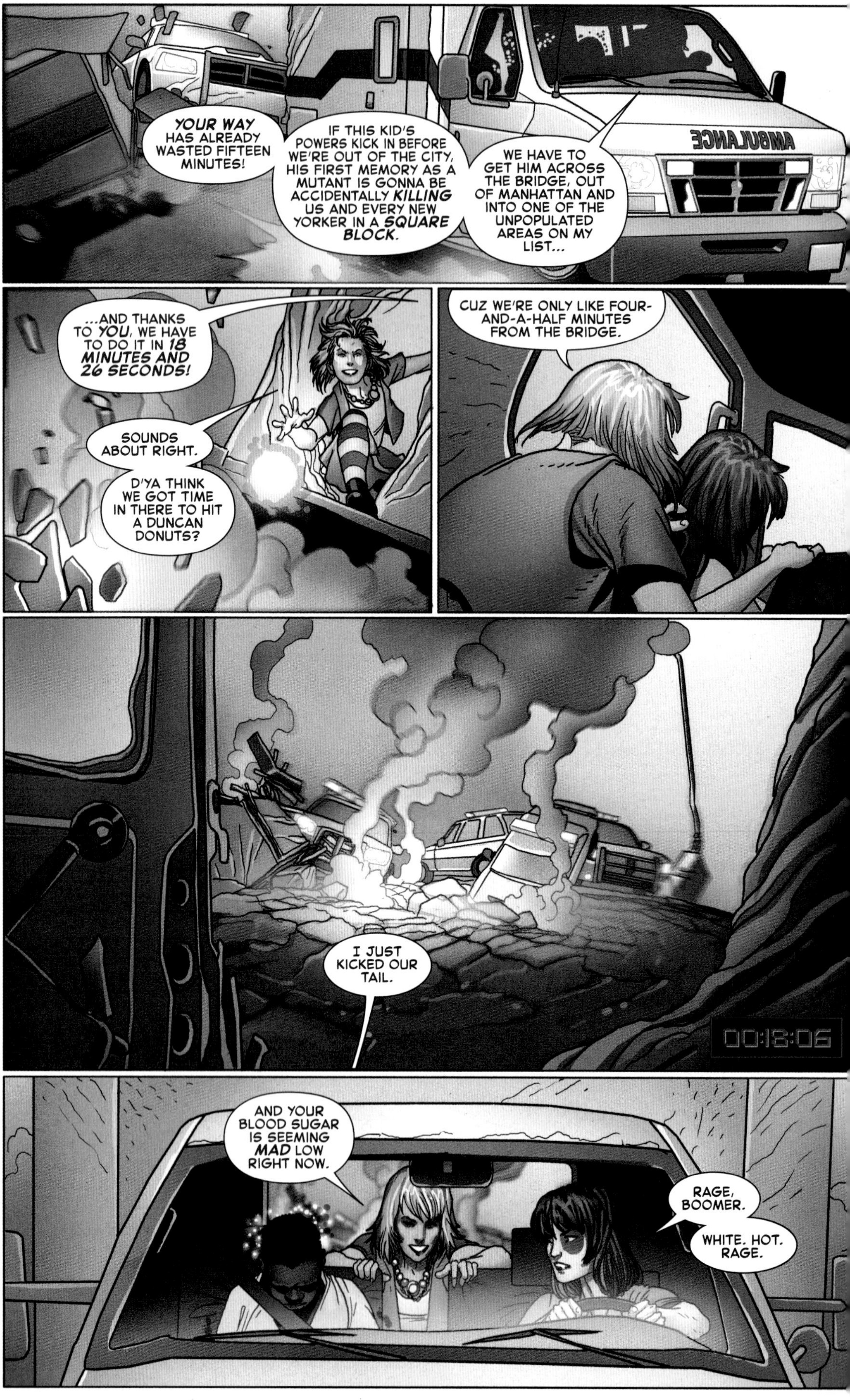
YOUR WAY HAS ALREADY WASTED FIFTEEN MINUTES!
IF THIS KID'S POWERS KICK IN BEFORE WE'RE OUT OF THE CITY, HIS FIRST MEMORY AS A MUTANT IS GONNA BE ACCIDENTALLY KILLING US AND EVERY NEW YORKER IN A SQUARE BLOCK.
WE HAVE TO GET HIM ACROSS THE BRIDGE, OUT OF MANHATTAN AND INTO ONE OF THE UNPOPULATED AREAS ON MY LIST...
AMBULANCE
...AND THANKS TO YOU, WE HAVE TO DO IT IN 18 MINUTES AND 26 SECONDS!
SOUNDS ABOUT RIGHT.
D'YA THINK WE GOT TIME IN THERE TO HIT A DUNCAN DONUTS?
CUZ WE'RE ONLY LIKE FOUR-AND-A-HALF MINUTES FROM THE BRIDGE.
I JUST KICKED OUR TAIL.
00:18:06
AND YOUR BLOOD SUGAR IS SEEMING MAD LOW RIGHT NOW.
RAGE, BOOMER.
WHITE. HOT. RAGE.

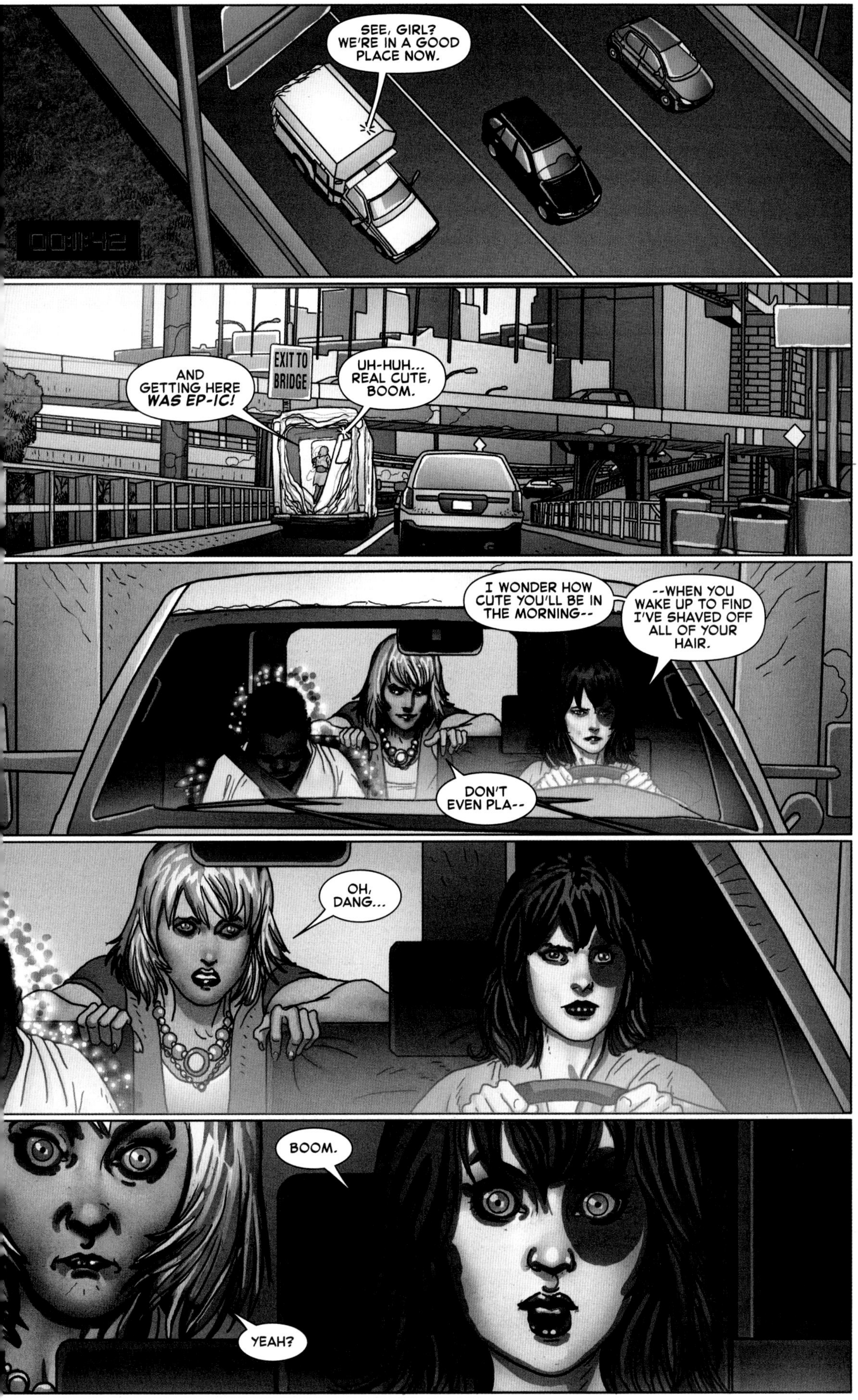
SEE, GIRL? WE'RE IN A GOOD PLACE NOW.
00:11:42
EXIT TO BRIDGE
AND GETTING HERE WAS EP-IC!
UH-HUH... REAL CUTE, BOOM.
I WONDER HOW CUTE YOU'LL BE IN THE MORNING--
--WHEN YOU WAKE UP TO FIND I'VE SHAVED OFF ALL OF YOUR HAIR.
DON'T EVEN PLA--
OH, DANG...
BOOM.
YEAH?

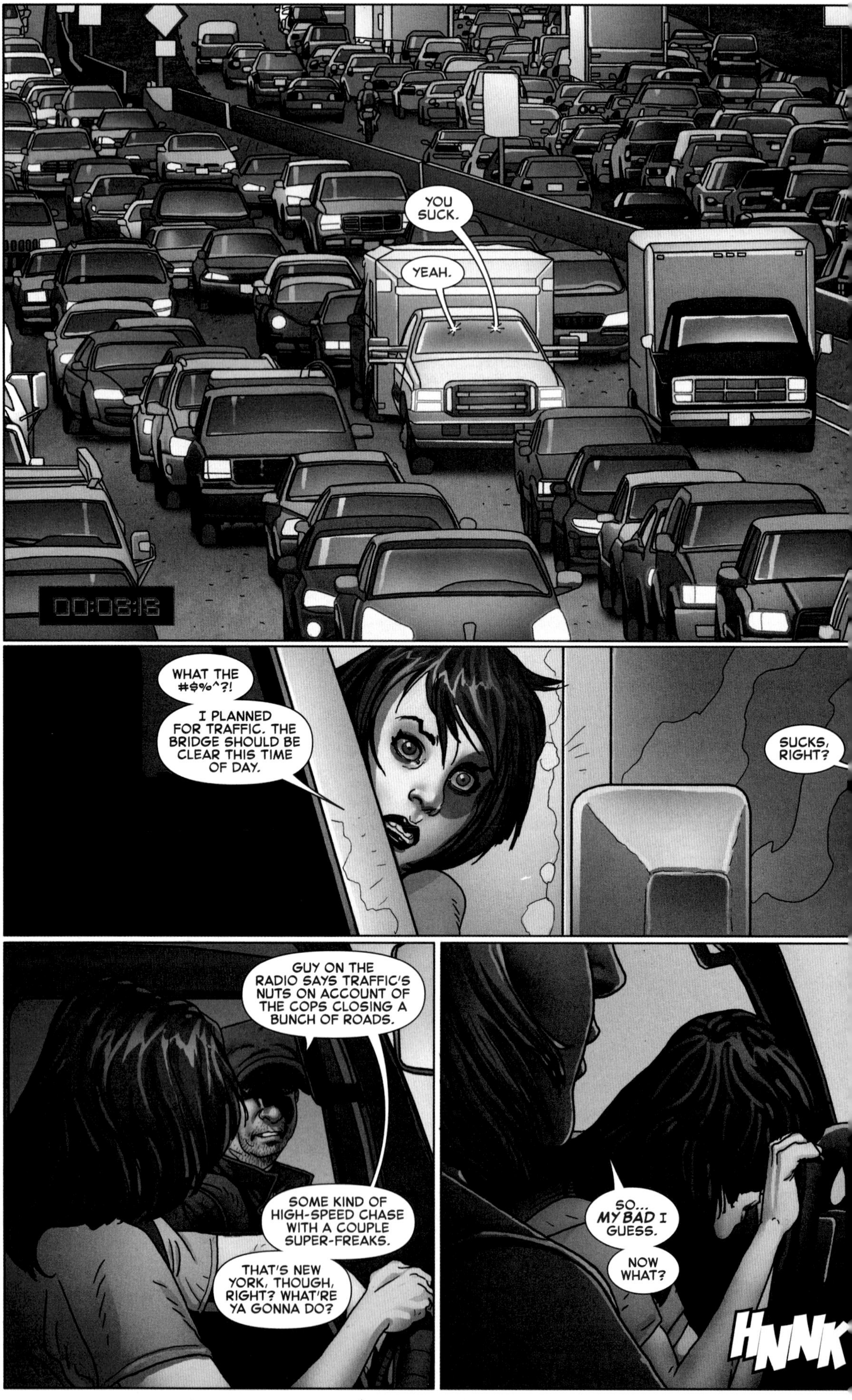
YOU SUCK.
YEAH.
00:08:18
WHAT THE #$%^?!
I PLANNED FOR TRAFFIC. THE BRIDGE SHOULD BE CLEAR THIS TIME OF DAY.
SUCKS, RIGHT?
GUY ON THE RADIO SAYS TRAFFIC'S NUTS ON ACCOUNT OF THE COPS CLOSING A BUNCH OF ROADS.
SOME KIND OF HIGH-SPEED CHASE WITH A COUPLE SUPER-FREAKS.
THAT'S NEW YORK, THOUGH, RIGHT? WHAT'RE YA GONNA DO?
SO... MY BAD I GUESS.
NOW WHAT?
HNNK

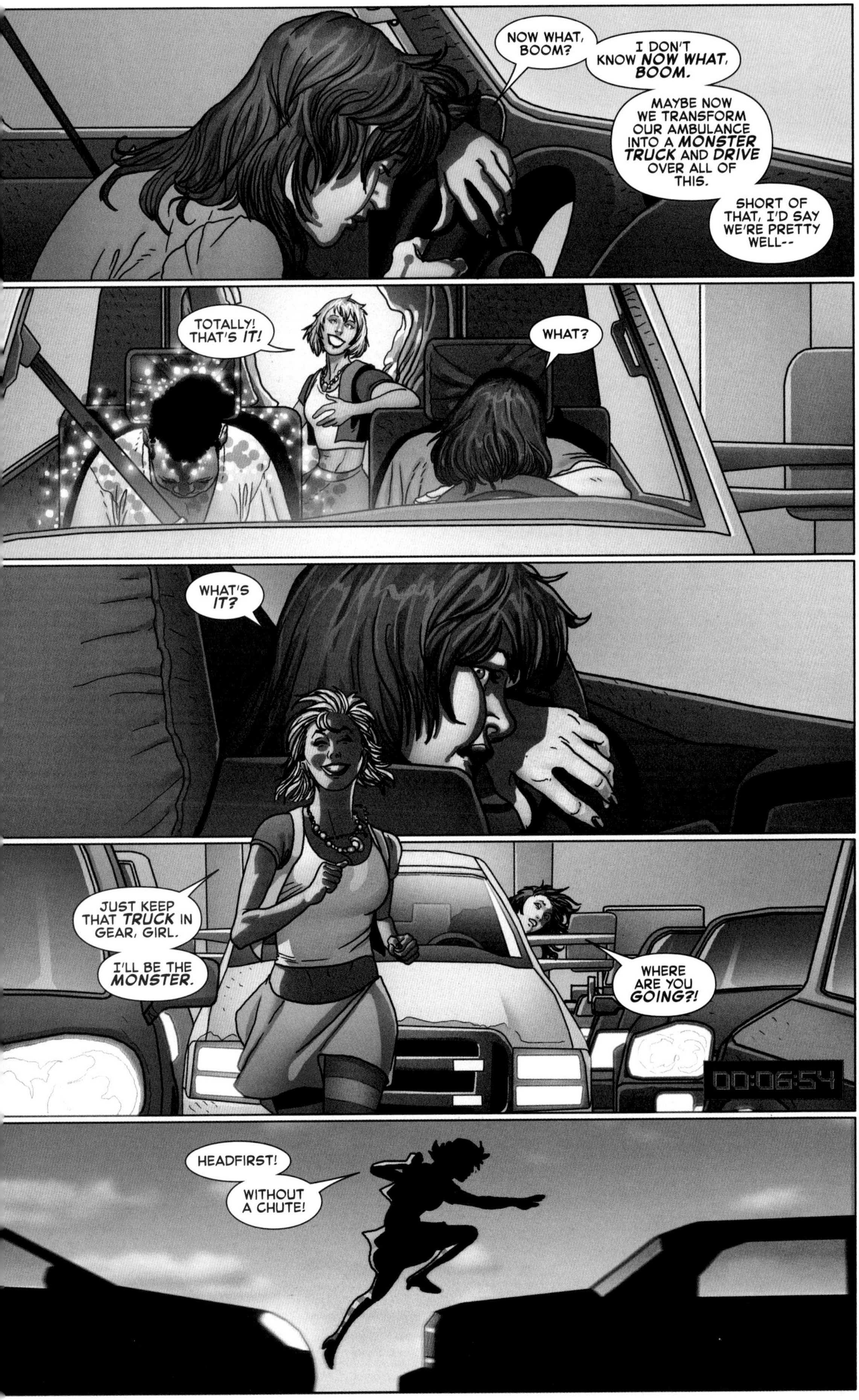
NOW WHAT, BOOM?
I DON'T KNOW NOW WHAT, BOOM.
MAYBE NOW WE TRANSFORM OUR AMBULANCE INTO A MONSTER TRUCK AND DRIVE OVER ALL OF THIS.
SHORT OF THAT, I'D SAY WE'RE PRETTY WELL--
TOTALLY! THAT'S IT!
WHAT?
WHAT'S IT?
JUST KEEP THAT TRUCK IN GEAR, GIRL.
I'LL BE THE MONSTER.
WHERE ARE YOU GOING?!
00:06:54
HEADFIRST!
WITHOUT A CHUTE!

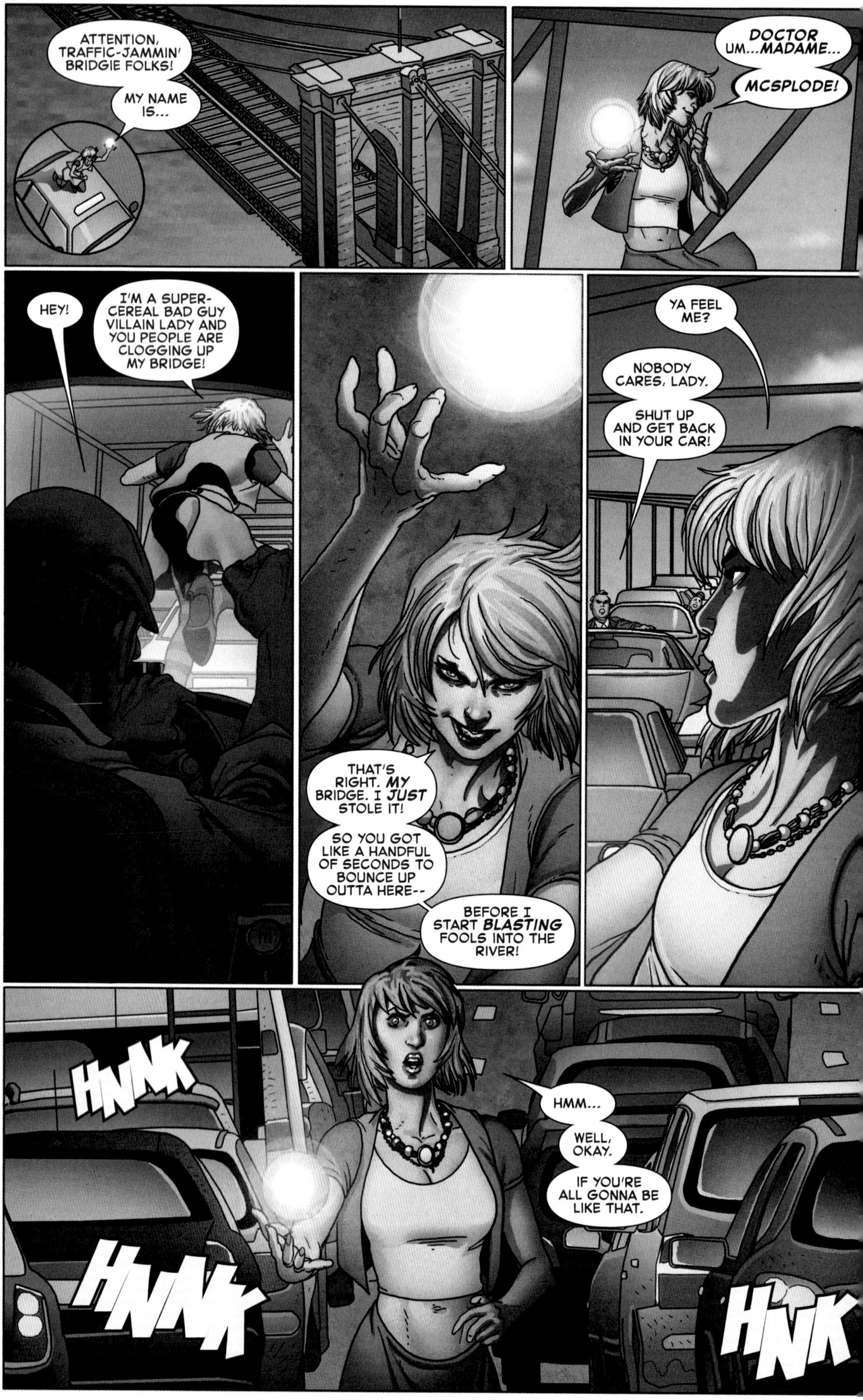
ATTENTION, TRAFFIC-JAMMIN' BRIDGIE FOLKS!
MY NAME IS...
DOCTOR UM...MADAME...
MCSPLODE!
HEY!
I'M A SUPER-CEREAL BAD GUY VILLAIN LADY AND YOU PEOPLE ARE CLOGGING UP MY BRIDGE!
THAT'S RIGHT. MY BRIDGE. I JUST STOLE IT!
SO YOU GOT LIKE A HANDFUL OF SECONDS TO BOUNCE UP OUTTA HERE--
BEFORE I START BLASTING FOOLS INTO THE RIVER!
YA FEEL ME?
NOBODY CARES, LADY.
SHUT UP AND GET BACK IN YOUR CAR!
HNNK
HMM...
WELL, OKAY.
IF YOU'RE ALL GONNA BE LIKE THAT.
HNNK
HNK

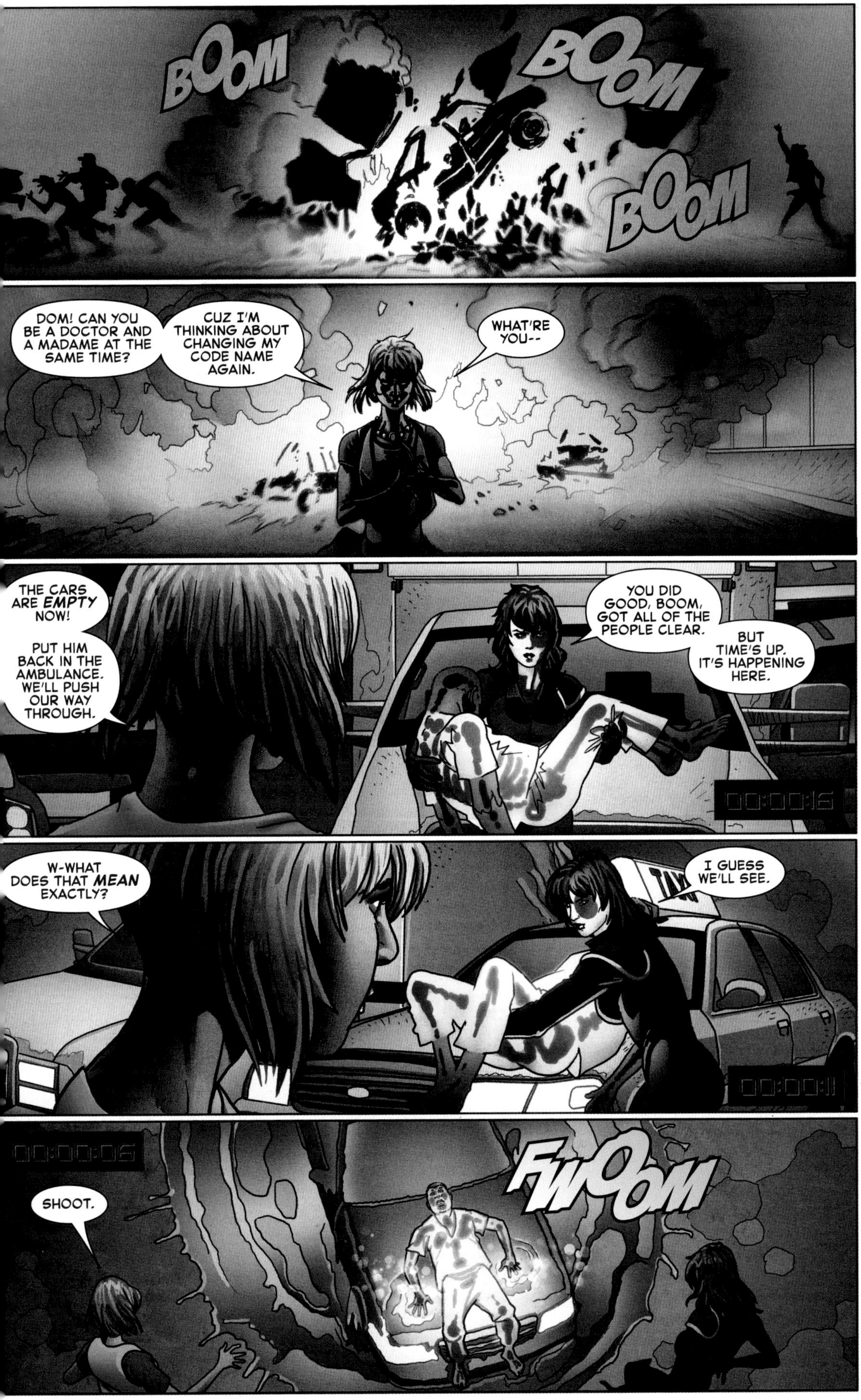
BOOM
BOOM
BOOM
DOM! CAN YOU BE A DOCTOR AND A MADAME AT THE SAME TIME?
CUZ I'M THINKING ABOUT CHANGING MY CODE NAME AGAIN.
WHAT'RE YOU--
THE CARS ARE EMPTY NOW!
PUT HIM BACK IN THE AMBULANCE. WE'LL PUSH OUR WAY THROUGH.
YOU DID GOOD, BOOM, GOT ALL OF THE PEOPLE CLEAR.
BUT TIME'S UP. IT'S HAPPENING HERE.
00:00:16
W-WHAT DOES THAT MEAN EXACTLY?
I GUESS WE'LL SEE.
00:00:11
00:00:06
FWOOM
SHOOT.

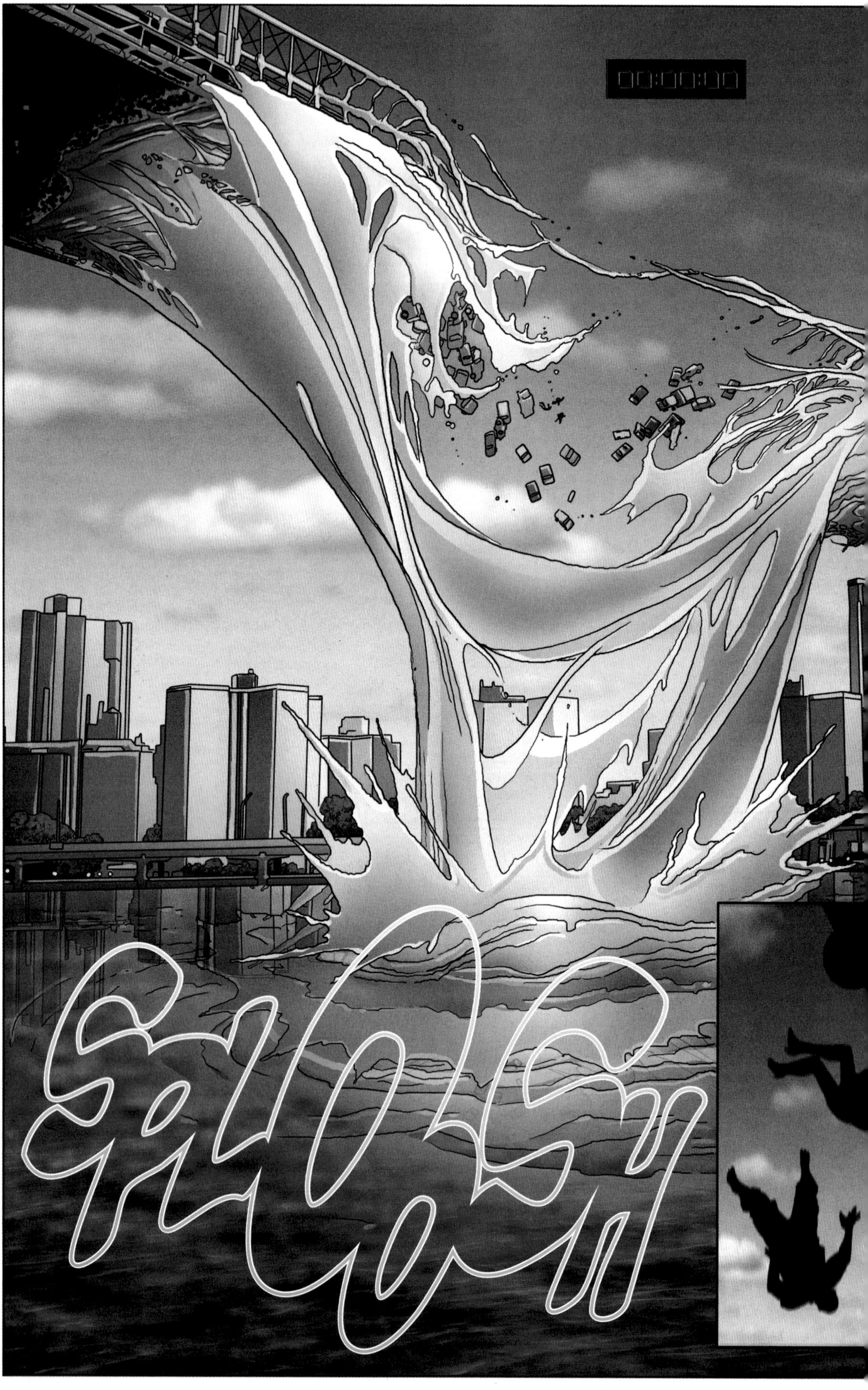
00:00:00

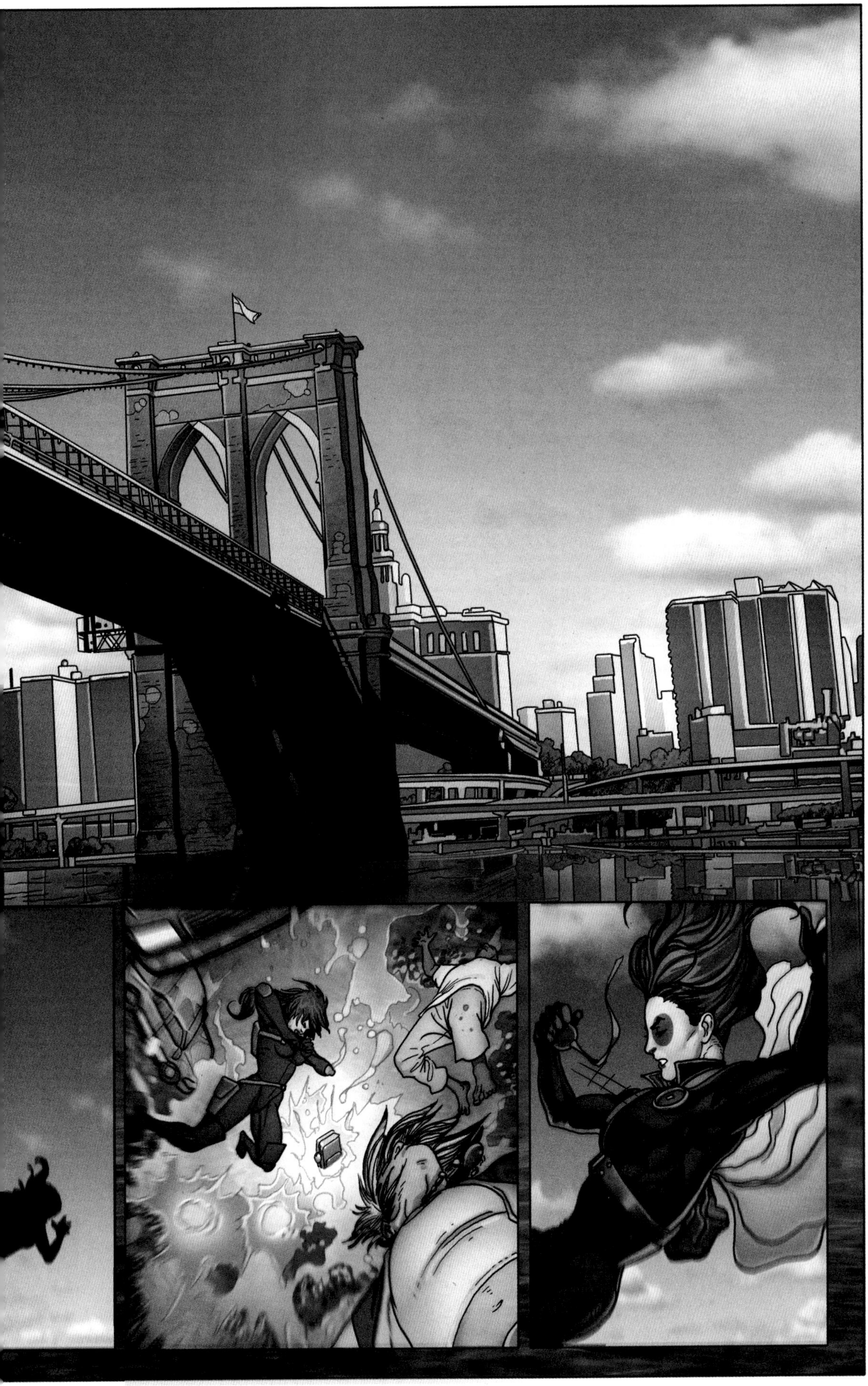

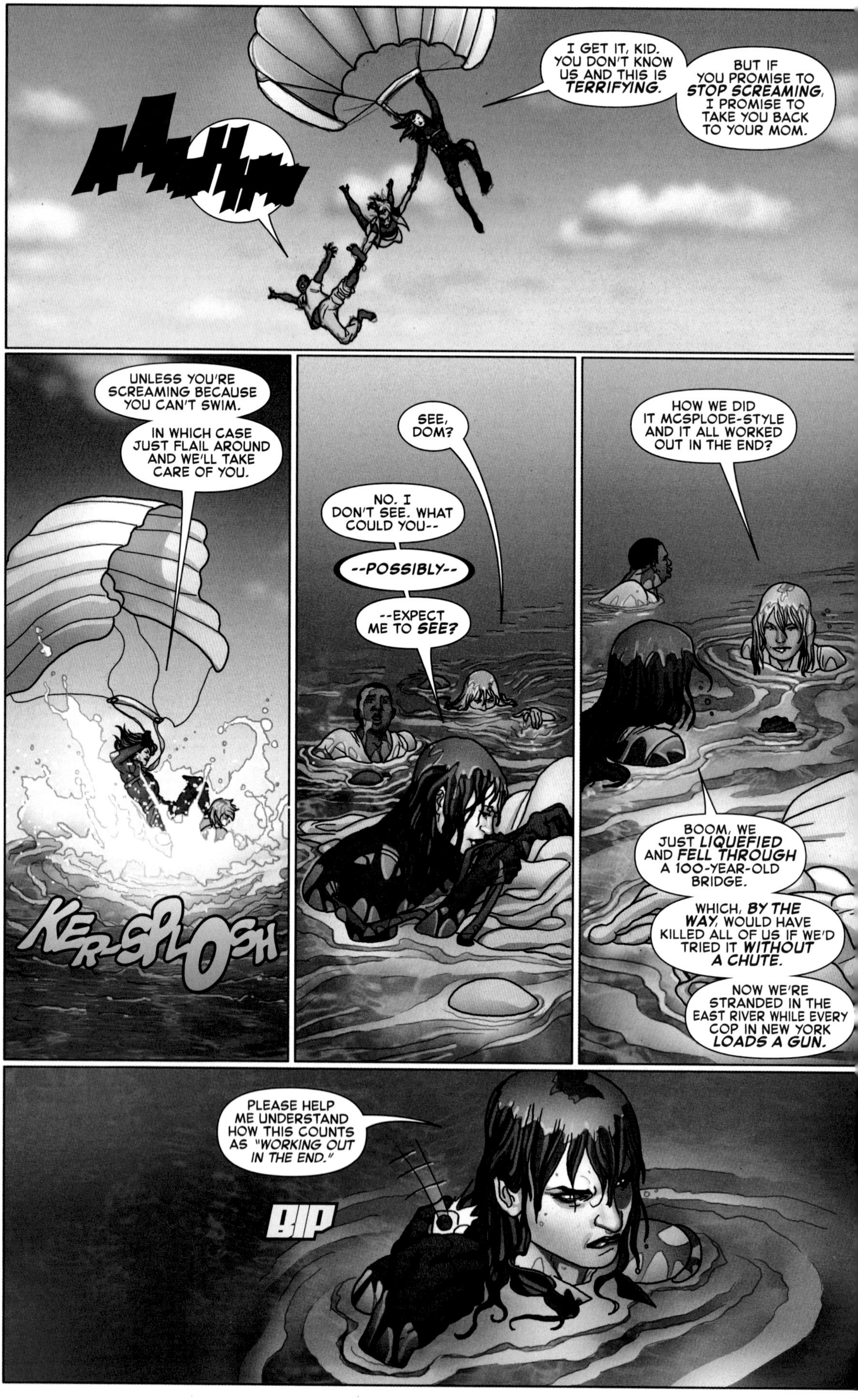
AAAHHHH
I GET IT, KID. YOU DON'T KNOW US AND THIS IS *TERRIFYING.*
BUT IF YOU PROMISE TO *STOP SCREAMING,* I PROMISE TO TAKE YOU BACK TO YOUR MOM.
UNLESS YOU'RE SCREAMING BECAUSE YOU CAN'T SWIM.
IN WHICH CASE JUST FLAIL AROUND AND WE'LL TAKE CARE OF YOU.
KER-SPLOSH
SEE, DOM?
NO. I DON'T SEE. WHAT COULD YOU--
--POSSIBLY--
--EXPECT ME TO *SEE?*
HOW WE DID IT MCSPLODE-STYLE AND IT ALL WORKED OUT IN THE END?
BOOM, WE JUST *LIQUEFIED* AND *FELL THROUGH* A 100-YEAR-OLD BRIDGE.
WHICH, *BY THE WAY,* WOULD HAVE KILLED ALL OF US IF WE'D TRIED IT *WITHOUT A CHUTE.*
NOW WE'RE STRANDED IN THE EAST RIVER WHILE EVERY COP IN NEW YORK *LOADS A GUN.*
PLEASE HELP ME UNDERSTAND HOW THIS COUNTS AS *"WORKING OUT IN THE END."*
BIP

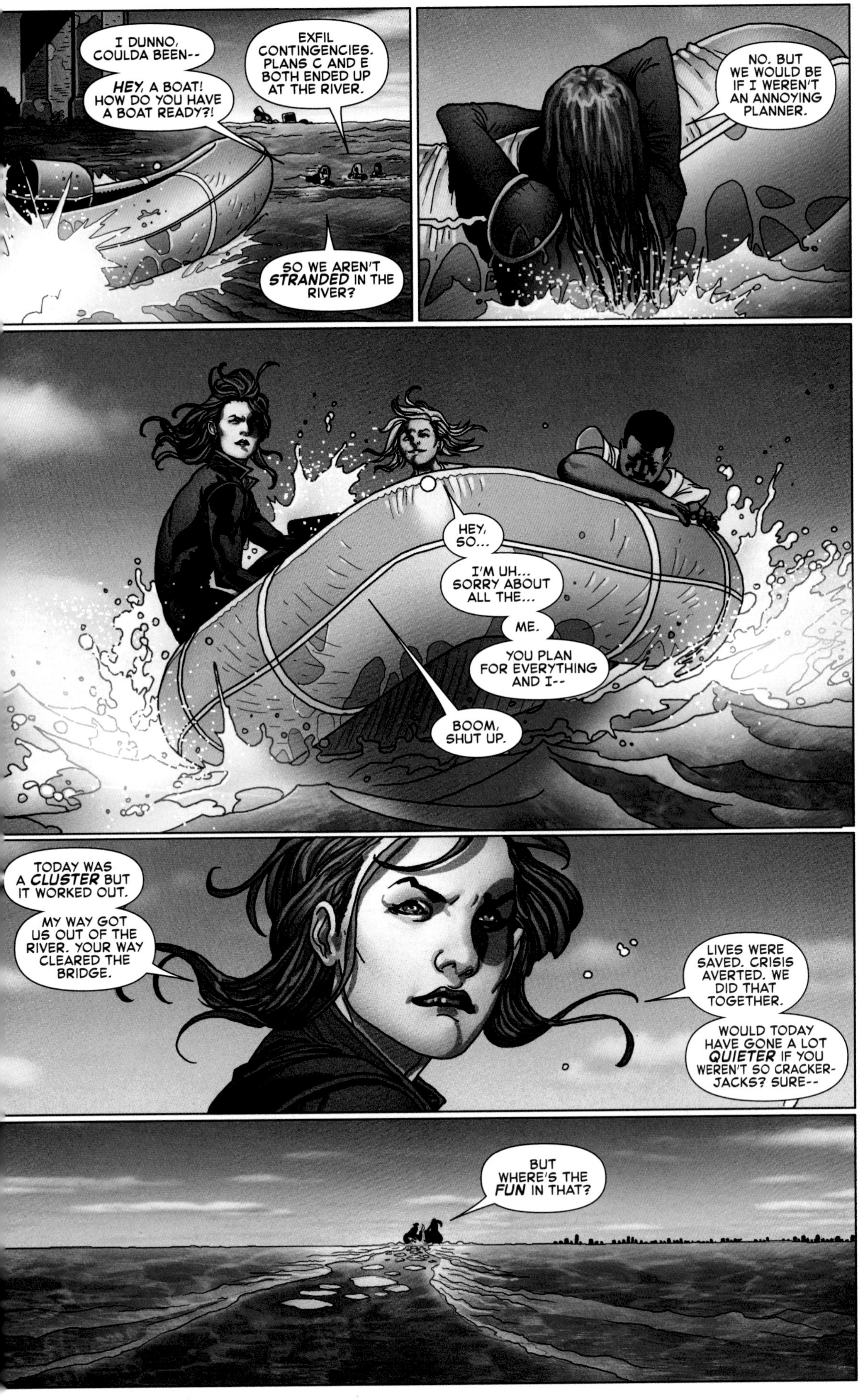

I DUNNO, COULDA BEEN--
HEY, A BOAT! HOW DO YOU HAVE A BOAT READY?!
EXFIL CONTINGENCIES. PLANS C AND E BOTH ENDED UP AT THE RIVER.
SO WE AREN'T *STRANDED* IN THE RIVER?
NO. BUT WE WOULD BE IF I WEREN'T AN ANNOYING PLANNER.
HEY, SO...
I'M UH... SORRY ABOUT ALL THE...
ME.
YOU PLAN FOR EVERYTHING AND I--
BOOM, SHUT UP.
TODAY WAS A *CLUSTER* BUT IT WORKED OUT.
MY WAY GOT US OUT OF THE RIVER. YOUR WAY CLEARED THE BRIDGE.
LIVES WERE SAVED. CRISIS AVERTED. WE DID THAT TOGETHER.
WOULD TODAY HAVE GONE A LOT *QUIETER* IF YOU WEREN'T SO CRACKER-JACKS? SURE--
BUT WHERE'S THE *FUN* IN THAT?

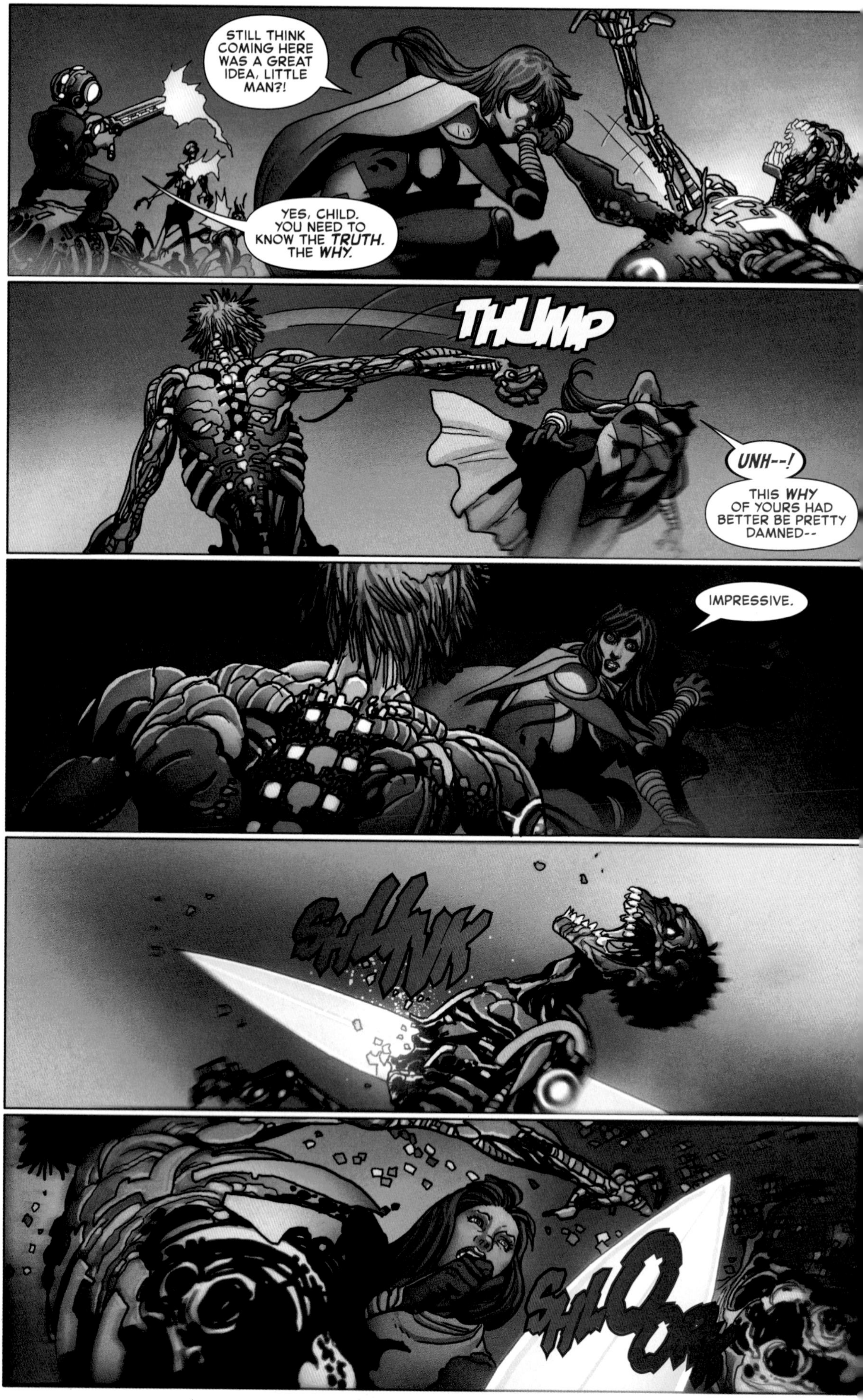
STILL THINK COMING HERE WAS A GREAT IDEA, LITTLE MAN?!
YES, CHILD. YOU NEED TO KNOW THE TRUTH. THE WHY.
THUMP
UNH--!
THIS WHY OF YOURS HAD BETTER BE PRETTY DAMNED--
IMPRESSIVE.
SHUNK

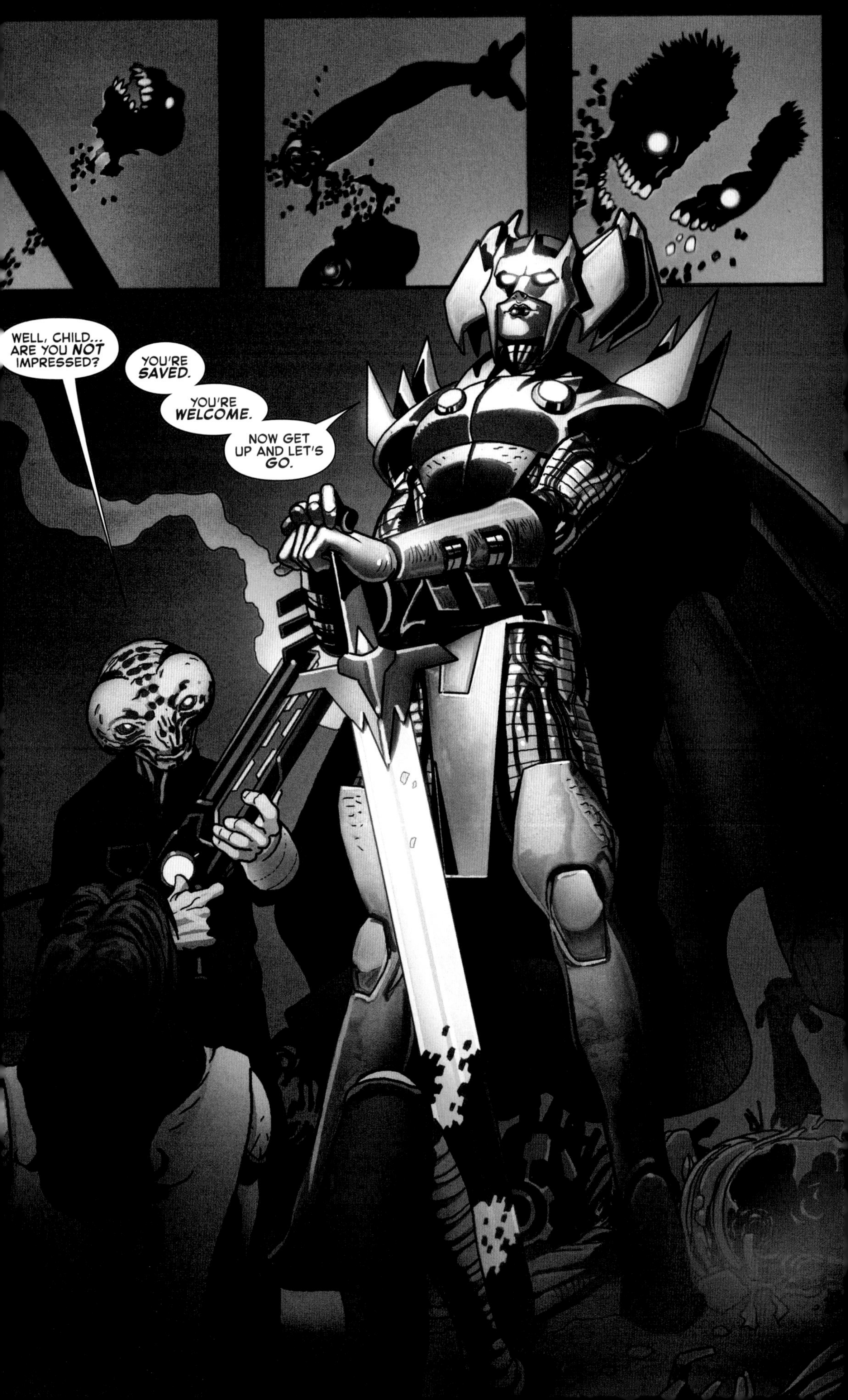
WELL, CHILD... ARE YOU NOT IMPRESSED?
YOU'RE SAVED.
YOU'RE WELCOME.
NOW GET UP AND LET'S GO.

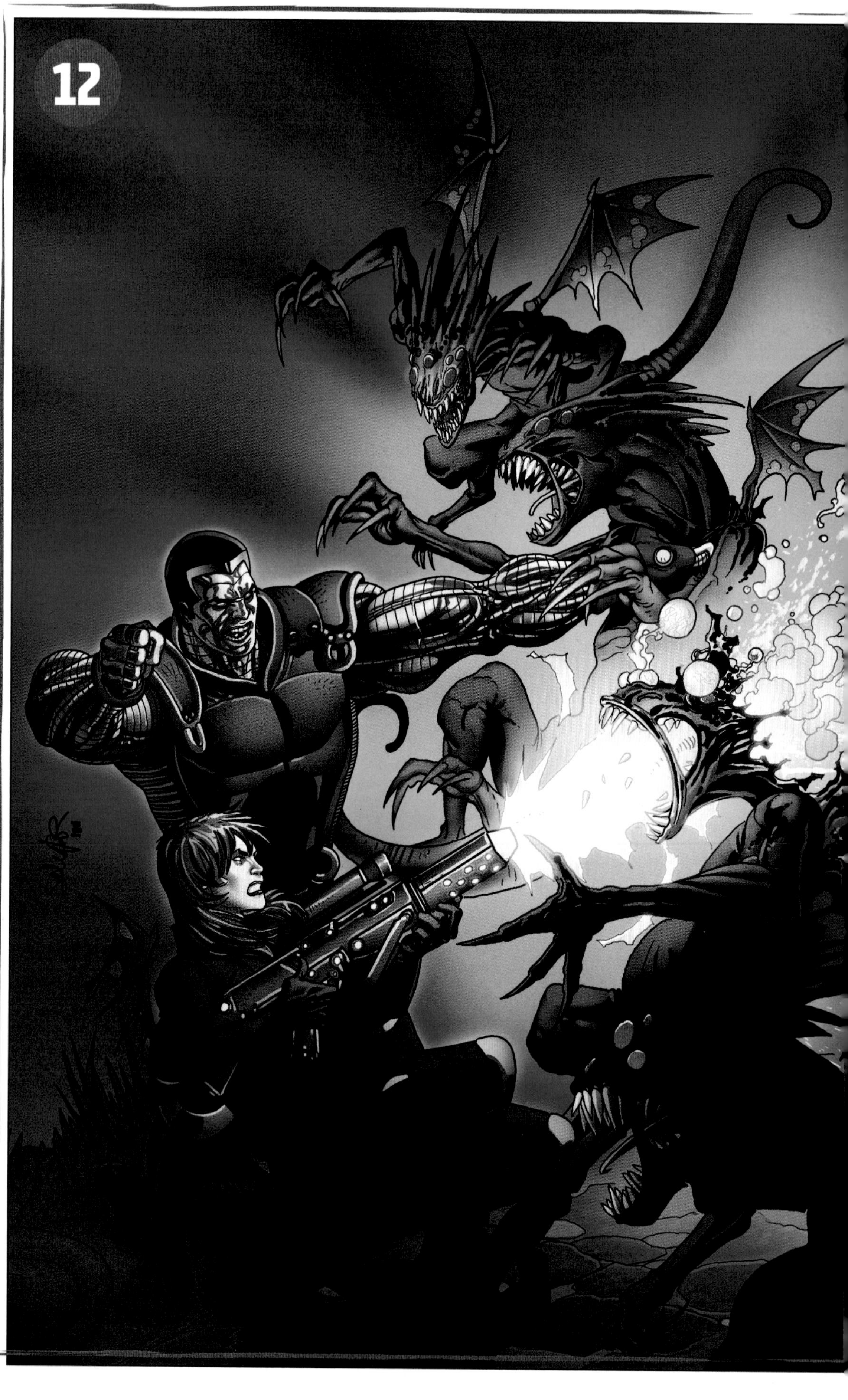
12

ZURICH.

RBS FINANCIAL HOLDINGS.

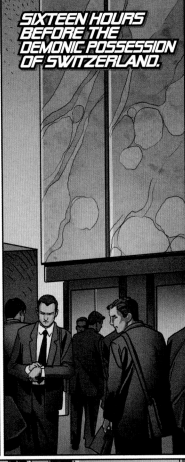

SIXTEEN HOURS BEFORE THE DEMONIC POSSESSION OF SWITZERLAND.

I'M *SORRY* FOR THIS, MY FRIEND.

HRRG...

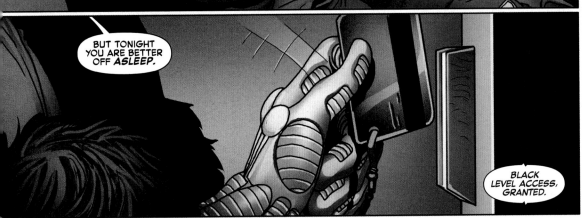

BUT TONIGHT YOU ARE BETTER OFF *ASLEEP.*

BLACK LEVEL ACCESS, GRANTED.

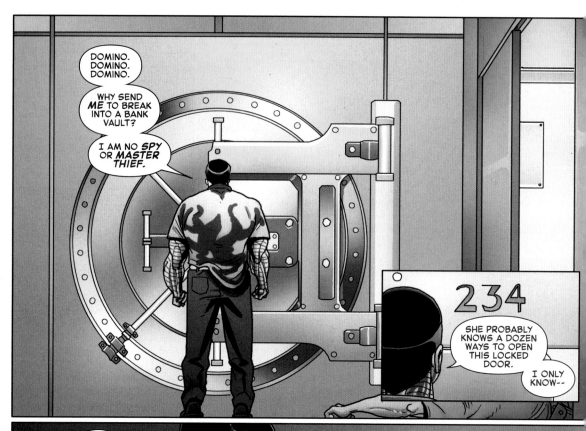

DOMINO. DOMINO. DOMINO.

WHY SEND *ME* TO BREAK INTO A BANK VAULT?

I AM NO *SPY* OR *MASTER THIEF.*

234

SHE PROBABLY KNOWS A DOZEN WAYS TO OPEN THIS LOCKED DOOR.

I ONLY KNOW--

--THE ONE.

WHOOM

WHOOM

MUCH AS I LOVE WATCHING YOU PUNCH THINGS, PETE...

WHY DON'T YOU COOL YOUR JETS?

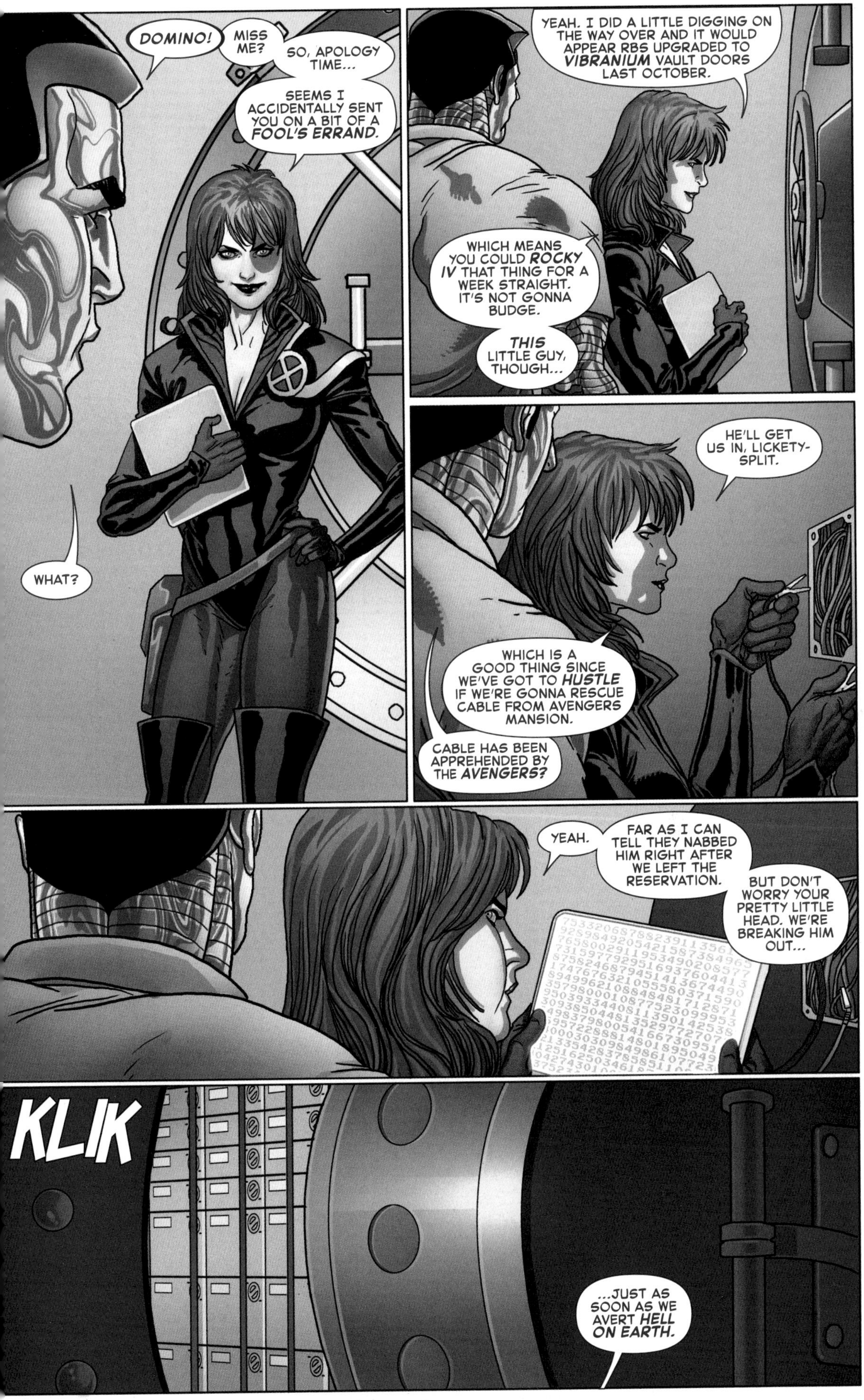
DOMINO!
MISS ME?
SO, APOLOGY TIME...
SEEMS I ACCIDENTALLY SENT YOU ON A BIT OF A FOOL'S ERRAND.
WHAT?
YEAH. I DID A LITTLE DIGGING ON THE WAY OVER AND IT WOULD APPEAR RBS UPGRADED TO VIBRANIUM VAULT DOORS LAST OCTOBER.
WHICH MEANS YOU COULD ROCKY IV THAT THING FOR A WEEK STRAIGHT. IT'S NOT GONNA BUDGE.
THIS LITTLE GUY, THOUGH...
HE'LL GET US IN, LICKETY-SPLIT.
WHICH IS A GOOD THING SINCE WE'VE GOT TO HUSTLE IF WE'RE GONNA RESCUE CABLE FROM AVENGERS MANSION.
CABLE HAS BEEN APPREHENDED BY THE AVENGERS?
YEAH.
FAR AS I CAN TELL THEY NABBED HIM RIGHT AFTER WE LEFT THE RESERVATION.
BUT DON'T WORRY YOUR PRETTY LITTLE HEAD. WE'RE BREAKING HIM OUT...
KLIK
...JUST AS SOON AS WE AVERT HELL ON EARTH.

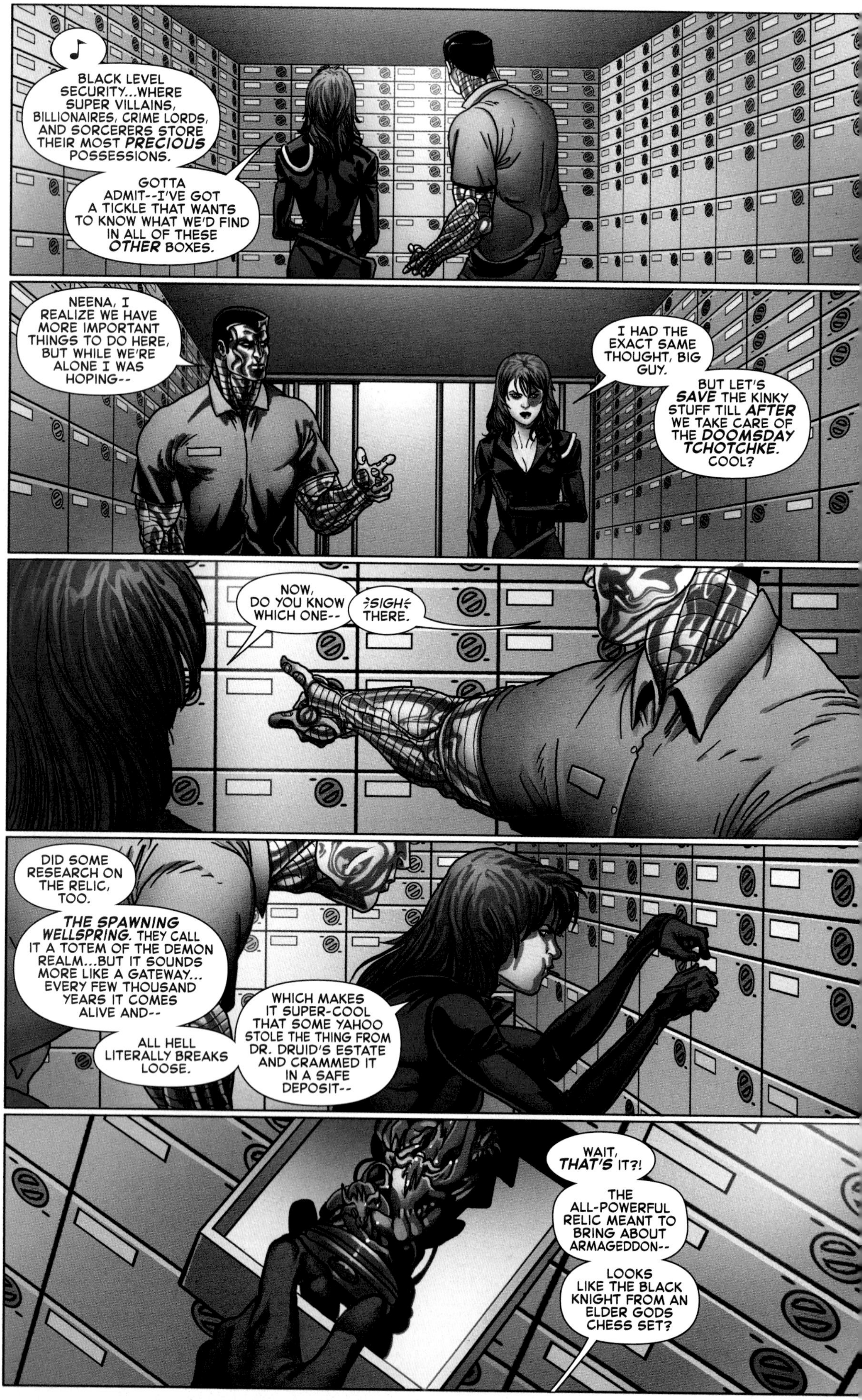
♪
BLACK LEVEL SECURITY...WHERE SUPER VILLAINS, BILLIONAIRES, CRIME LORDS, AND SORCERERS STORE THEIR MOST PRECIOUS POSSESSIONS.
GOTTA ADMIT--I'VE GOT A TICKLE THAT WANTS TO KNOW WHAT WE'D FIND IN ALL OF THESE OTHER BOXES.
NEENA, I REALIZE WE HAVE MORE IMPORTANT THINGS TO DO HERE, BUT WHILE WE'RE ALONE I WAS HOPING--
I HAD THE EXACT SAME THOUGHT, BIG GUY.
BUT LET'S SAVE THE KINKY STUFF TILL AFTER WE TAKE CARE OF THE DOOMSDAY TCHOTCHKE. COOL?
NOW, DO YOU KNOW WHICH ONE--
SIGH THERE.
DID SOME RESEARCH ON THE RELIC, TOO.
THE SPAWNING WELLSPRING. THEY CALL IT A TOTEM OF THE DEMON REALM...BUT IT SOUNDS MORE LIKE A GATEWAY... EVERY FEW THOUSAND YEARS IT COMES ALIVE AND--
ALL HELL LITERALLY BREAKS LOOSE.
WHICH MAKES IT SUPER-COOL THAT SOME YAHOO STOLE THE THING FROM DR. DRUID'S ESTATE AND CRAMMED IT IN A SAFE DEPOSIT--
WAIT, THAT'S IT?!
THE ALL-POWERFUL RELIC MEANT TO BRING ABOUT ARMAGEDDON--
LOOKS LIKE THE BLACK KNIGHT FROM AN ELDER GODS CHESS SET?

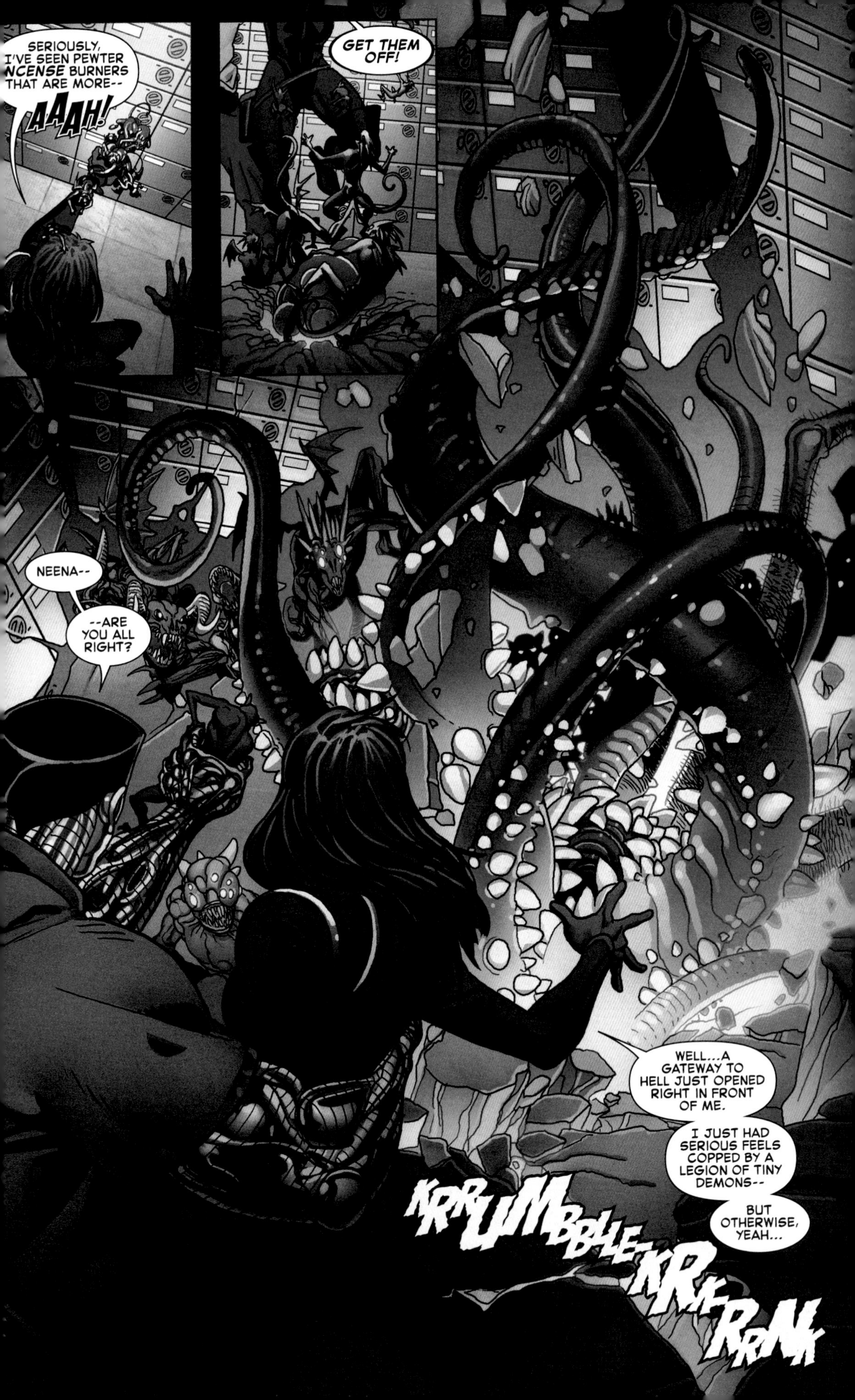

SERIOUSLY, I'VE SEEN PEWTER NCENSE BURNERS THAT ARE MORE--
AAAH!
GET THEM OFF!
NEENA--
--ARE YOU ALL RIGHT?
WELL...A GATEWAY TO HELL JUST OPENED RIGHT IN FRONT OF ME.
I JUST HAD SERIOUS FEELS COPPED BY A LEGION OF TINY DEMONS--
BUT OTHERWISE, YEAH...
KRRUMBBLE-KRKRRNK

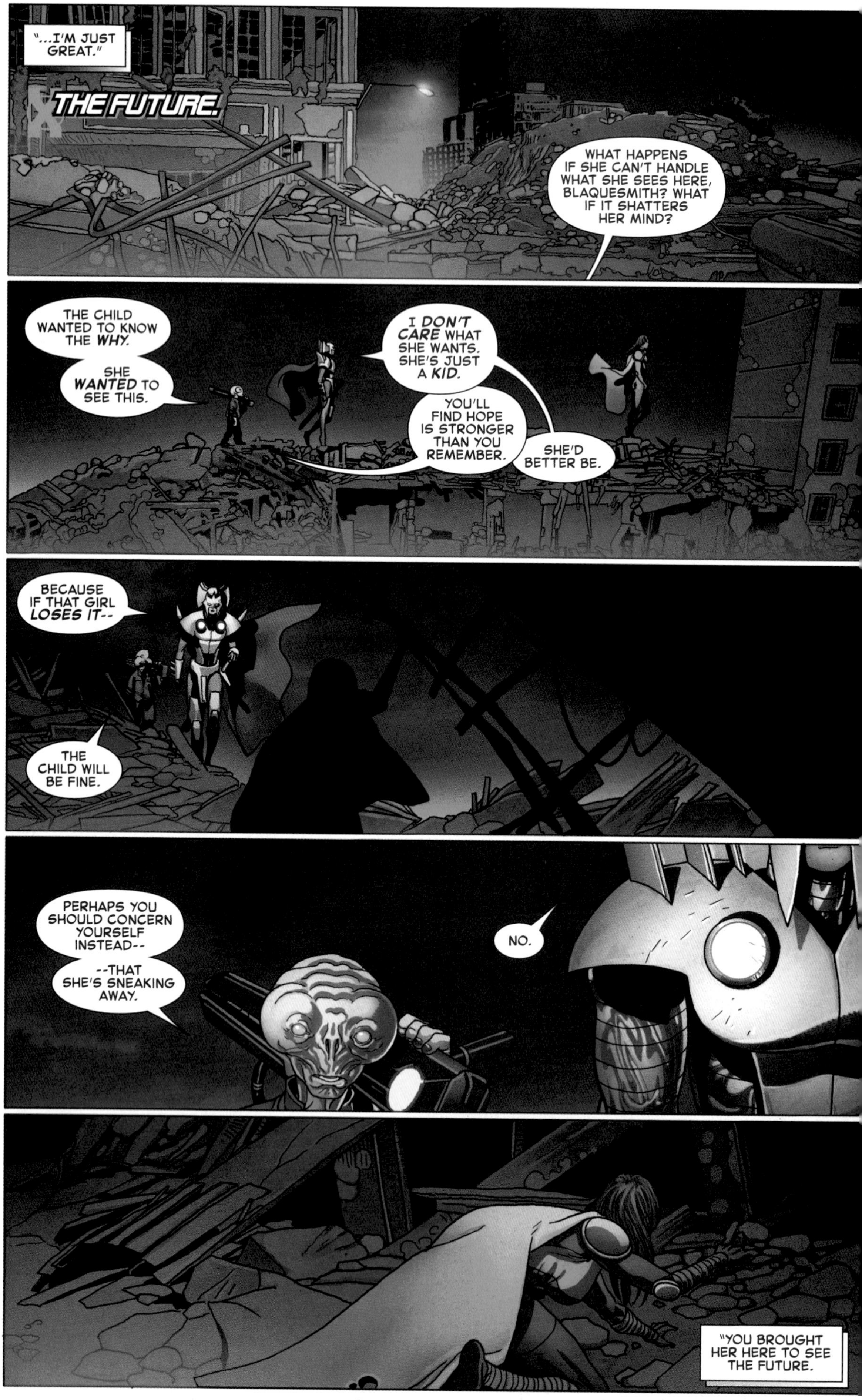
"...I'M JUST GREAT."
THE FUTURE.
WHAT HAPPENS IF SHE CAN'T HANDLE WHAT SHE SEES HERE, BLAQUESMITH? WHAT IF IT SHATTERS HER MIND?
THE CHILD WANTED TO KNOW THE WHY.
SHE WANTED TO SEE THIS.
I DON'T CARE WHAT SHE WANTS. SHE'S JUST A KID.
YOU'LL FIND HOPE IS STRONGER THAN YOU REMEMBER.
SHE'D BETTER BE.
BECAUSE IF THAT GIRL LOSES IT--
THE CHILD WILL BE FINE.
PERHAPS YOU SHOULD CONCERN YOURSELF INSTEAD--
--THAT SHE'S SNEAKING AWAY.
NO.
"YOU BROUGHT HER HERE TO SEE THE FUTURE.

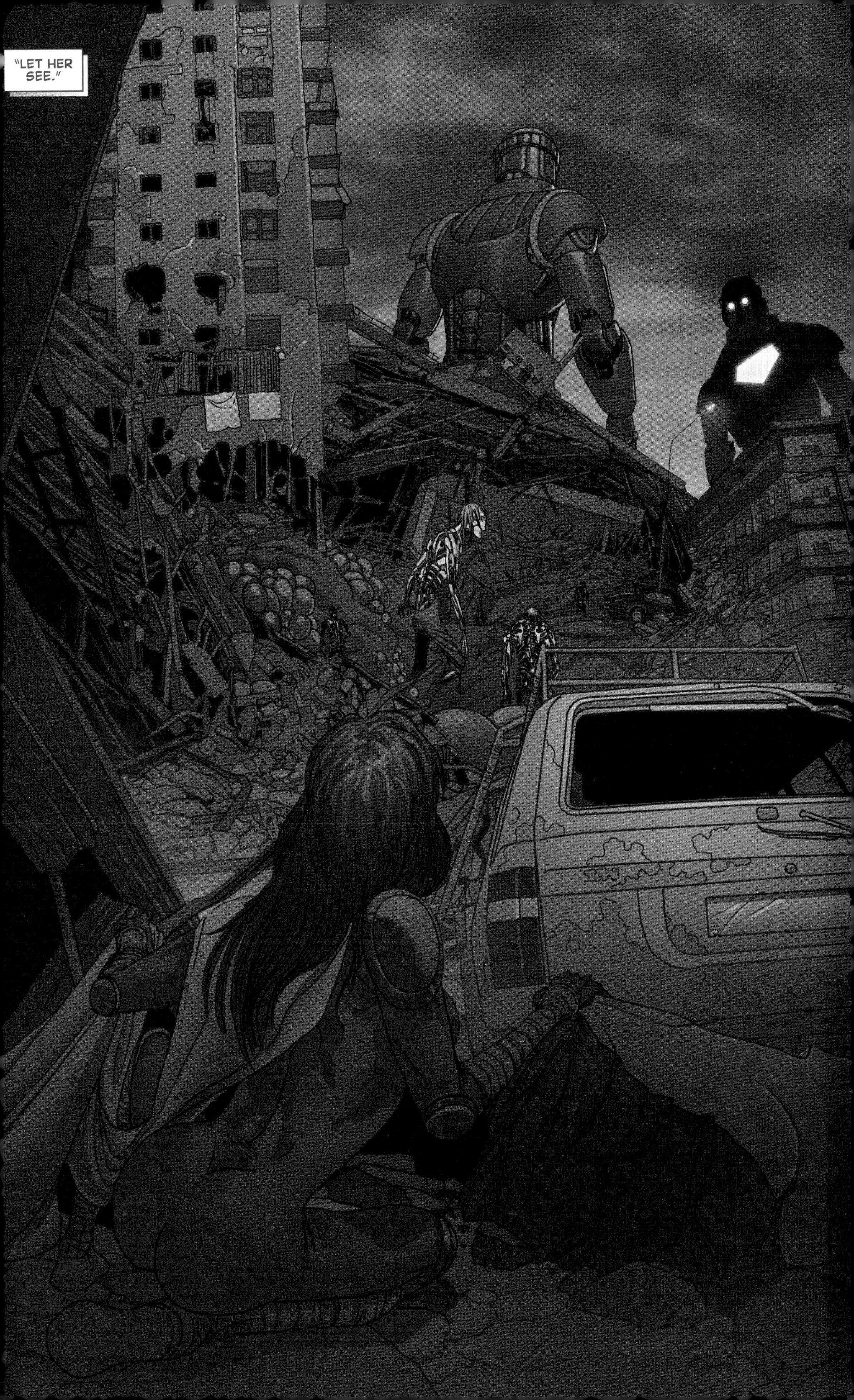
"LET HER SEE."

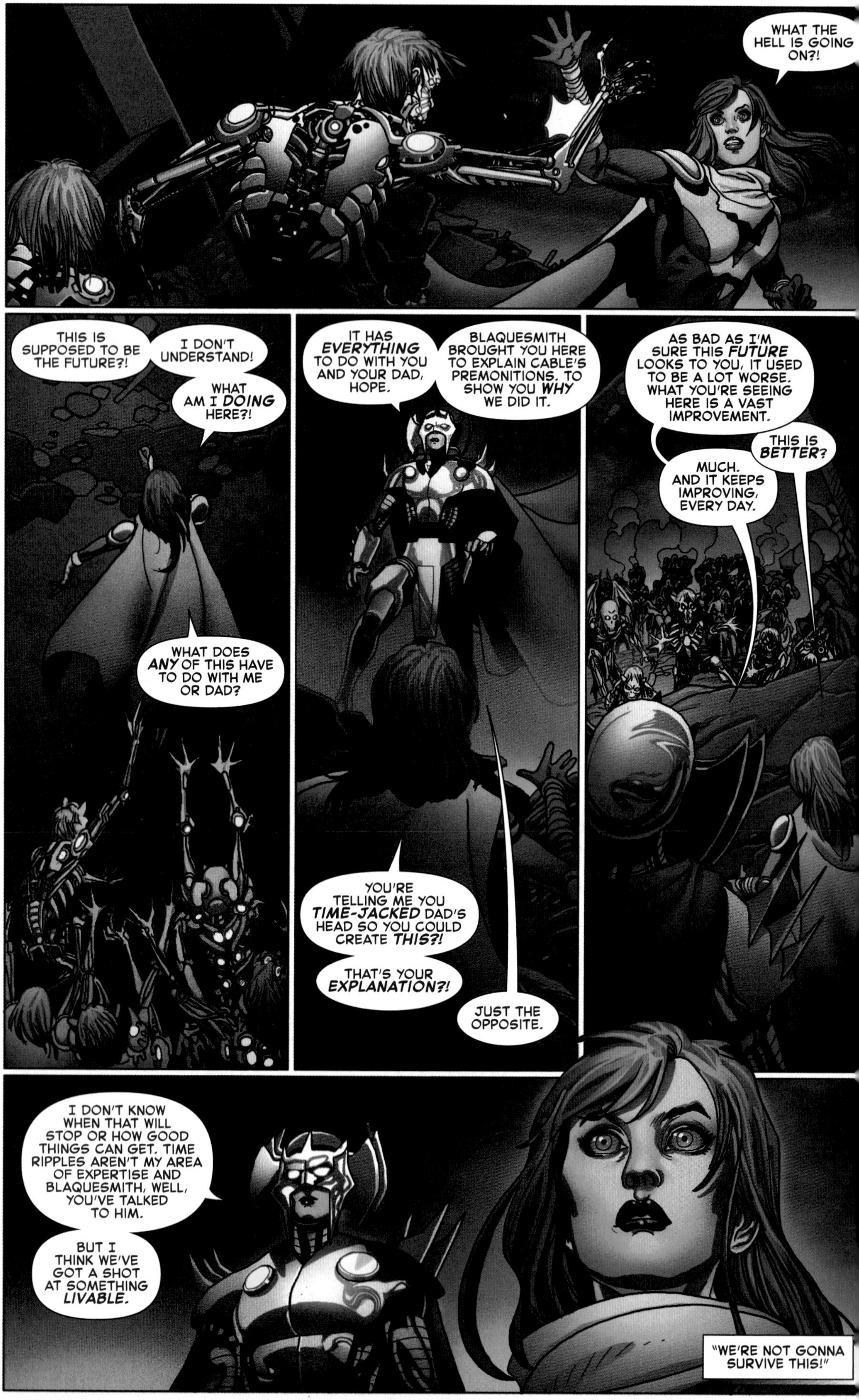

WHAT THE HELL IS GOING ON?!
THIS IS SUPPOSED TO BE THE FUTURE?!
I DON'T UNDERSTAND!
WHAT AM I DOING HERE?!
WHAT DOES ANY OF THIS HAVE TO DO WITH ME OR DAD?
IT HAS EVERYTHING TO DO WITH YOU AND YOUR DAD, HOPE.
BLAQUESMITH BROUGHT YOU HERE TO EXPLAIN CABLE'S PREMONITIONS. TO SHOW YOU WHY WE DID IT.
YOU'RE TELLING ME YOU TIME-JACKED DAD'S HEAD SO YOU COULD CREATE THIS?!
THAT'S YOUR EXPLANATION?!
JUST THE OPPOSITE.
AS BAD AS I'M SURE THIS FUTURE LOOKS TO YOU, IT USED TO BE A LOT WORSE. WHAT YOU'RE SEEING HERE IS A VAST IMPROVEMENT.
THIS IS BETTER?
MUCH. AND IT KEEPS IMPROVING, EVERY DAY.
I DON'T KNOW WHEN THAT WILL STOP OR HOW GOOD THINGS CAN GET. TIME RIPPLES AREN'T MY AREA OF EXPERTISE AND BLAQUESMITH, WELL, YOU'VE TALKED TO HIM.
BUT I THINK WE'VE GOT A SHOT AT SOMETHING LIVABLE.
"WE'RE NOT GONNA SURVIVE THIS!"

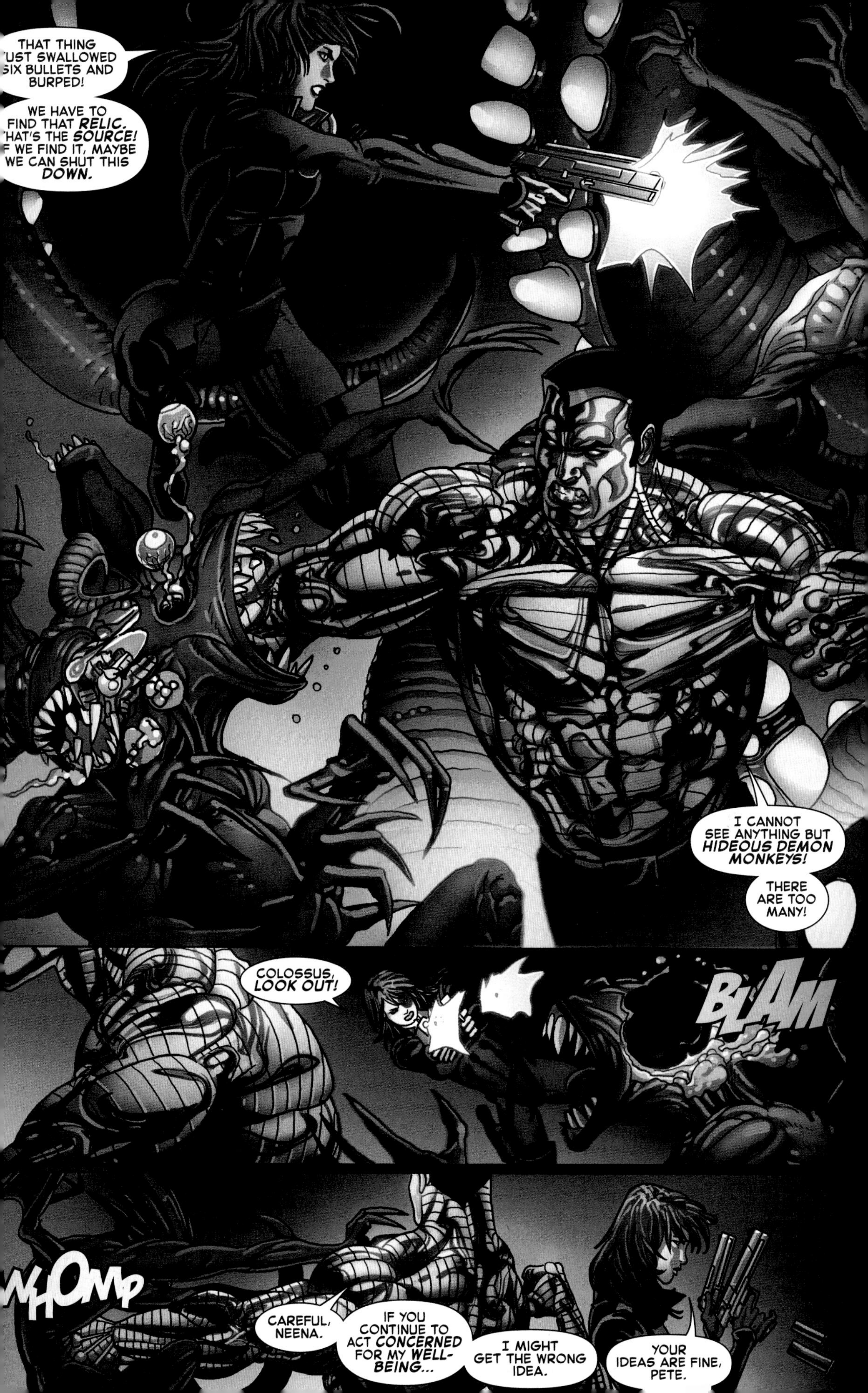
THAT THING 'UST SWALLOWED SIX BULLETS AND BURPED!
WE HAVE TO FIND THAT RELIC. 'HAT'S THE SOURCE! 'F WE FIND IT, MAYBE WE CAN SHUT THIS DOWN.
I CANNOT SEE ANYTHING BUT HIDEOUS DEMON MONKEYS!
THERE ARE TOO MANY!
COLOSSUS, LOOK OUT!
BLAM
WHOMP
CAREFUL, NEENA.
IF YOU CONTINUE TO ACT CONCERNED FOR MY WELL-BEING...
I MIGHT GET THE WRONG IDEA.
YOUR IDEAS ARE FINE, PETE.

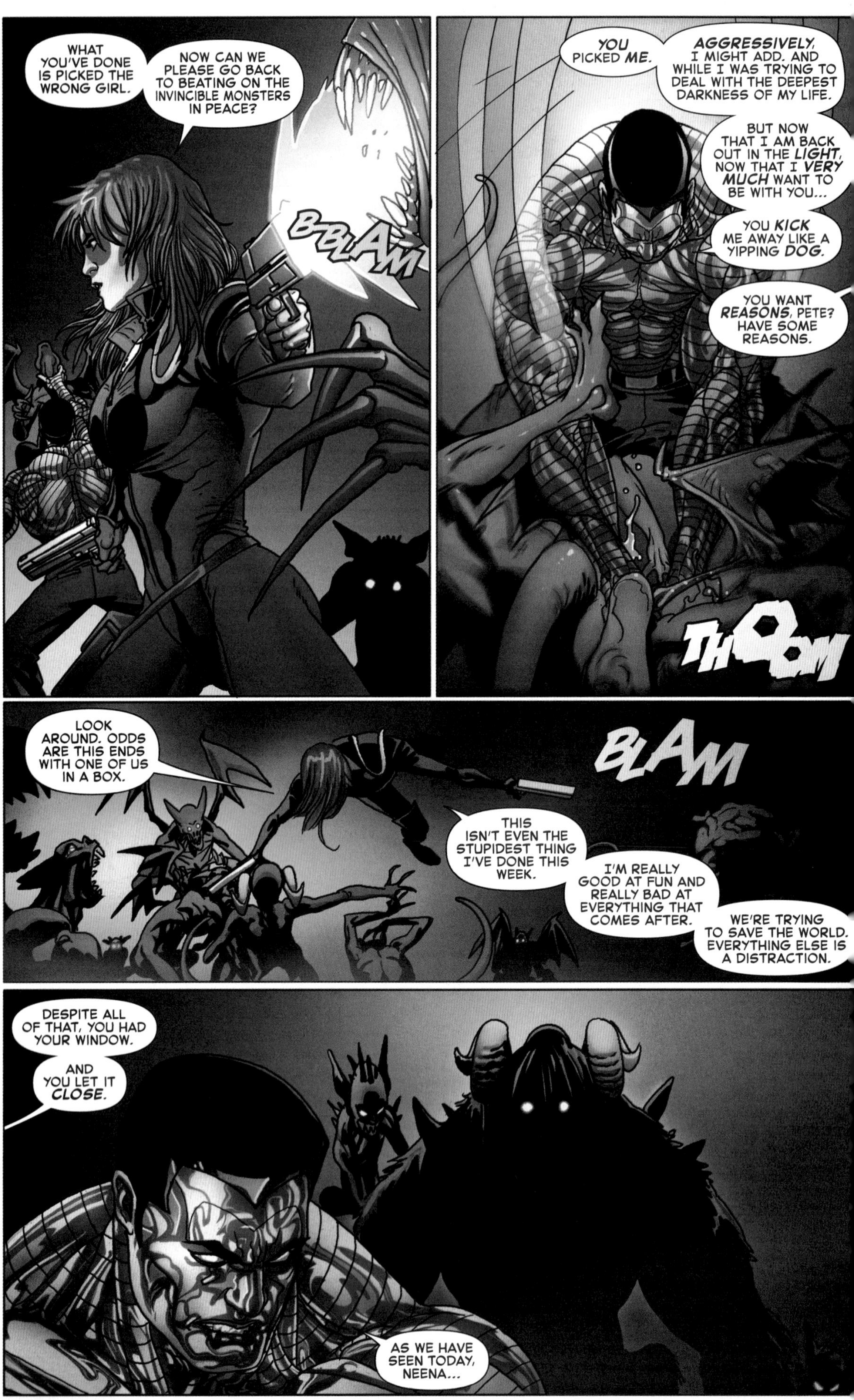
WHAT YOU'VE DONE IS PICKED THE WRONG GIRL.
NOW CAN WE PLEASE GO BACK TO BEATING ON THE INVINCIBLE MONSTERS IN PEACE?
B-BLAM
YOU PICKED ME.
AGGRESSIVELY, I MIGHT ADD. AND WHILE I WAS TRYING TO DEAL WITH THE DEEPEST DARKNESS OF MY LIFE.
BUT NOW THAT I AM BACK OUT IN THE LIGHT, NOW THAT I VERY MUCH WANT TO BE WITH YOU...
YOU KICK ME AWAY LIKE A YIPPING DOG.
YOU WANT REASONS, PETE? HAVE SOME REASONS.
THOOM
LOOK AROUND. ODDS ARE THIS ENDS WITH ONE OF US IN A BOX.
BLAM
THIS ISN'T EVEN THE STUPIDEST THING I'VE DONE THIS WEEK.
I'M REALLY GOOD AT FUN AND REALLY BAD AT EVERYTHING THAT COMES AFTER.
WE'RE TRYING TO SAVE THE WORLD. EVERYTHING ELSE IS A DISTRACTION.
DESPITE ALL OF THAT, YOU HAD YOUR WINDOW.
AND YOU LET IT CLOSE.
AS WE HAVE SEEN TODAY, NEENA...

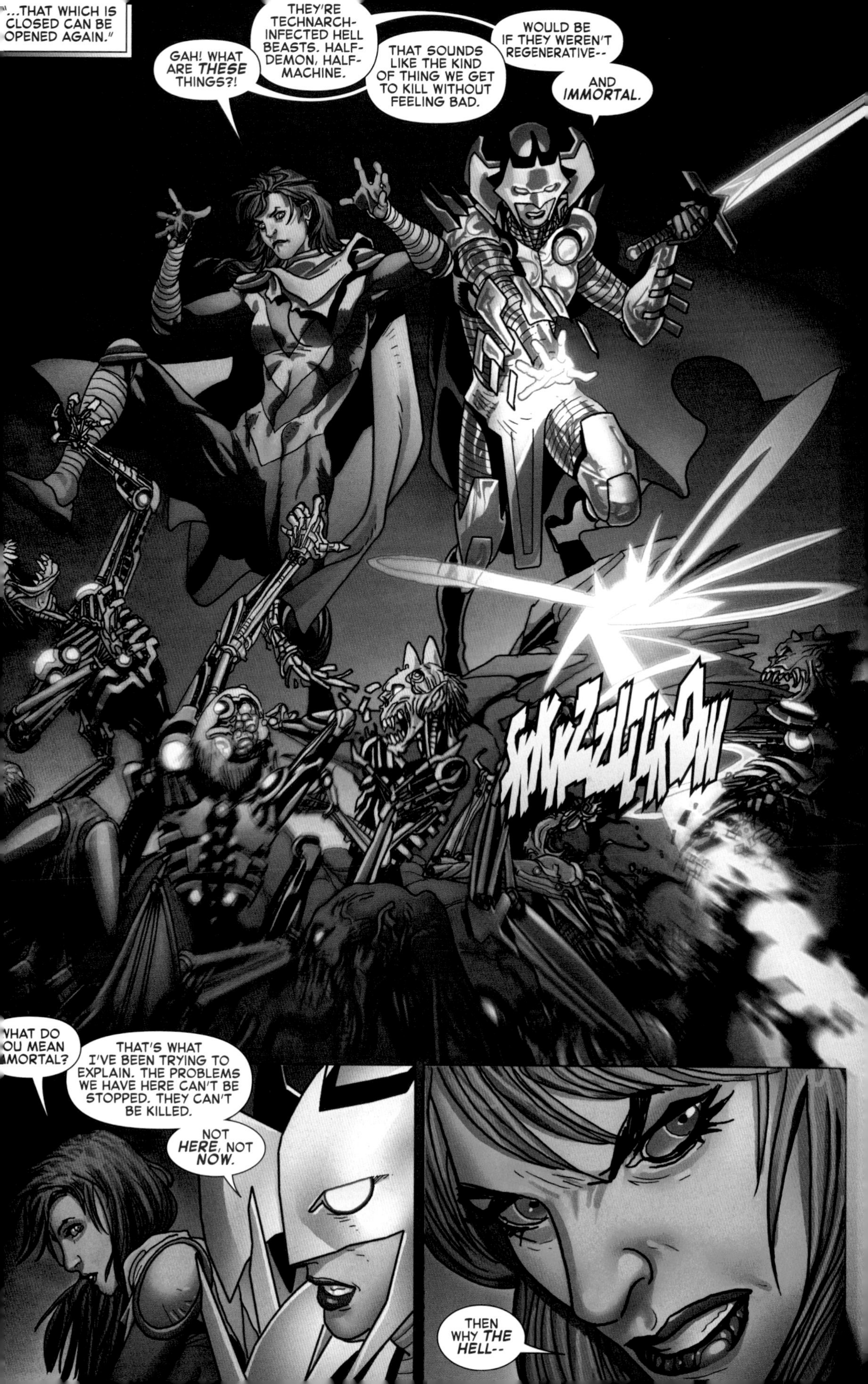
"...THAT WHICH IS CLOSED CAN BE OPENED AGAIN."
GAH! WHAT ARE THESE THINGS?!
THEY'RE TECHNARCH-INFECTED HELL BEASTS. HALF-DEMON, HALF-MACHINE.
THAT SOUNDS LIKE THE KIND OF THING WE GET TO KILL WITHOUT FEELING BAD.
WOULD BE IF THEY WEREN'T REGENERATIVE--
AND IMMORTAL.
SCHKZZZLLLKOW
WHAT DO OU MEAN MORTAL?
THAT'S WHAT I'VE BEEN TRYING TO EXPLAIN. THE PROBLEMS WE HAVE HERE CAN'T BE STOPPED. THEY CAN'T BE KILLED.
NOT HERE, NOT NOW.
THEN WHY THE HELL--

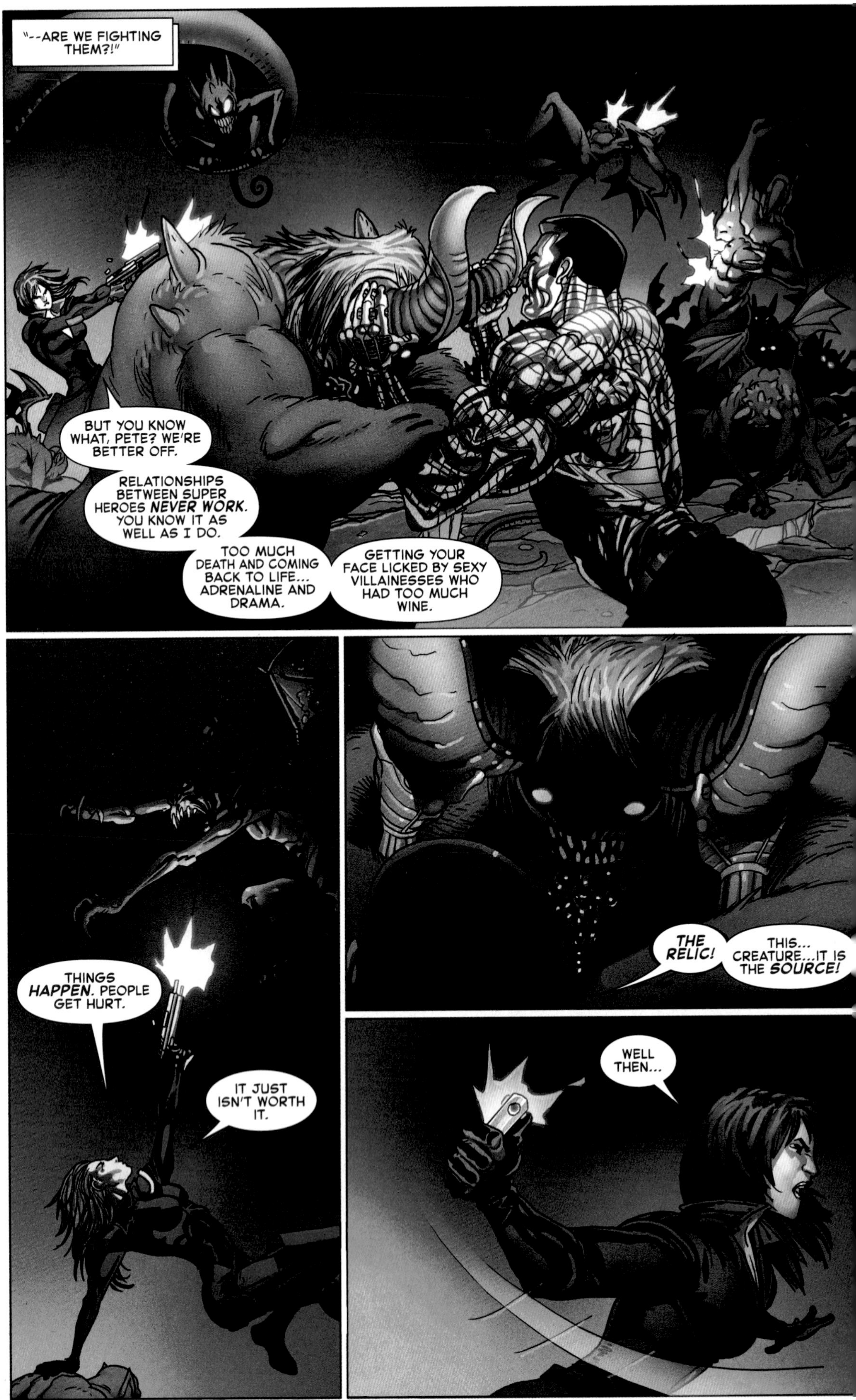
"--ARE WE FIGHTING THEM?!"
BUT YOU KNOW WHAT, PETE? WE'RE BETTER OFF.
RELATIONSHIPS BETWEEN SUPER HEROES NEVER WORK. YOU KNOW IT AS WELL AS I DO.
TOO MUCH DEATH AND COMING BACK TO LIFE... ADRENALINE AND DRAMA.
GETTING YOUR FACE LICKED BY SEXY VILLAINESSES WHO HAD TOO MUCH WINE.
THINGS HAPPEN. PEOPLE GET HURT.
IT JUST ISN'T WORTH IT.
THE RELIC!
THIS... CREATURE...IT IS THE SOURCE!
WELL THEN...

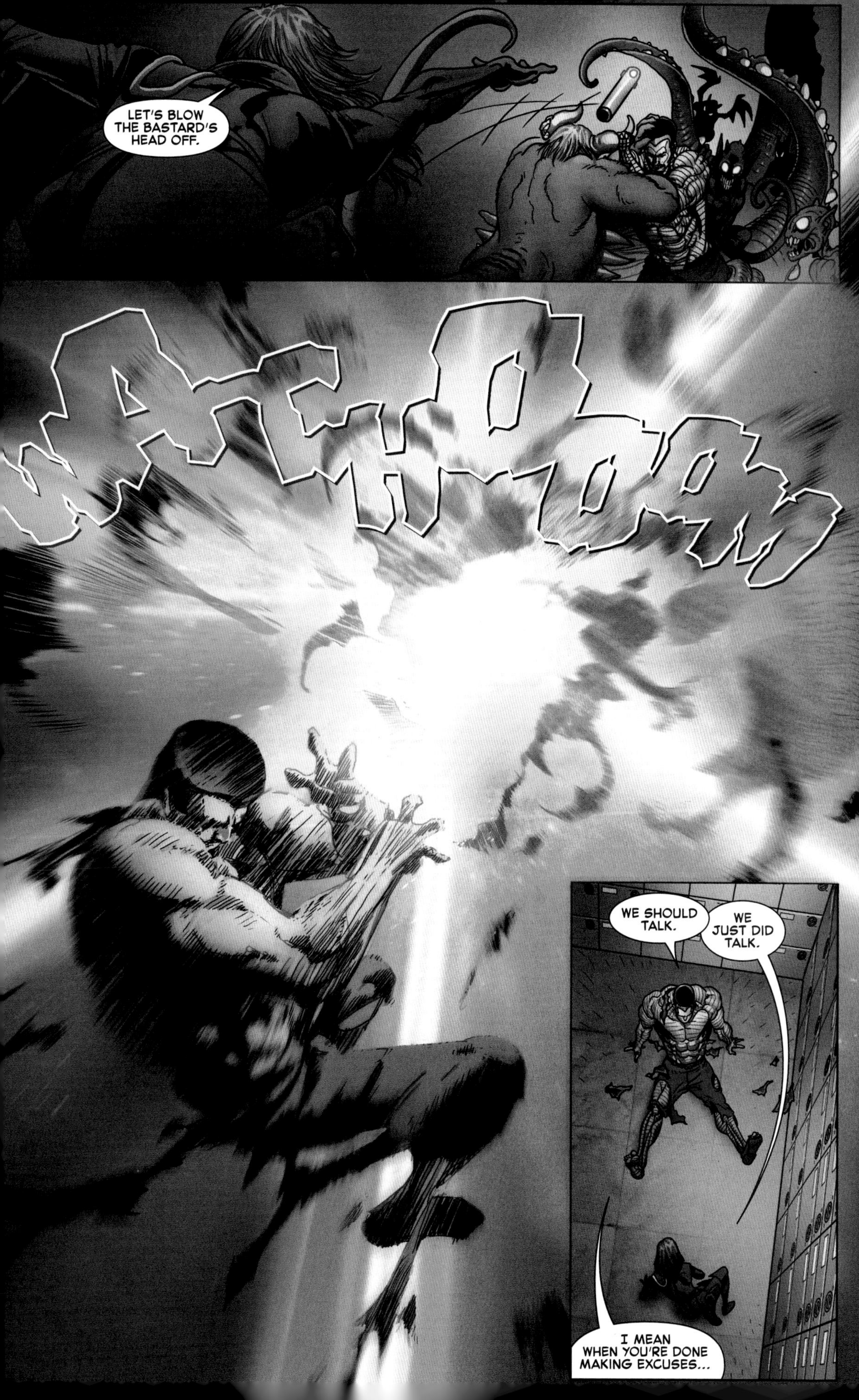
LET'S BLOW THE BASTARD'S HEAD OFF.
WE SHOULD TALK.
WE JUST DID TALK.
I MEAN WHEN YOU'RE DONE MAKING EXCUSES...

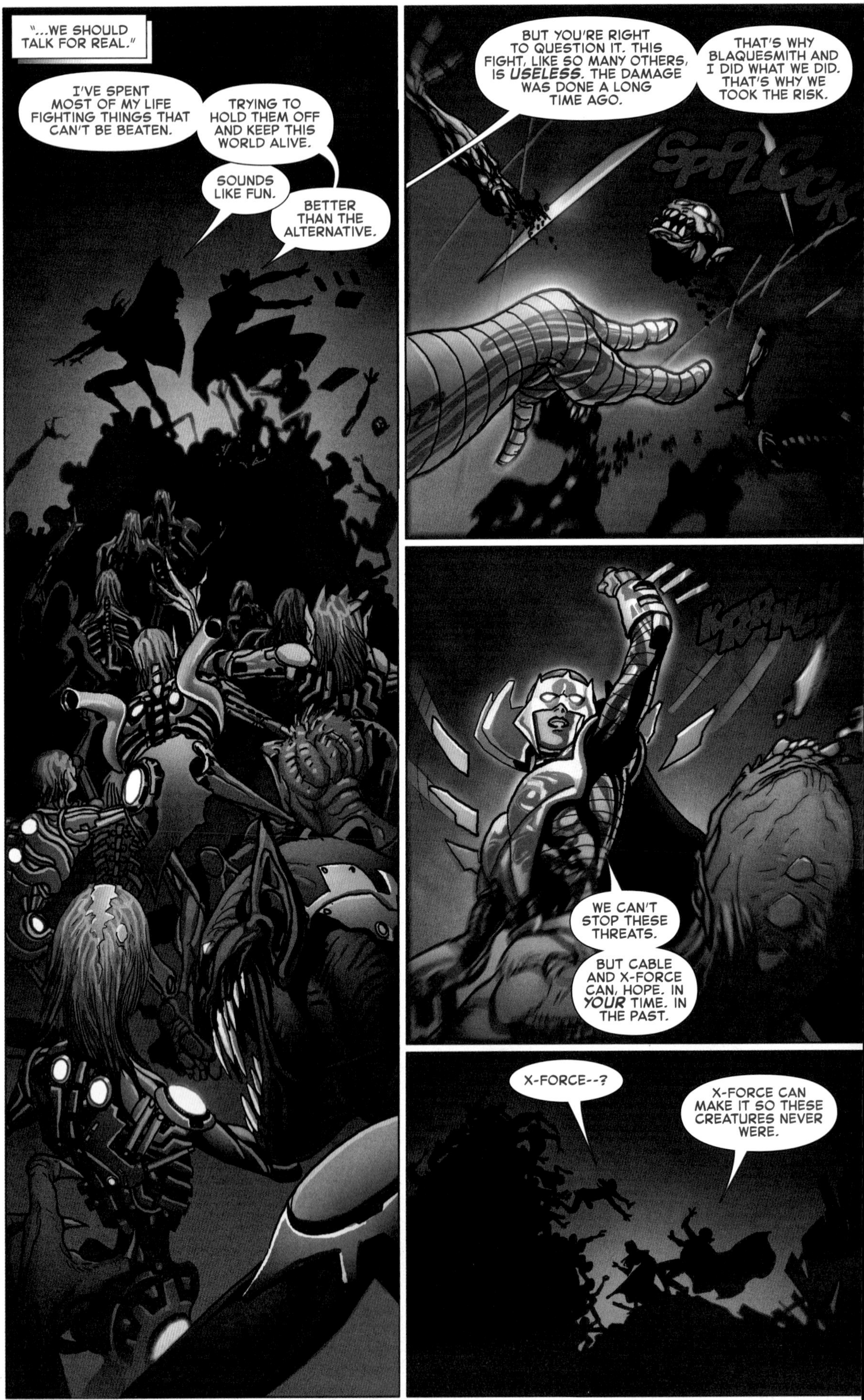
"...WE SHOULD TALK FOR REAL."
I'VE SPENT MOST OF MY LIFE FIGHTING THINGS THAT CAN'T BE BEATEN.
TRYING TO HOLD THEM OFF AND KEEP THIS WORLD ALIVE.
SOUNDS LIKE FUN.
BETTER THAN THE ALTERNATIVE.
BUT YOU'RE RIGHT TO QUESTION IT. THIS FIGHT, LIKE SO MANY OTHERS, IS USELESS. THE DAMAGE WAS DONE A LONG TIME AGO.
THAT'S WHY BLAQUESMITH AND I DID WHAT WE DID. THAT'S WHY WE TOOK THE RISK.
WE CAN'T STOP THESE THREATS.
BUT CABLE AND X-FORCE CAN, HOPE. IN YOUR TIME. IN THE PAST.
X-FORCE--?
X-FORCE CAN MAKE IT SO THESE CREATURES NEVER WERE.

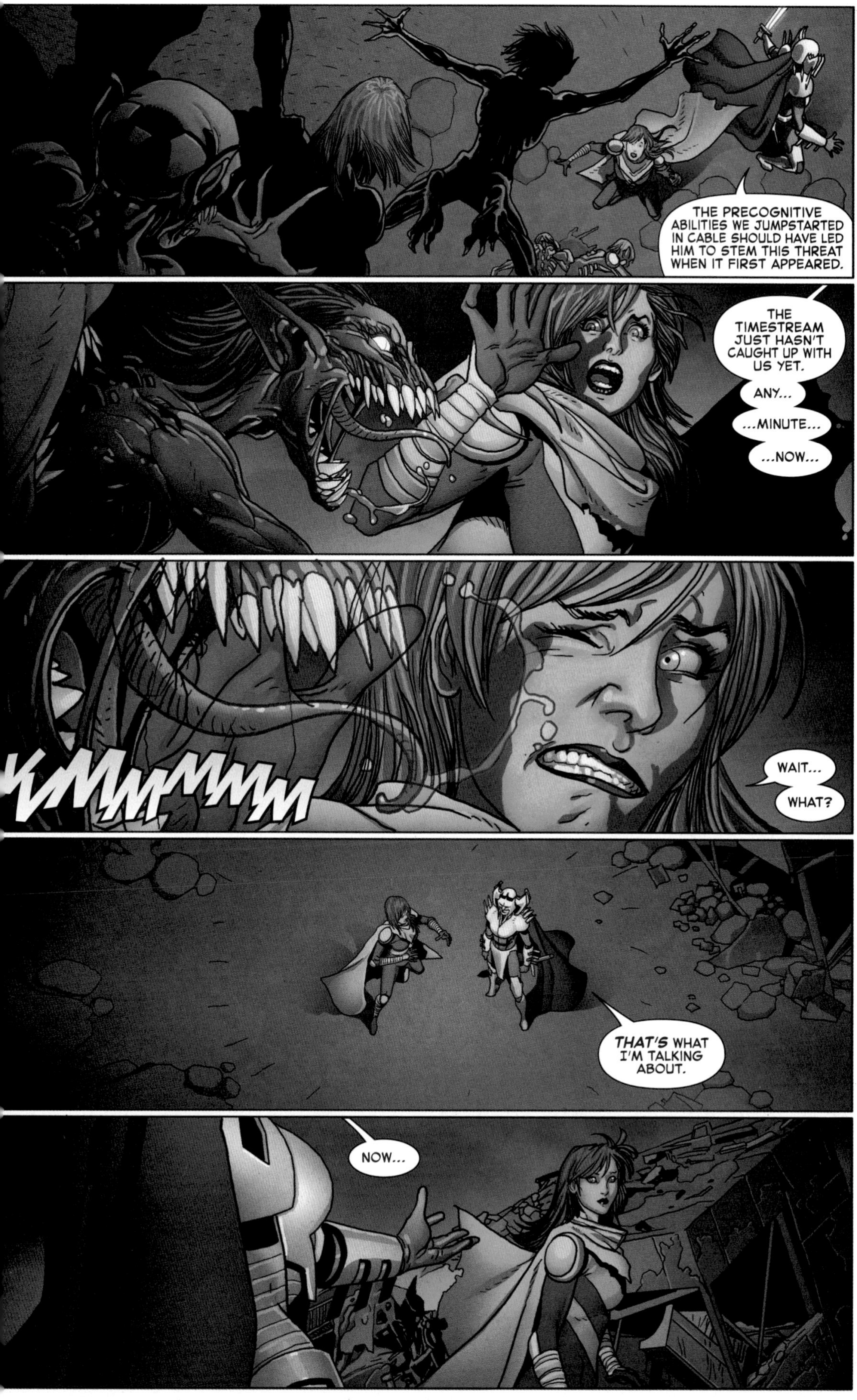
THE PRECOGNITIVE ABILITIES WE JUMPSTARTED IN CABLE SHOULD HAVE LED HIM TO STEM THIS THREAT WHEN IT FIRST APPEARED.
THE TIMESTREAM JUST HASN'T CAUGHT UP WITH US YET.
ANY...
...MINUTE...
...NOW...
KVMMMMMM
WAIT...
WHAT?
THAT'S WHAT I'M TALKING ABOUT.
NOW...

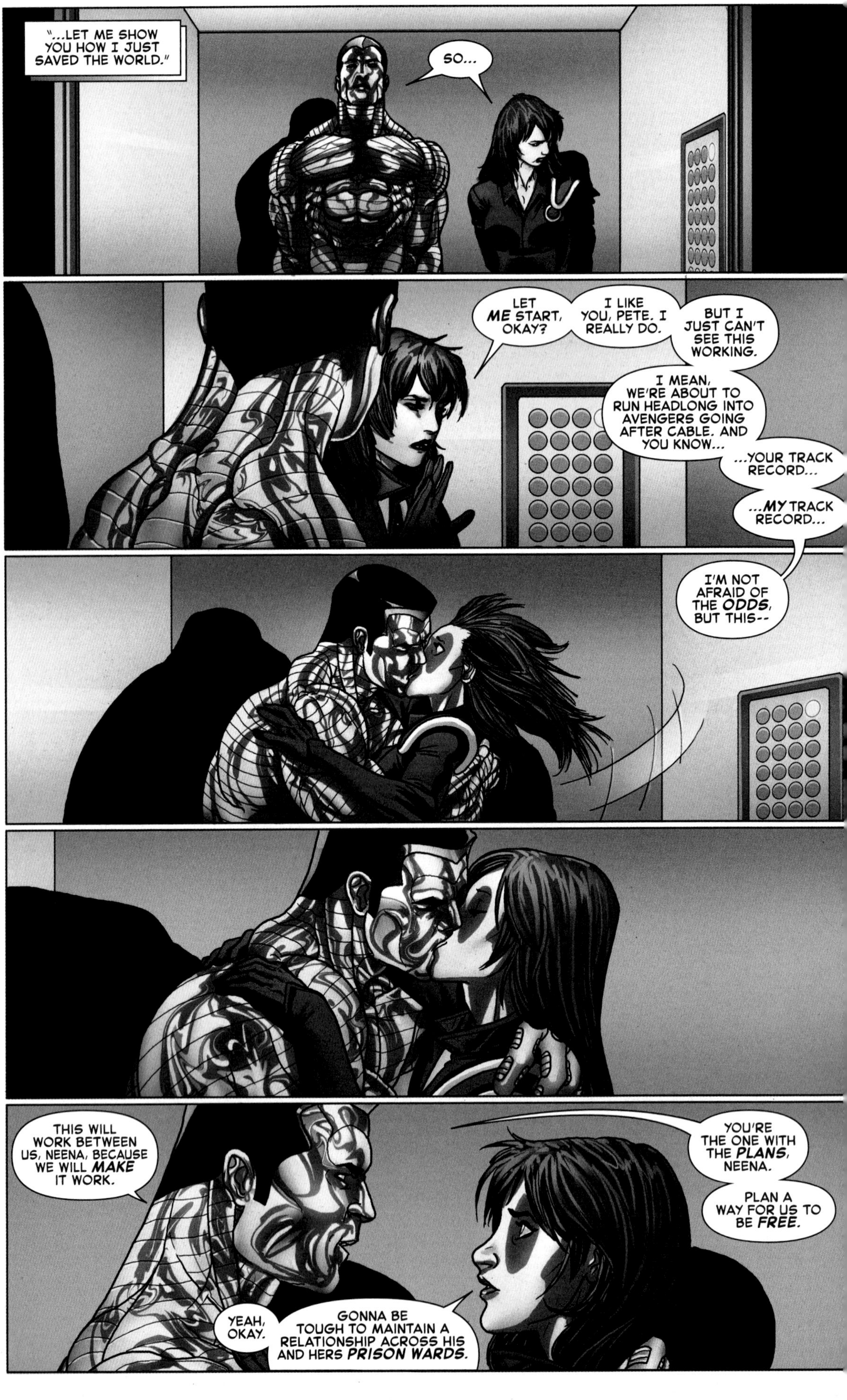
"...LET ME SHOW YOU HOW I JUST SAVED THE WORLD."
SO...
LET *ME* START, OKAY?
I LIKE YOU, PETE. I REALLY DO.
BUT I JUST CAN'T SEE THIS WORKING.
I MEAN, WE'RE ABOUT TO RUN HEADLONG INTO AVENGERS GOING AFTER CABLE. AND YOU KNOW...
...YOUR TRACK RECORD...
...*MY* TRACK RECORD...
I'M NOT AFRAID OF THE *ODDS*, BUT THIS--
THIS WILL WORK BETWEEN US, NEENA, BECAUSE WE WILL *MAKE* IT WORK.
YOU'RE THE ONE WITH THE *PLANS*, NEENA.
PLAN A WAY FOR US TO BE *FREE*.
YEAH, OKAY.
GONNA BE TOUGH TO MAINTAIN A RELATIONSHIP ACROSS HIS AND HERS *PRISON WARDS*.

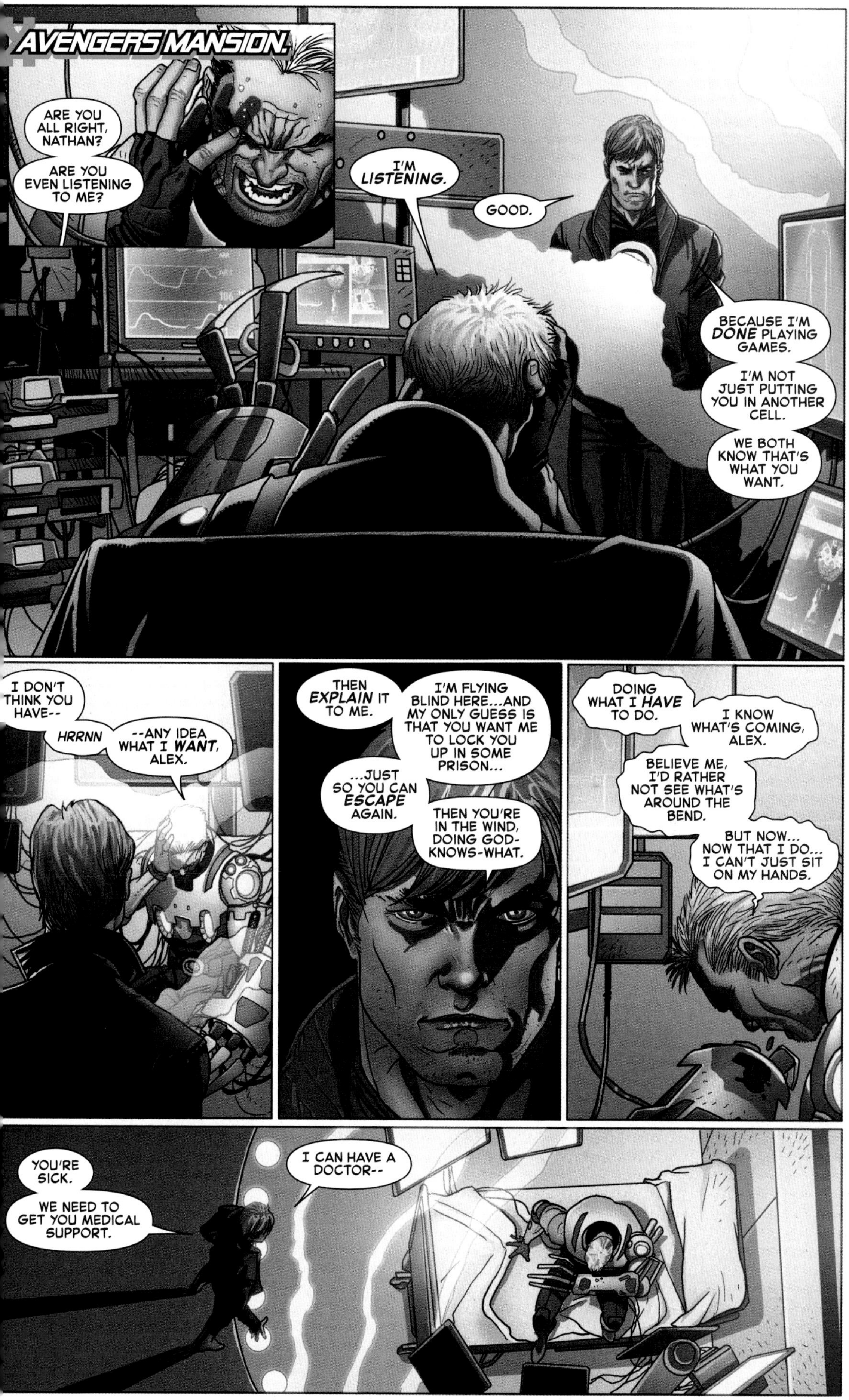
AVENGERS MANSION.
ARE YOU ALL RIGHT, NATHAN?
ARE YOU EVEN LISTENING TO ME?
I'M LISTENING.
GOOD.
BECAUSE I'M DONE PLAYING GAMES.
I'M NOT JUST PUTTING YOU IN ANOTHER CELL.
WE BOTH KNOW THAT'S WHAT YOU WANT.
I DON'T THINK YOU HAVE--
HRRNN
--ANY IDEA WHAT I WANT, ALEX.
THEN EXPLAIN IT TO ME.
I'M FLYING BLIND HERE...AND MY ONLY GUESS IS THAT YOU WANT ME TO LOCK YOU UP IN SOME PRISON...
...JUST SO YOU CAN ESCAPE AGAIN.
THEN YOU'RE IN THE WIND, DOING GOD-KNOWS-WHAT.
DOING WHAT I HAVE TO DO.
I KNOW WHAT'S COMING, ALEX.
BELIEVE ME, I'D RATHER NOT SEE WHAT'S AROUND THE BEND.
BUT NOW... NOW THAT I DO... I CAN'T JUST SIT ON MY HANDS.
YOU'RE SICK.
WE NEED TO GET YOU MEDICAL SUPPORT.
I CAN HAVE A DOCTOR--

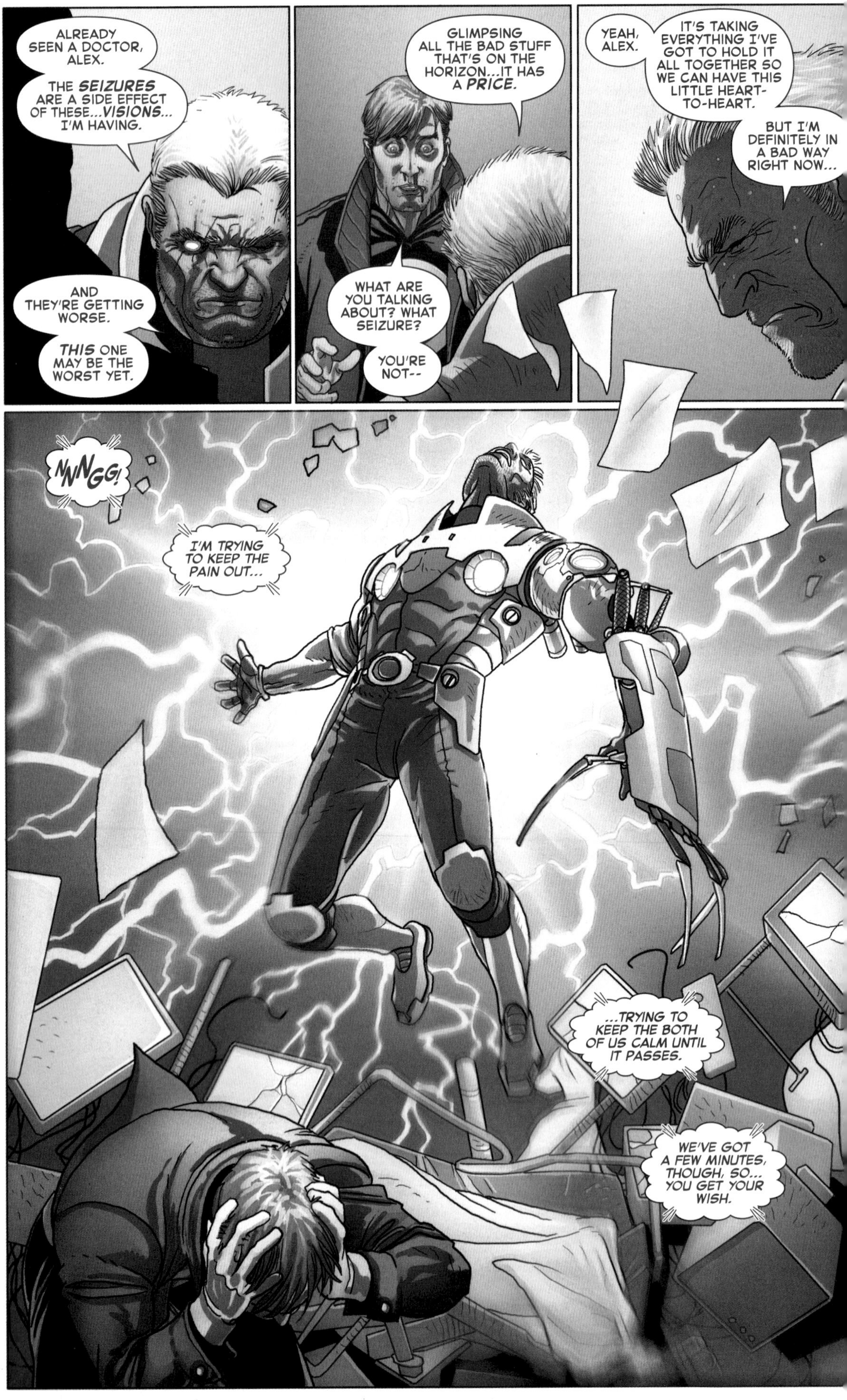
ALREADY SEEN A DOCTOR, ALEX.
THE SEIZURES ARE A SIDE EFFECT OF THESE...VISIONS... I'M HAVING.
AND THEY'RE GETTING WORSE.
THIS ONE MAY BE THE WORST YET.
GLIMPSING ALL THE BAD STUFF THAT'S ON THE HORIZON...IT HAS A PRICE.
WHAT ARE YOU TALKING ABOUT? WHAT SEIZURE?
YOU'RE NOT--
YEAH, ALEX.
IT'S TAKING EVERYTHING I'VE GOT TO HOLD IT ALL TOGETHER SO WE CAN HAVE THIS LITTLE HEART-TO-HEART.
BUT I'M DEFINITELY IN A BAD WAY RIGHT NOW...
NNNGG!
I'M TRYING TO KEEP THE PAIN OUT...
...TRYING TO KEEP THE BOTH OF US CALM UNTIL IT PASSES.
WE'VE GOT A FEW MINUTES, THOUGH, SO... YOU GET YOUR WISH.

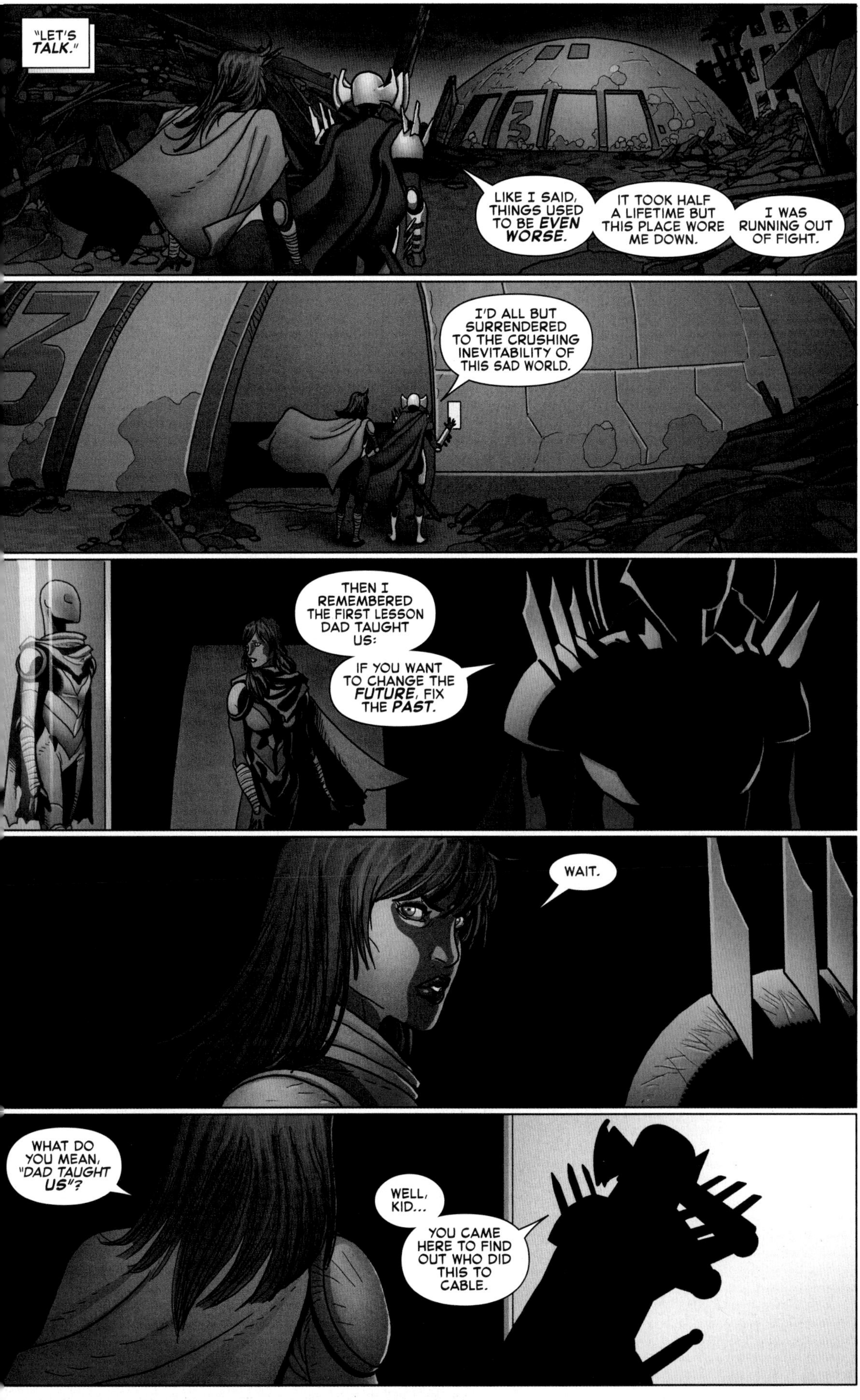
"LET'S TALK."
LIKE I SAID, THINGS USED TO BE EVEN WORSE.
IT TOOK HALF A LIFETIME BUT THIS PLACE WORE ME DOWN.
I WAS RUNNING OUT OF FIGHT.
I'D ALL BUT SURRENDERED TO THE CRUSHING INEVITABILITY OF THIS SAD WORLD.
THEN I REMEMBERED THE FIRST LESSON DAD TAUGHT US:
IF YOU WANT TO CHANGE THE FUTURE, FIX THE PAST.
WAIT.
WHAT DO YOU MEAN, "DAD TAUGHT US"?
WELL, KID...
YOU CAME HERE TO FIND OUT WHO DID THIS TO CABLE.

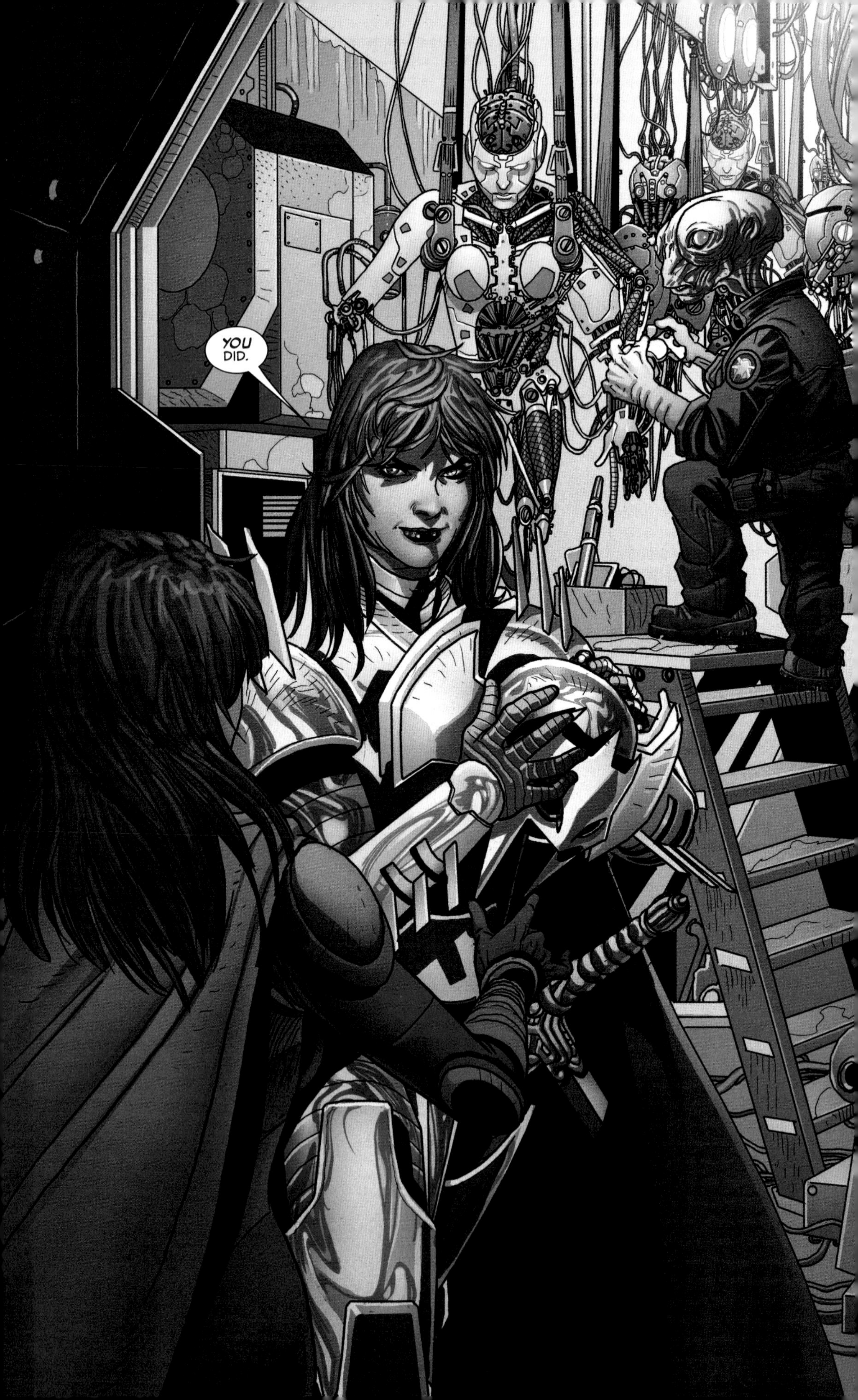
YOU DID.

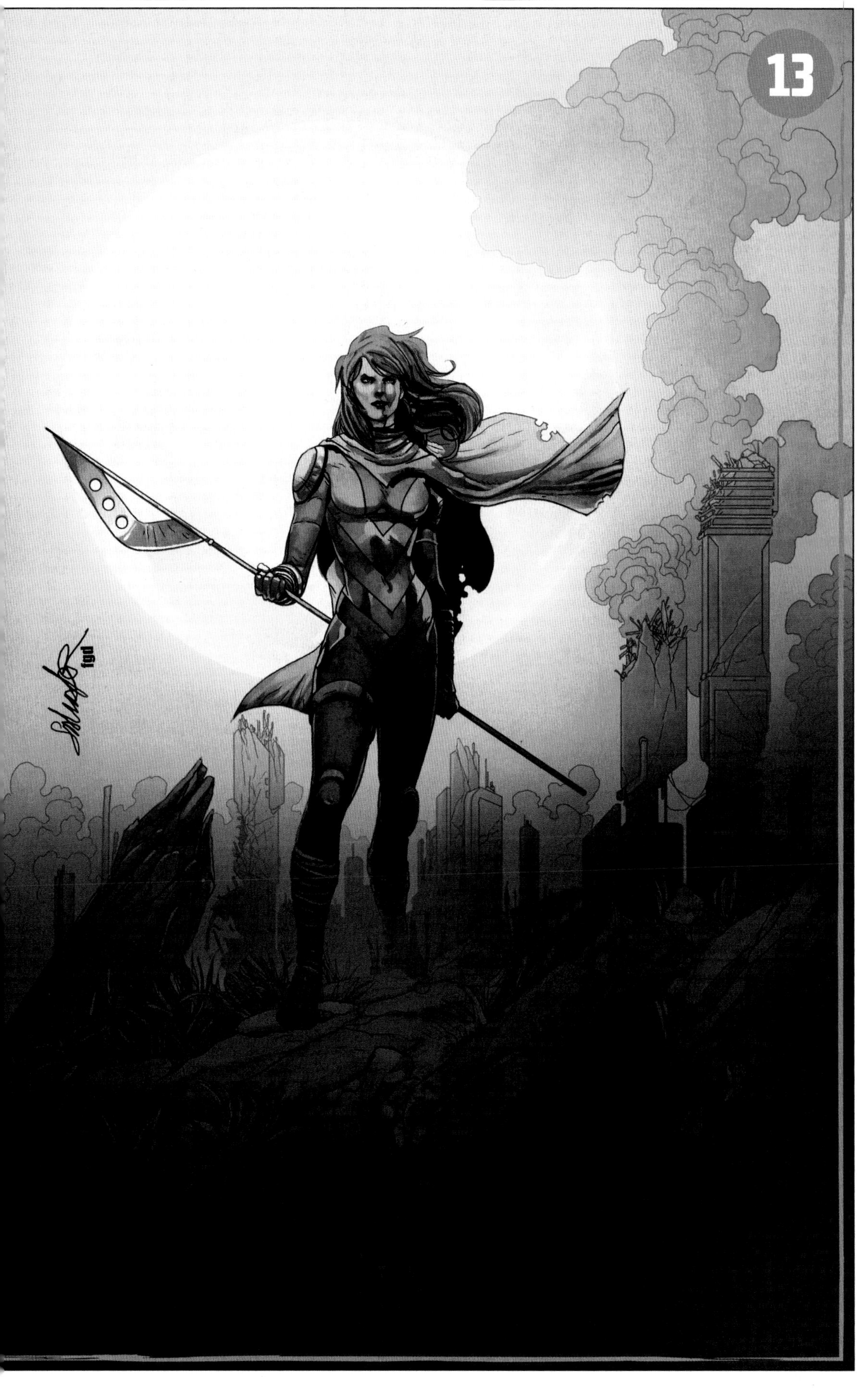
13

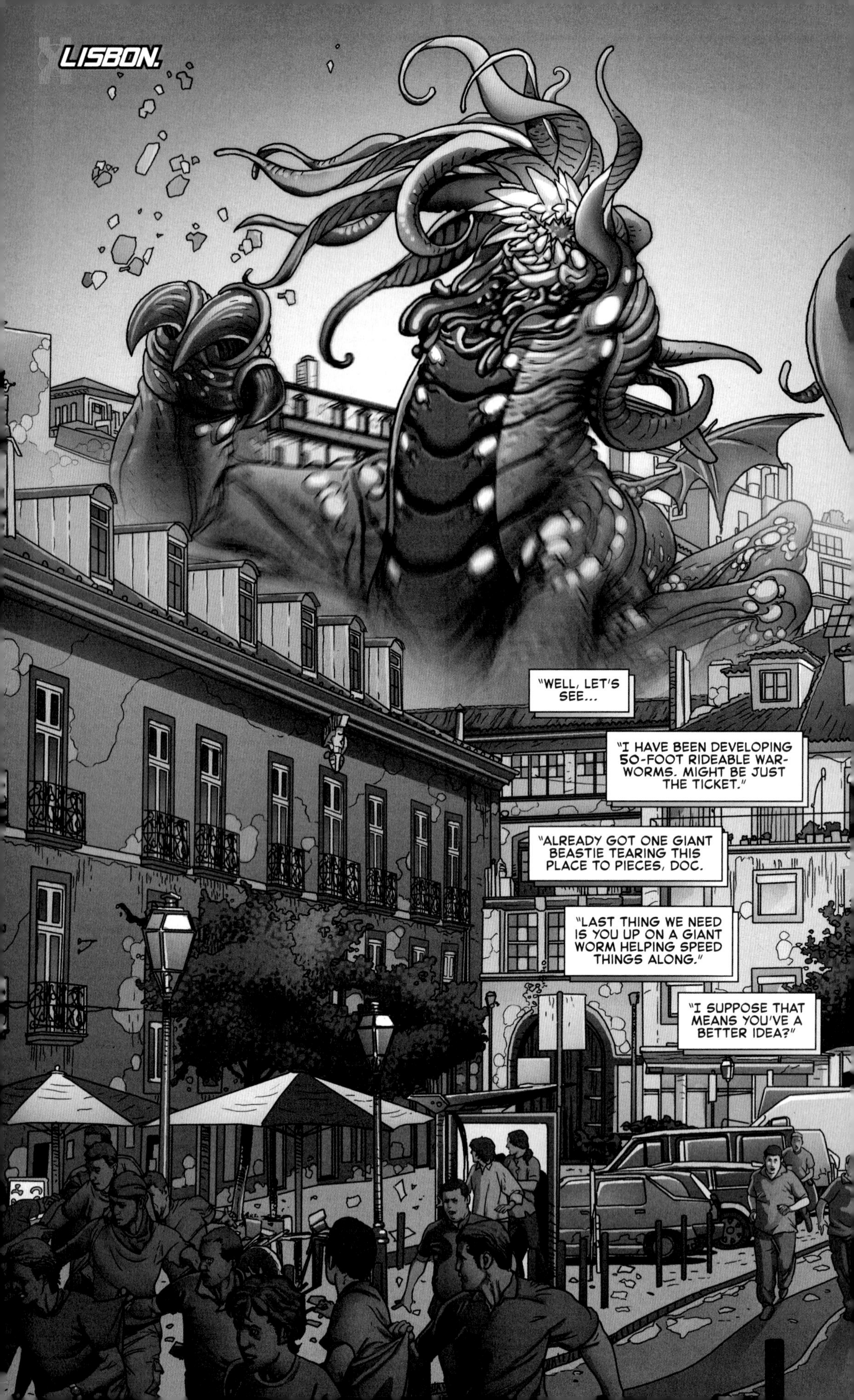
LISBON.
"WELL, LET'S SEE...
"I HAVE BEEN DEVELOPING 50-FOOT RIDEABLE WAR-WORMS. MIGHT BE JUST THE TICKET."
"ALREADY GOT ONE GIANT BEASTIE TEARING THIS PLACE TO PIECES, DOC.
"LAST THING WE NEED IS YOU UP ON A GIANT WORM HELPING SPEED THINGS ALONG."
"I SUPPOSE THAT MEANS YOU'VE A BETTER IDEA?"

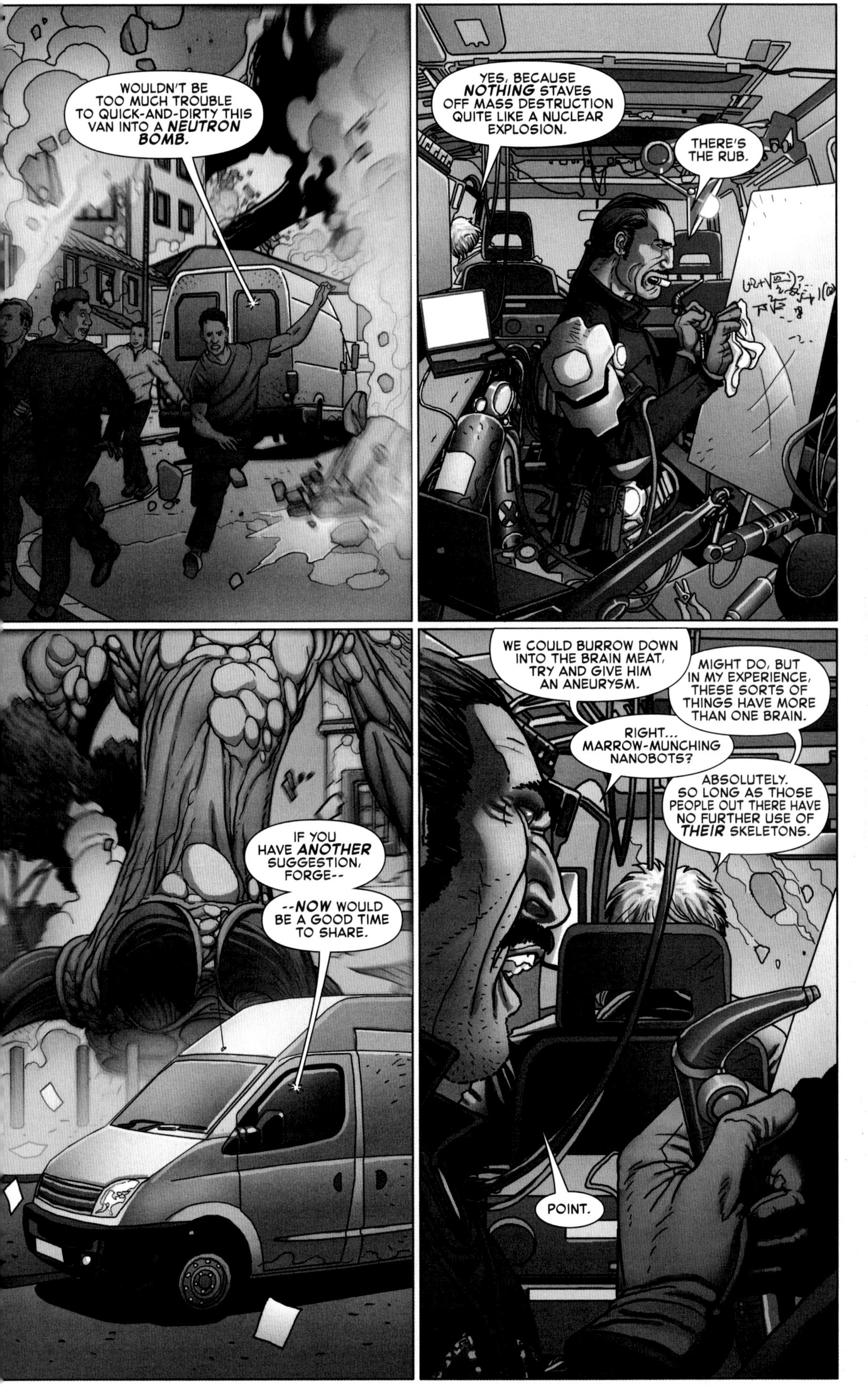
WOULDN'T BE TOO MUCH TROUBLE TO QUICK-AND-DIRTY THIS VAN INTO A ***NEUTRON BOMB.***
YES, BECAUSE ***NOTHING*** STAVES OFF MASS DESTRUCTION QUITE LIKE A NUCLEAR EXPLOSION.
THERE'S THE RUB.
IF YOU HAVE ***ANOTHER*** SUGGESTION, FORGE--
--***NOW*** WOULD BE A GOOD TIME TO SHARE.
WE COULD BURROW DOWN INTO THE BRAIN MEAT, TRY AND GIVE HIM AN ANEURYSM.
MIGHT DO, BUT IN MY EXPERIENCE, THESE SORTS OF THINGS HAVE MORE THAN ONE BRAIN.
RIGHT... MARROW-MUNCHING NANOBOTS?
ABSOLUTELY. SO LONG AS THOSE PEOPLE OUT THERE HAVE NO FURTHER USE OF ***THEIR*** SKELETONS.
POINT.

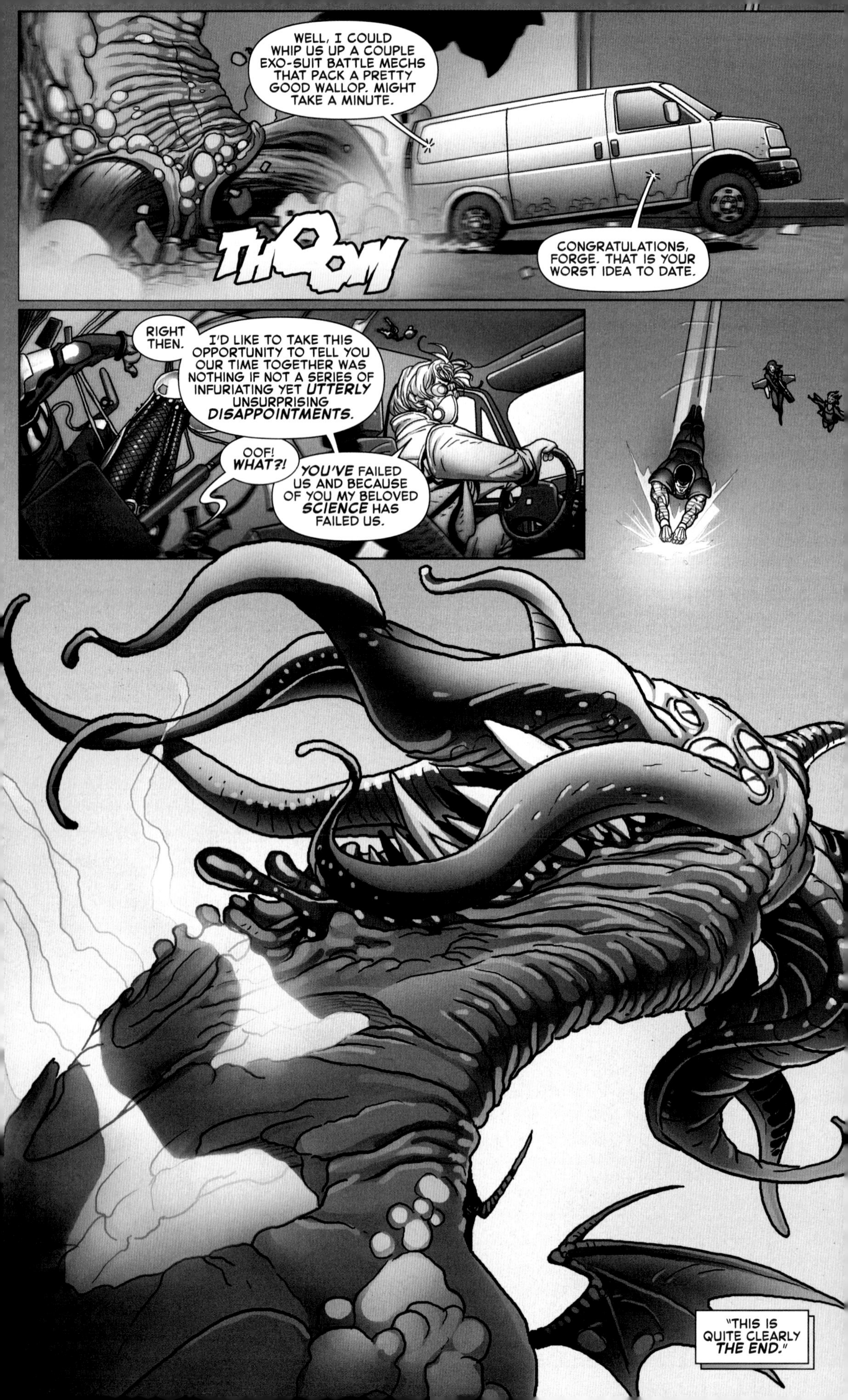
WELL, I COULD WHIP US UP A COUPLE EXO-SUIT BATTLE MECHS THAT PACK A PRETTY GOOD WALLOP. MIGHT TAKE A MINUTE.
THOOM
CONGRATULATIONS, FORGE. THAT IS YOUR WORST IDEA TO DATE.
RIGHT THEN.
I'D LIKE TO TAKE THIS OPPORTUNITY TO TELL YOU OUR TIME TOGETHER WAS NOTHING IF NOT A SERIES OF INFURIATING YET UTTERLY UNSURPRISING DISAPPOINTMENTS.
OOF! WHAT?!
YOU'VE FAILED US AND BECAUSE OF YOU MY BELOVED SCIENCE HAS FAILED US.
"THIS IS QUITE CLEARLY THE END."

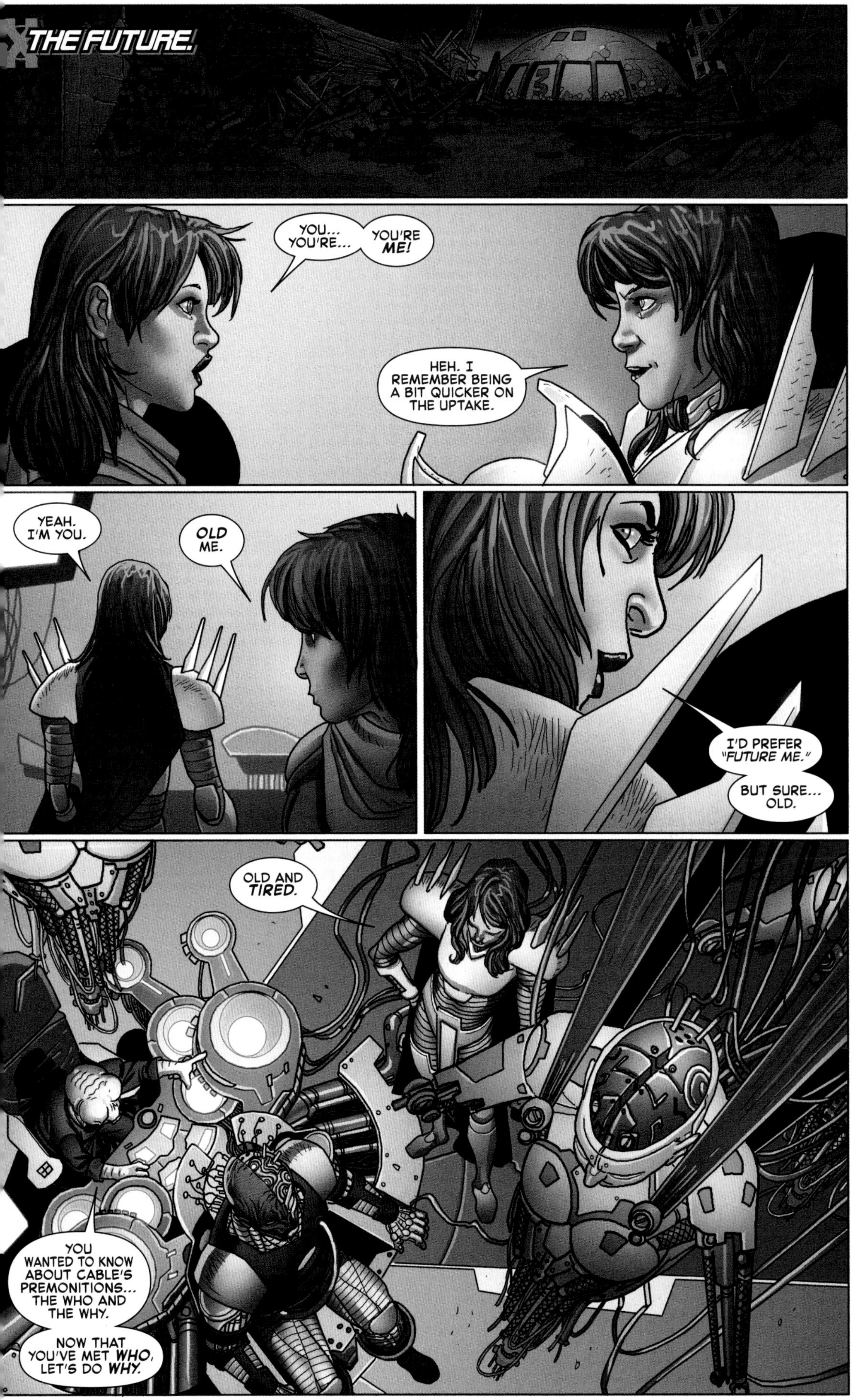
THE FUTURE.
YOU... YOU'RE...
YOU'RE ME!
HEH. I REMEMBER BEING A BIT QUICKER ON THE UPTAKE.
YEAH. I'M YOU.
OLD ME.
I'D PREFER "FUTURE ME."
BUT SURE... OLD.
OLD AND TIRED.
YOU WANTED TO KNOW ABOUT CABLE'S PREMONITIONS... THE WHO AND THE WHY.
NOW THAT YOU'VE MET WHO, LET'S DO WHY.

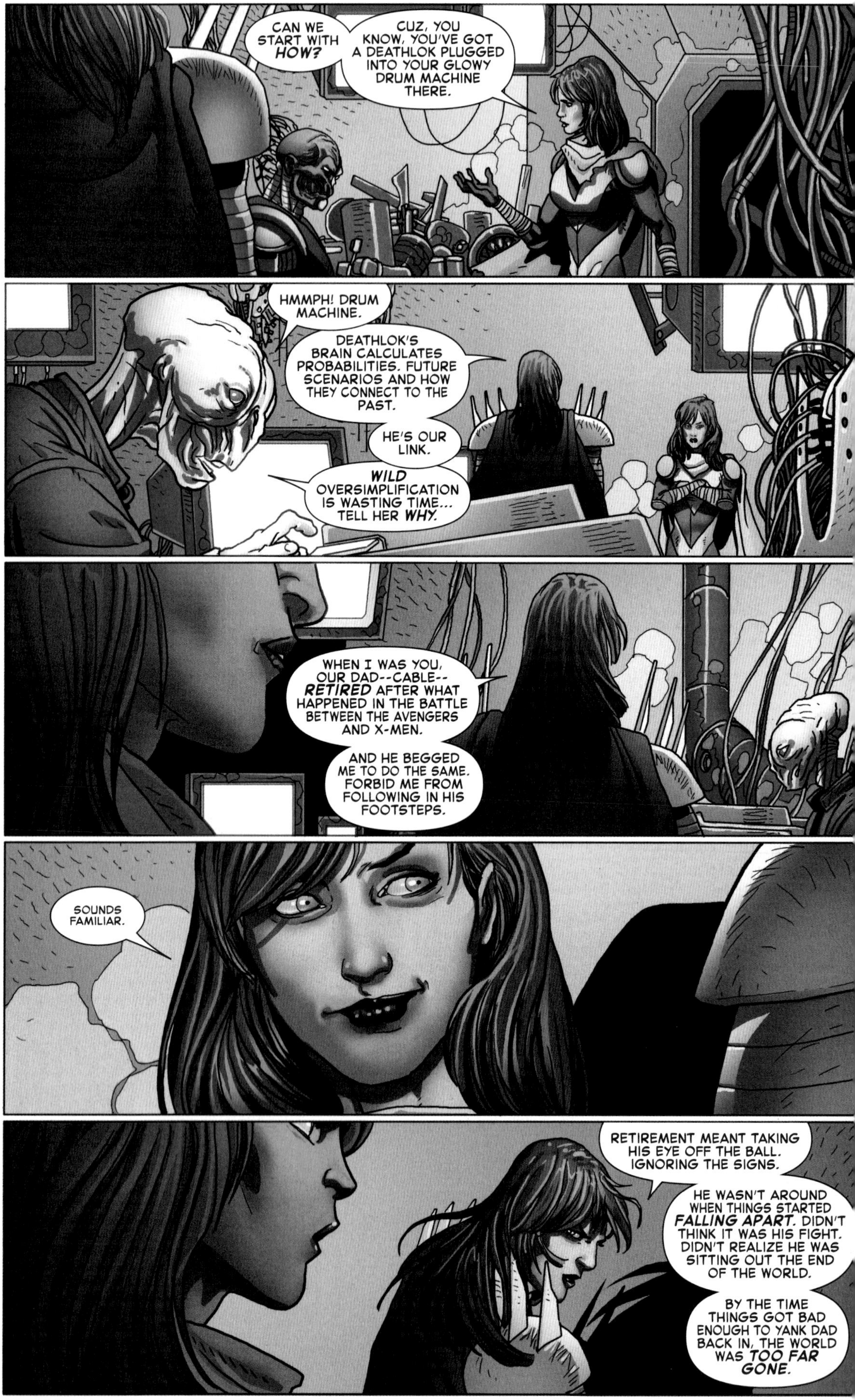
CAN WE START WITH *HOW?*
CUZ, YOU KNOW, YOU'VE GOT A DEATHLOK PLUGGED INTO YOUR GLOWY DRUM MACHINE THERE.
HMMPH! DRUM MACHINE.
DEATHLOK'S BRAIN CALCULATES PROBABILITIES. FUTURE SCENARIOS AND HOW THEY CONNECT TO THE PAST.
HE'S OUR LINK.
WILD OVERSIMPLIFICATION IS WASTING TIME... TELL HER *WHY.*
WHEN I WAS YOU, OUR DAD--CABLE-- *RETIRED* AFTER WHAT HAPPENED IN THE BATTLE BETWEEN THE AVENGERS AND X-MEN.
AND HE BEGGED ME TO DO THE SAME. FORBID ME FROM FOLLOWING IN HIS FOOTSTEPS.
SOUNDS FAMILIAR.
RETIREMENT MEANT TAKING HIS EYE OFF THE BALL. IGNORING THE SIGNS.
HE WASN'T AROUND WHEN THINGS STARTED *FALLING APART.* DIDN'T THINK IT WAS HIS FIGHT. DIDN'T REALIZE HE WAS SITTING OUT THE END OF THE WORLD.
BY THE TIME THINGS GOT BAD ENOUGH TO YANK DAD BACK IN, THE WORLD WAS *TOO FAR GONE.*

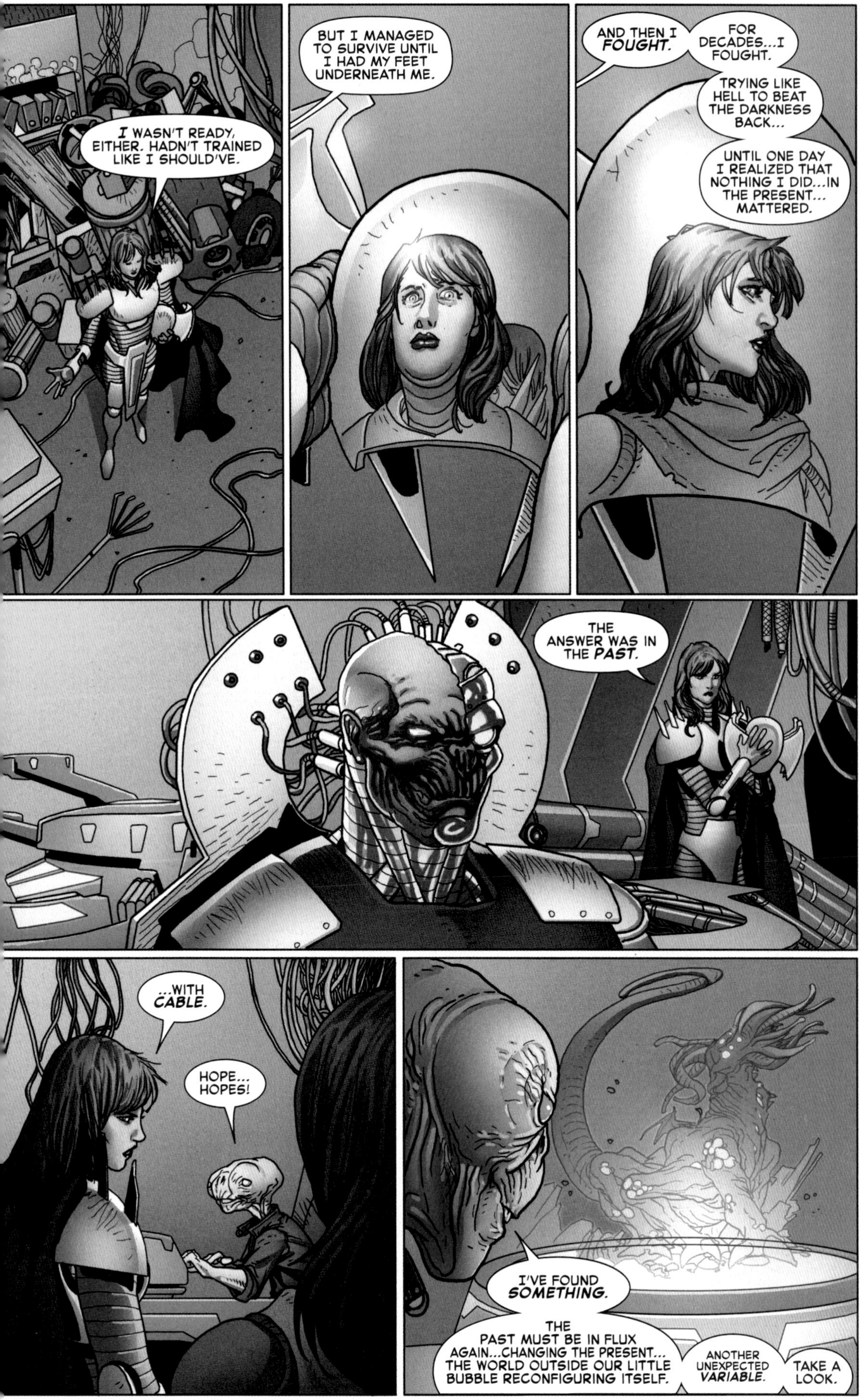
I WASN'T READY, EITHER. HADN'T TRAINED LIKE I SHOULD'VE.
BUT I MANAGED TO SURVIVE UNTIL I HAD MY FEET UNDERNEATH ME.
AND THEN I FOUGHT.
FOR DECADES...I FOUGHT.
TRYING LIKE HELL TO BEAT THE DARKNESS BACK...
UNTIL ONE DAY I REALIZED THAT NOTHING I DID...IN THE PRESENT... MATTERED.
THE ANSWER WAS IN THE PAST.
...WITH CABLE.
HOPE... HOPES!
I'VE FOUND SOMETHING.
THE PAST MUST BE IN FLUX AGAIN...CHANGING THE PRESENT... THE WORLD OUTSIDE OUR LITTLE BUBBLE RECONFIGURING ITSELF.
ANOTHER UNEXPECTED VARIABLE.
TAKE A LOOK.

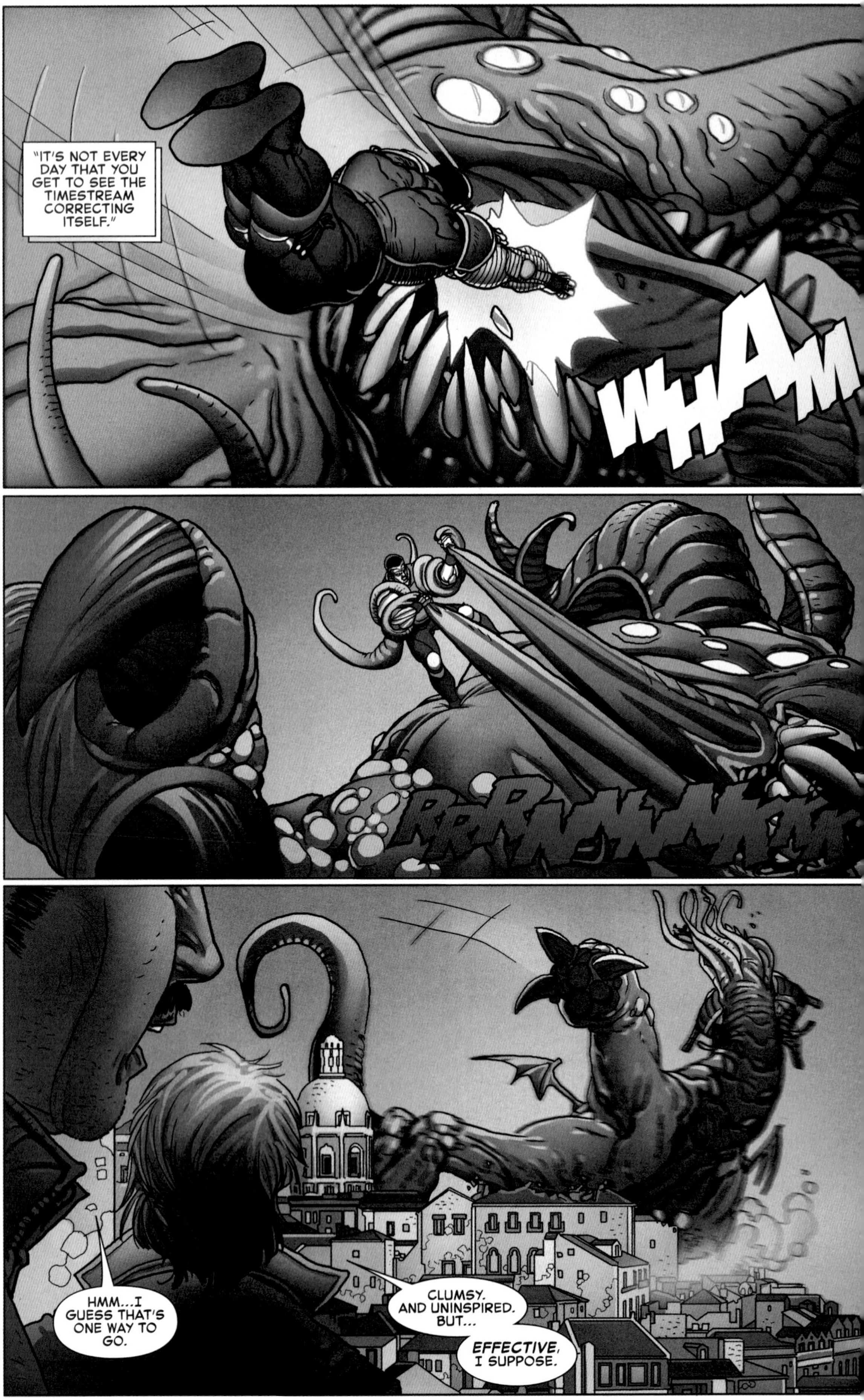
"IT'S NOT EVERY DAY THAT YOU GET TO SEE THE TIMESTREAM CORRECTING ITSELF."
WHAM
RRRUMMMM
HMM...I GUESS THAT'S ONE WAY TO GO.
CLUMSY. AND UNINSPIRED. BUT...
EFFECTIVE, I SUPPOSE.

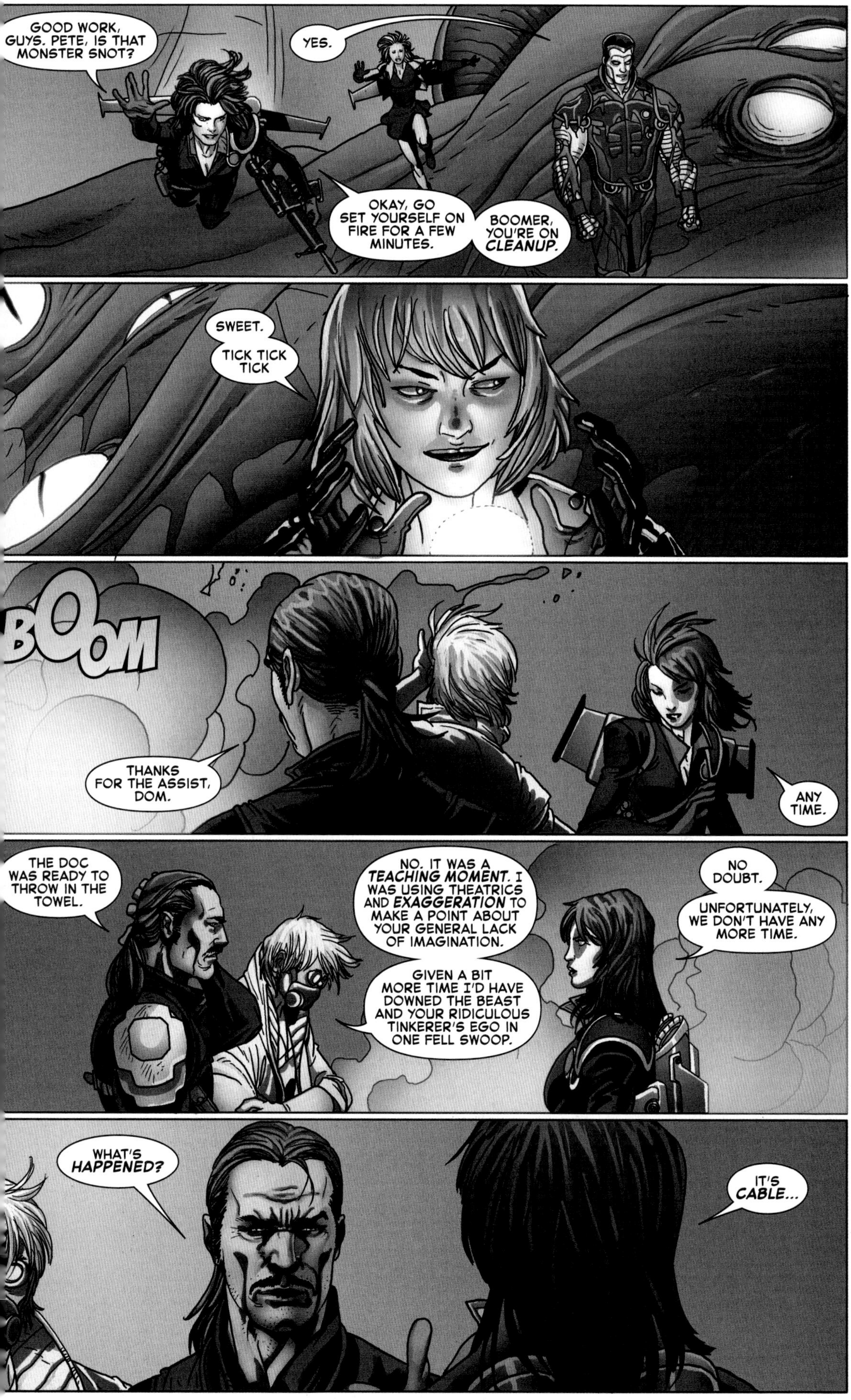

GOOD WORK, GUYS. PETE, IS THAT MONSTER SNOT?
YES.
OKAY, GO SET YOURSELF ON FIRE FOR A FEW MINUTES.
BOOMER, YOU'RE ON CLEANUP.
SWEET.
TICK TICK TICK
BOOM
THANKS FOR THE ASSIST, DOM.
ANY TIME.
THE DOC WAS READY TO THROW IN THE TOWEL.
NO. IT WAS A TEACHING MOMENT. I WAS USING THEATRICS AND EXAGGERATION TO MAKE A POINT ABOUT YOUR GENERAL LACK OF IMAGINATION.
GIVEN A BIT MORE TIME I'D HAVE DOWNED THE BEAST AND YOUR RIDICULOUS TINKERER'S EGO IN ONE FELL SWOOP.
NO DOUBT.
UNFORTUNATELY, WE DON'T HAVE ANY MORE TIME.
WHAT'S HAPPENED?
IT'S CABLE...

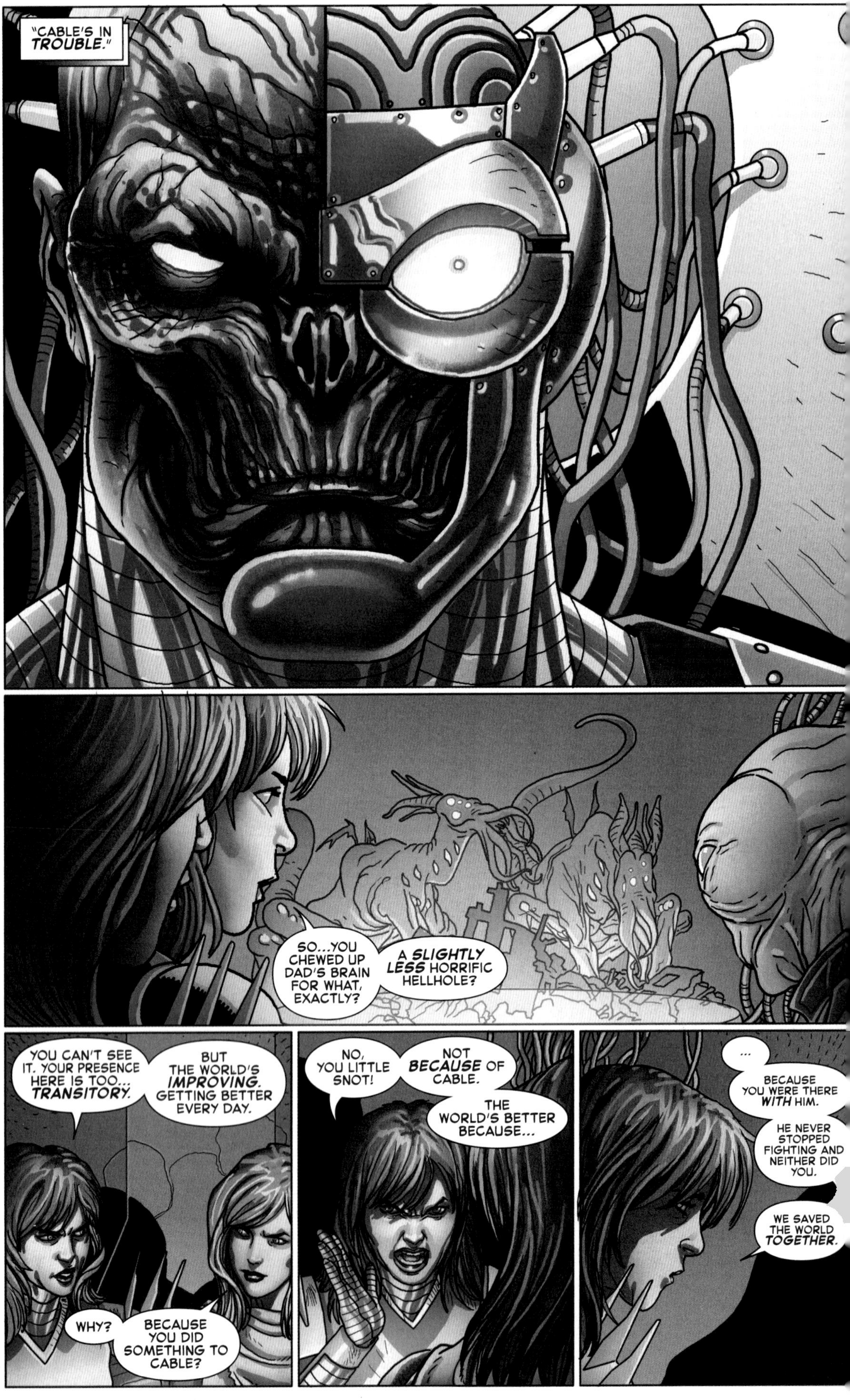
"CABLE'S IN TROUBLE."
SO...YOU CHEWED UP DAD'S BRAIN FOR WHAT, EXACTLY?
A SLIGHTLY LESS HORRIFIC HELLHOLE?
YOU CAN'T SEE IT. YOUR PRESENCE HERE IS TOO... TRANSITORY.
BUT THE WORLD'S IMPROVING. GETTING BETTER EVERY DAY.
WHY?
BECAUSE YOU DID SOMETHING TO CABLE?
NO, YOU LITTLE SNOT!
NOT BECAUSE OF CABLE.
THE WORLD'S BETTER BECAUSE...
...
BECAUSE YOU WERE THERE WITH HIM.
HE NEVER STOPPED FIGHTING AND NEITHER DID YOU.
WE SAVED THE WORLD TOGETHER.

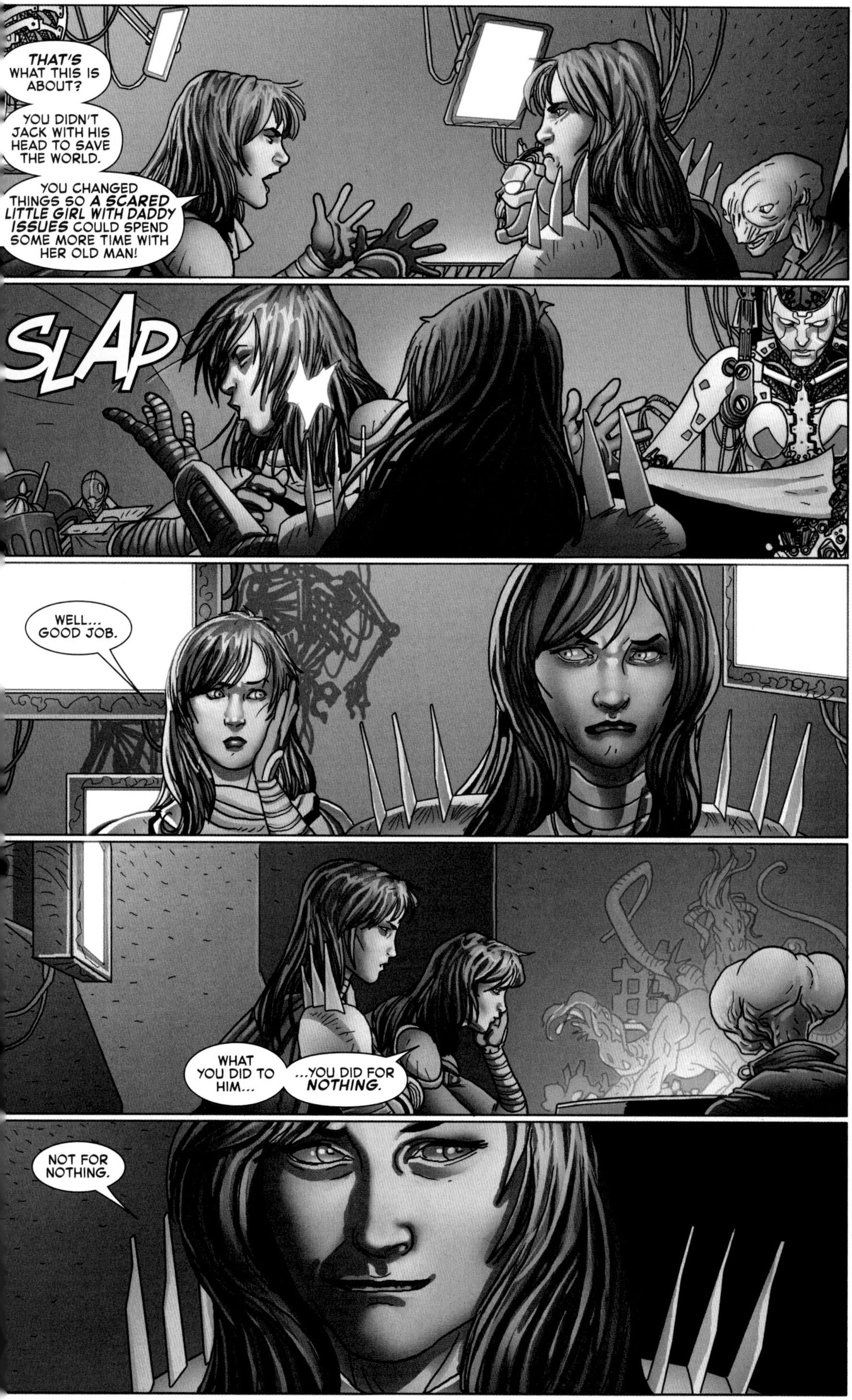
THAT'S WHAT THIS IS ABOUT?
YOU DIDN'T JACK WITH HIS HEAD TO SAVE THE WORLD.
YOU CHANGED THINGS SO A SCARED LITTLE GIRL WITH DADDY ISSUES COULD SPEND SOME MORE TIME WITH HER OLD MAN!
SLAP
WELL... GOOD JOB.
WHAT YOU DID TO HIM...
...YOU DID FOR NOTHING.
NOT FOR NOTHING.

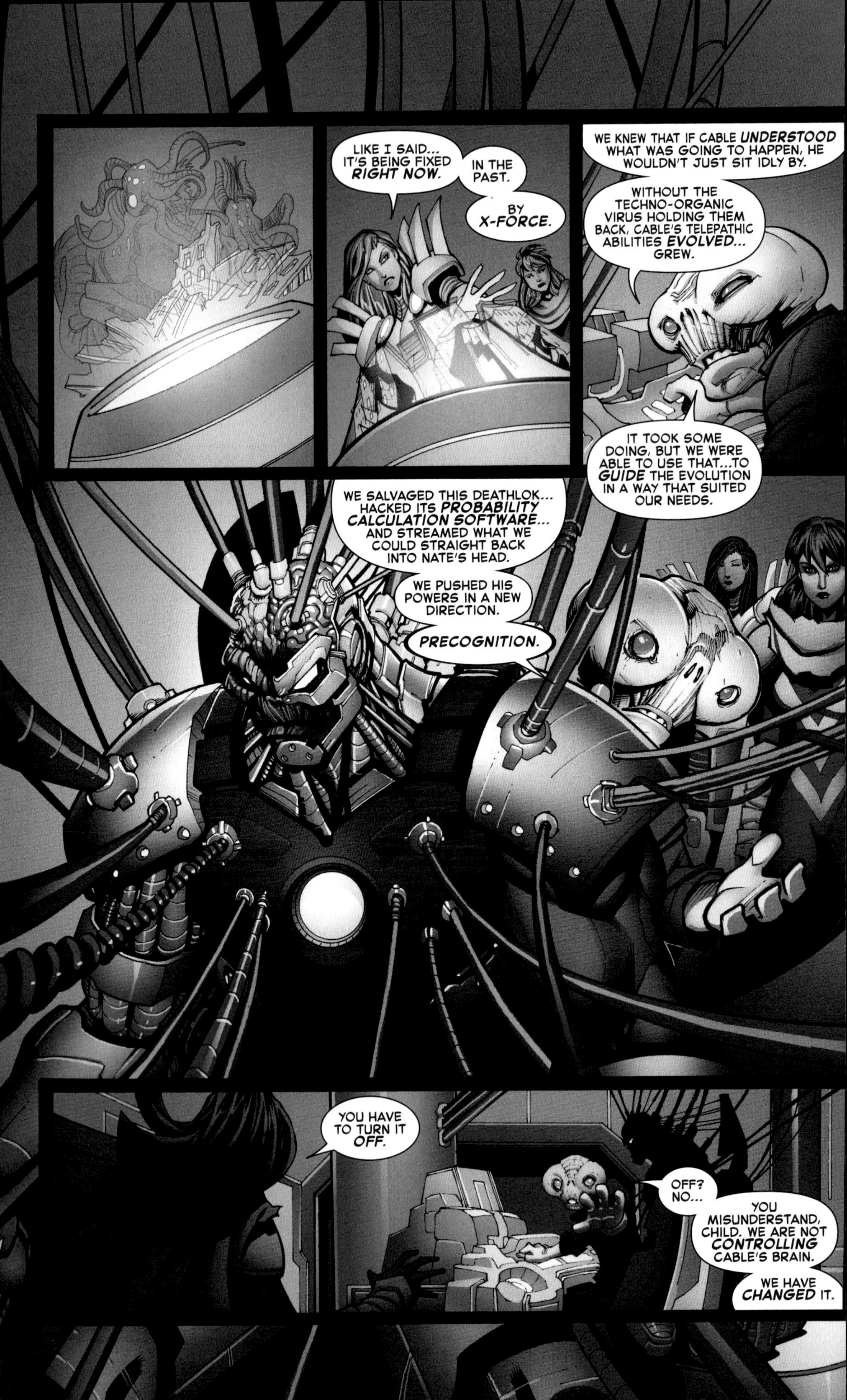

LIKE I SAID... IT'S BEING FIXED RIGHT NOW.
IN THE PAST.
BY X-FORCE.
WE KNEW THAT IF CABLE UNDERSTOOD WHAT WAS GOING TO HAPPEN, HE WOULDN'T JUST SIT IDLY BY.
WITHOUT THE TECHNO-ORGANIC VIRUS HOLDING THEM BACK, CABLE'S TELEPATHIC ABILITIES EVOLVED... GREW.
IT TOOK SOME DOING, BUT WE WERE ABLE TO USE THAT...TO GUIDE THE EVOLUTION IN A WAY THAT SUITED OUR NEEDS.
WE SALVAGED THIS DEATHLOK... HACKED ITS PROBABILITY CALCULATION SOFTWARE... AND STREAMED WHAT WE COULD STRAIGHT BACK INTO NATE'S HEAD.
WE PUSHED HIS POWERS IN A NEW DIRECTION.
PRECOGNITION.
YOU HAVE TO TURN IT OFF.
OFF? NO...
YOU MISUNDERSTAND, CHILD. WE ARE NOT CONTROLLING CABLE'S BRAIN.
WE HAVE CHANGED IT.

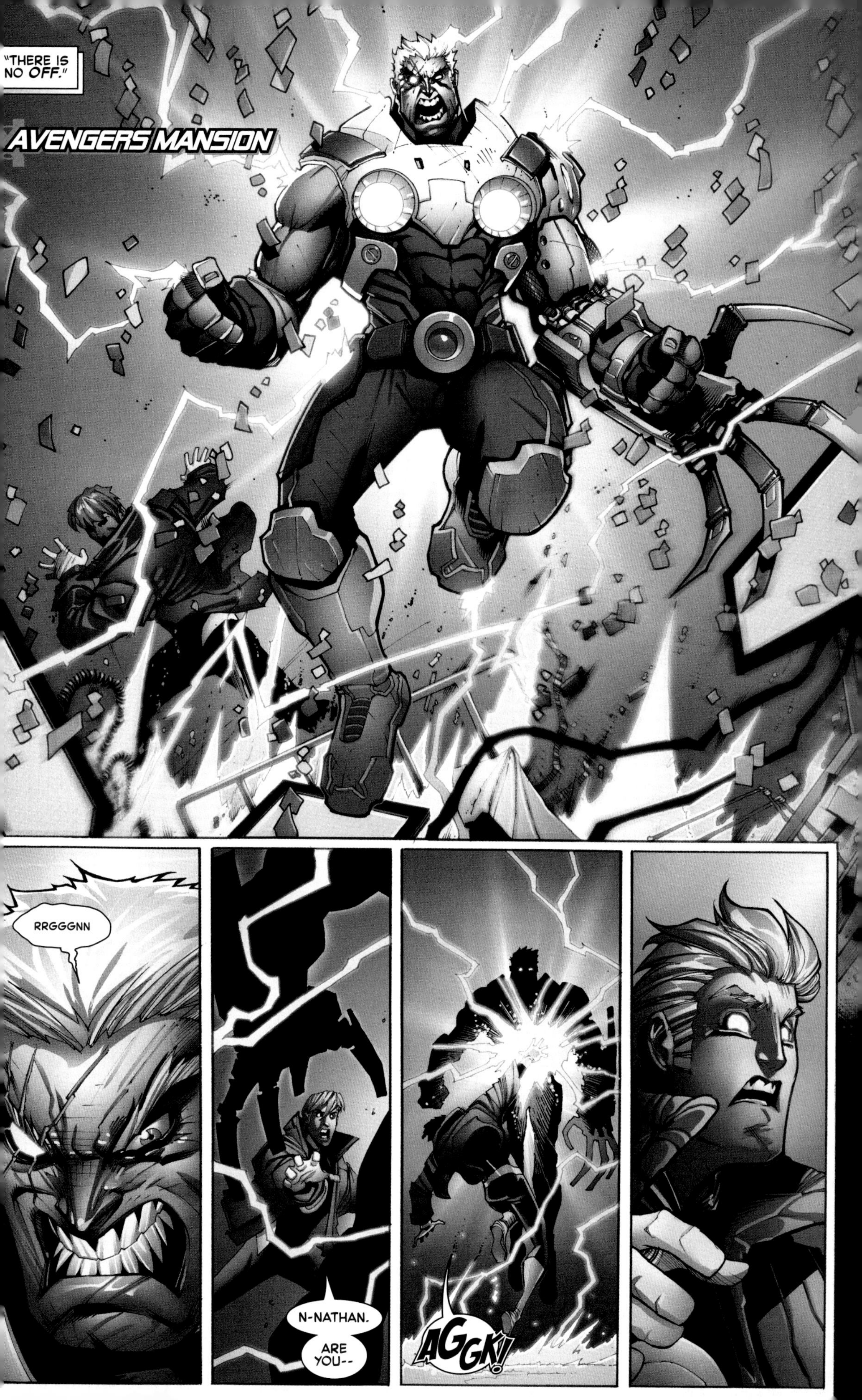
"THERE IS NO OFF."
AVENGERS MANSION
RRGGGNN
N-NATHAN.
ARE YOU--
AGGK!

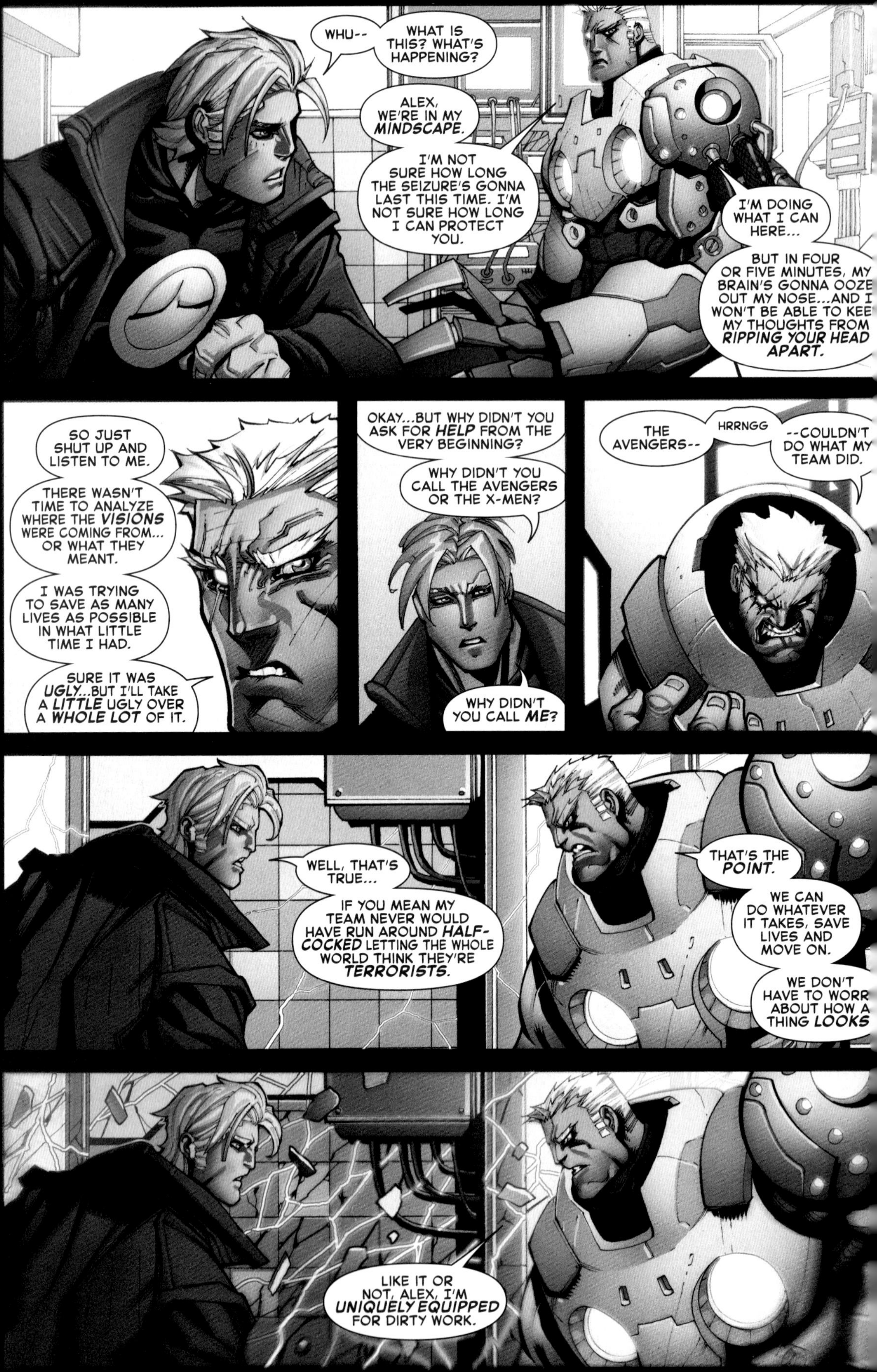
WHU--
WHAT IS THIS? WHAT'S HAPPENING?
ALEX, WE'RE IN MY MINDSCAPE.
I'M NOT SURE HOW LONG THE SEIZURE'S GONNA LAST THIS TIME. I'M NOT SURE HOW LONG I CAN PROTECT YOU.
I'M DOING WHAT I CAN HERE...
BUT IN FOUR OR FIVE MINUTES, MY BRAIN'S GONNA OOZE OUT MY NOSE...AND I WON'T BE ABLE TO KEE MY THOUGHTS FROM RIPPING YOUR HEAD APART.
SO JUST SHUT UP AND LISTEN TO ME.
THERE WASN'T TIME TO ANALYZE WHERE THE VISIONS WERE COMING FROM... OR WHAT THEY MEANT.
I WAS TRYING TO SAVE AS MANY LIVES AS POSSIBLE IN WHAT LITTLE TIME I HAD.
SURE IT WAS UGLY...BUT I'LL TAKE A LITTLE UGLY OVER A WHOLE LOT OF IT.
OKAY...BUT WHY DIDN'T YOU ASK FOR HELP FROM THE VERY BEGINNING?
WHY DIDN'T YOU CALL THE AVENGERS OR THE X-MEN?
WHY DIDN'T YOU CALL ME?
THE AVENGERS--
HRRNGG
--COULDN'T DO WHAT MY TEAM DID.
WELL, THAT'S TRUE...
IF YOU MEAN MY TEAM NEVER WOULD HAVE RUN AROUND HALF-COCKED LETTING THE WHOLE WORLD THINK THEY'RE TERRORISTS.
THAT'S THE POINT.
WE CAN DO WHATEVER IT TAKES, SAVE LIVES AND MOVE ON.
WE DON'T HAVE TO WORR ABOUT HOW A THING LOOKS
LIKE IT OR NOT, ALEX, I'M UNIQUELY EQUIPPED FOR DIRTY WORK.

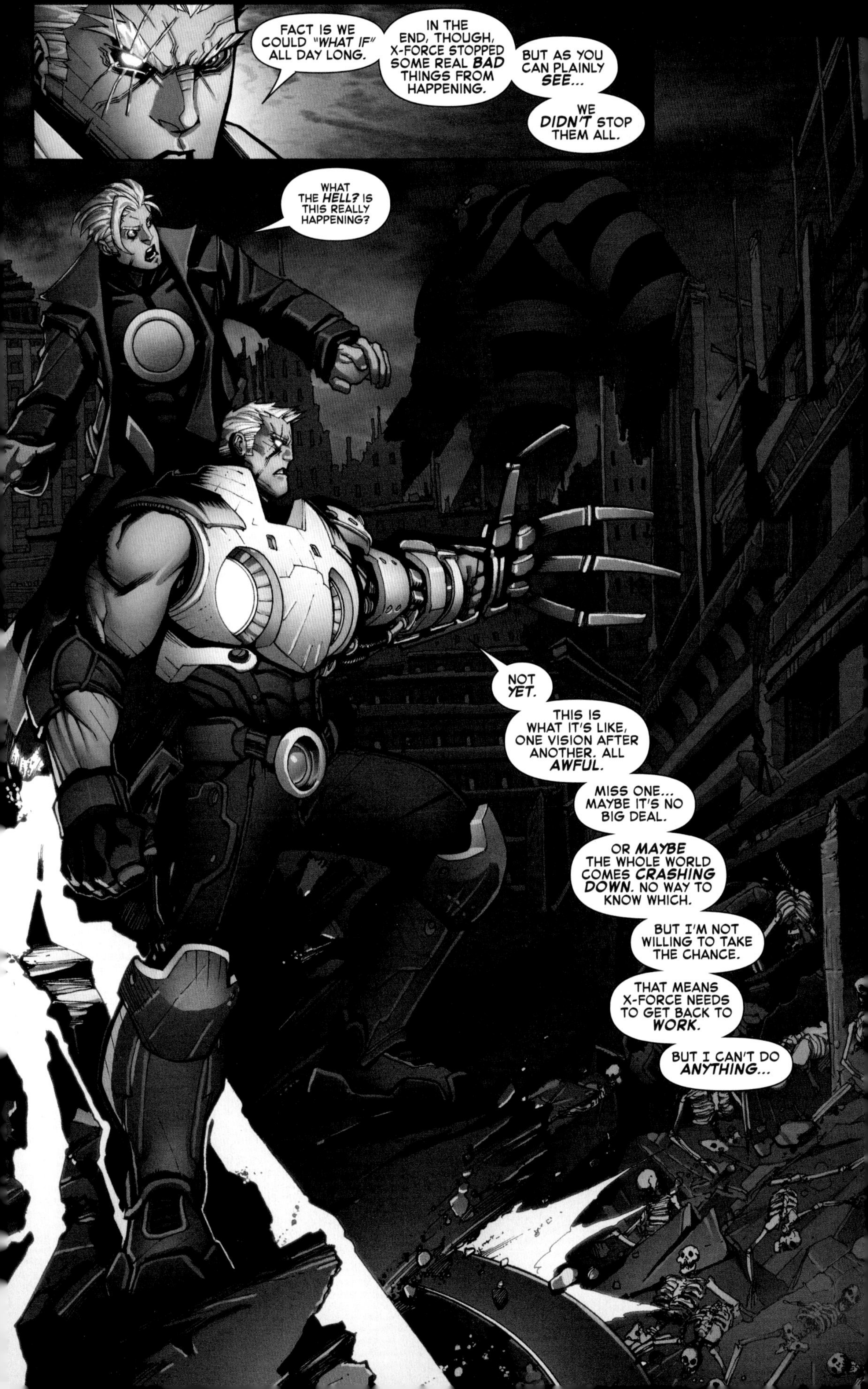
FACT IS WE COULD "WHAT IF" ALL DAY LONG.
IN THE END, THOUGH, X-FORCE STOPPED SOME REAL BAD THINGS FROM HAPPENING.
BUT AS YOU CAN PLAINLY SEE...
WE DIDN'T STOP THEM ALL.
WHAT THE HELL? IS THIS REALLY HAPPENING?
NOT YET.
THIS IS WHAT IT'S LIKE, ONE VISION AFTER ANOTHER. ALL AWFUL.
MISS ONE... MAYBE IT'S NO BIG DEAL.
OR MAYBE THE WHOLE WORLD COMES CRASHING DOWN. NO WAY TO KNOW WHICH.
BUT I'M NOT WILLING TO TAKE THE CHANCE.
THAT MEANS X-FORCE NEEDS TO GET BACK TO WORK.
BUT I CAN'T DO ANYTHING...

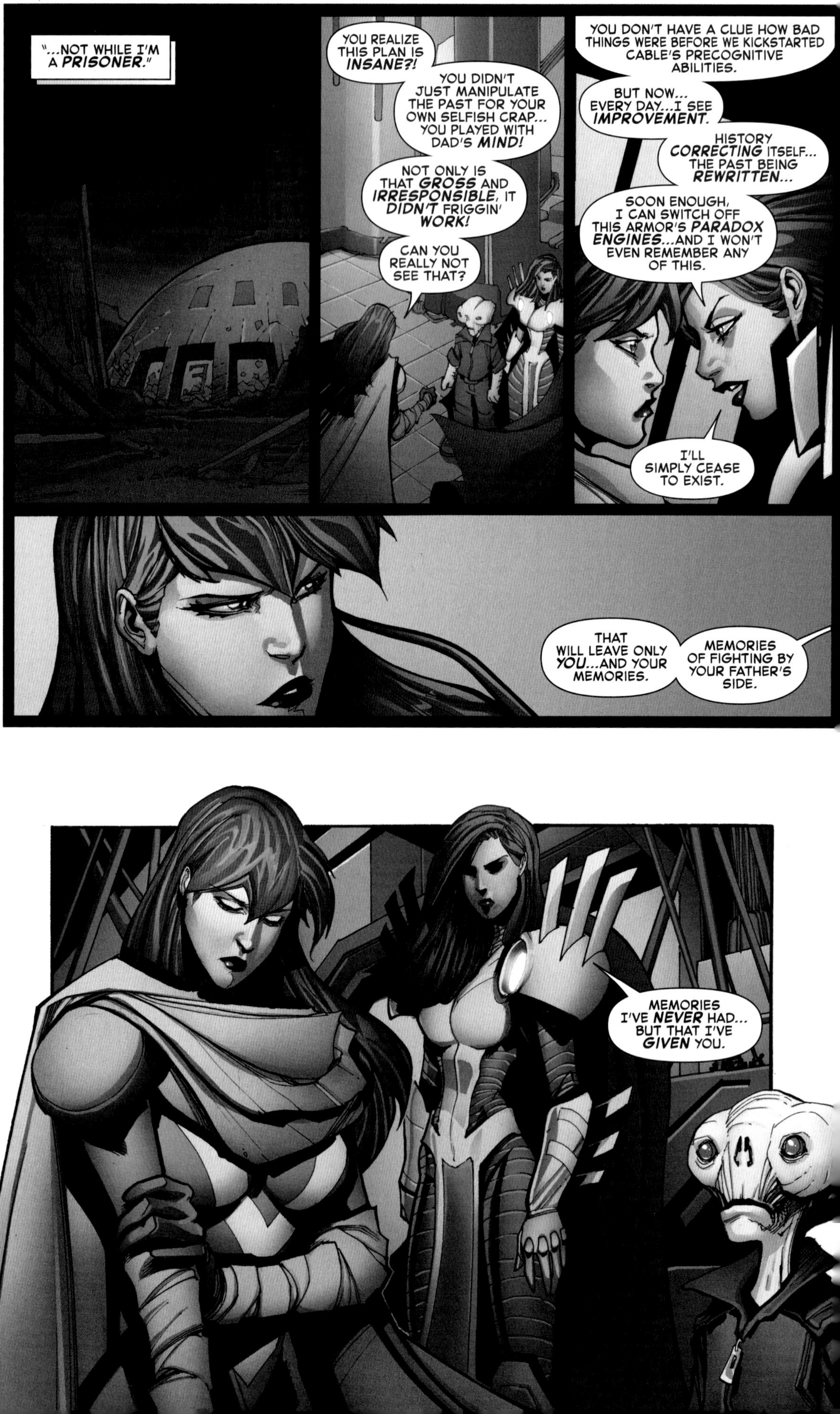
"...NOT WHILE I'M A *PRISONER*."
YOU REALIZE THIS PLAN IS *INSANE?!*
YOU DIDN'T JUST MANIPULATE THE PAST FOR YOUR OWN SELFISH CRAP... YOU PLAYED WITH DAD'S *MIND!*
NOT ONLY IS THAT *GROSS* AND *IRRESPONSIBLE*, IT *DIDN'T* FRIGGIN' *WORK!*
CAN YOU REALLY NOT SEE THAT?
YOU DON'T HAVE A CLUE HOW BAD THINGS WERE BEFORE WE KICKSTARTED CABLE'S PRECOGNITIVE ABILITIES.
BUT NOW... EVERY DAY...I SEE *IMPROVEMENT.*
HISTORY *CORRECTING* ITSELF... THE PAST BEING *REWRITTEN...*
SOON ENOUGH, I CAN SWITCH OFF THIS ARMOR'S *PARADOX ENGINES*...AND I WON'T EVEN REMEMBER ANY OF THIS.
I'LL SIMPLY CEASE TO EXIST.
THAT WILL LEAVE ONLY *YOU*...AND YOUR MEMORIES.
MEMORIES OF FIGHTING BY YOUR FATHER'S SIDE.
MEMORIES I'VE *NEVER* HAD... BUT THAT I'VE *GIVEN* YOU.

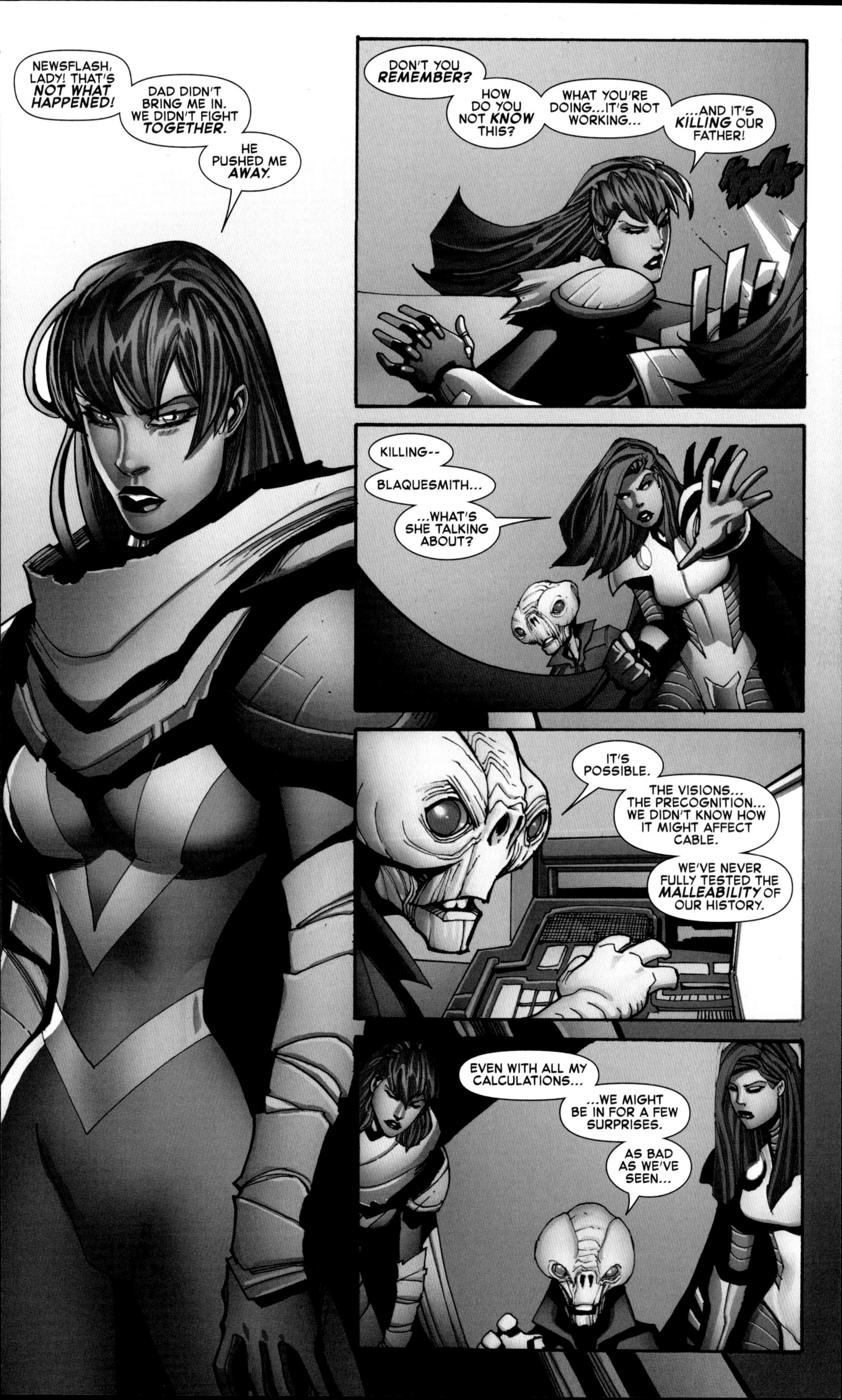
NEWSFLASH, LADY! THAT'S NOT WHAT HAPPENED!
DAD DIDN'T BRING ME IN. WE DIDN'T FIGHT TOGETHER.
HE PUSHED ME AWAY.
DON'T YOU REMEMBER?
HOW DO YOU NOT KNOW THIS?
WHAT YOU'RE DOING...IT'S NOT WORKING...
...AND IT'S KILLING OUR FATHER!
KILLING--
BLAQUESMITH...
...WHAT'S SHE TALKING ABOUT?
IT'S POSSIBLE.
THE VISIONS... THE PRECOGNITION... WE DIDN'T KNOW HOW IT MIGHT AFFECT CABLE.
WE'VE NEVER FULLY TESTED THE MALLEABILITY OF OUR HISTORY.
EVEN WITH ALL MY CALCULATIONS...
...WE MIGHT BE IN FOR A FEW SURPRISES.
AS BAD AS WE'VE SEEN...

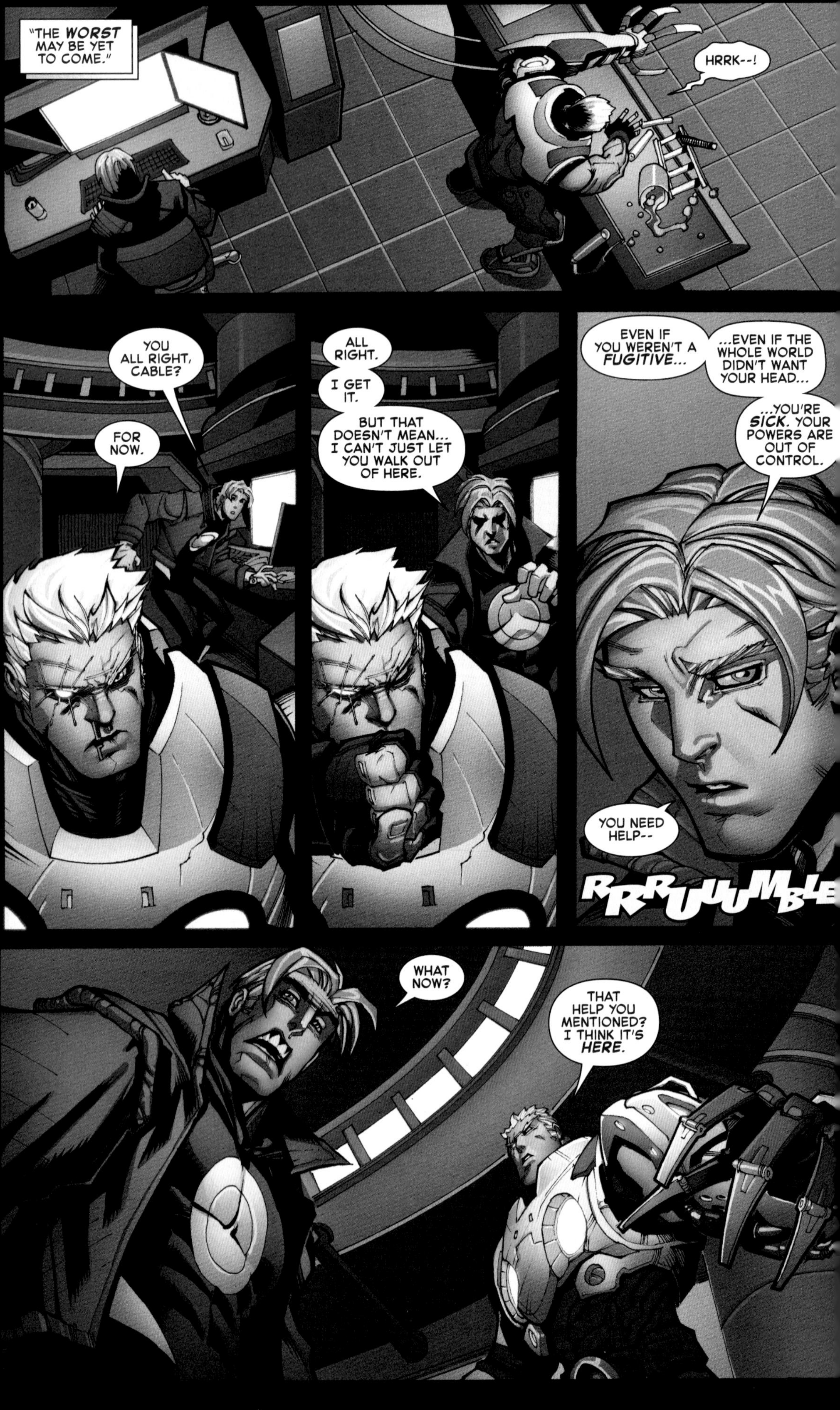
"THE WORST MAY BE YET TO COME."
HRRK--!
YOU ALL RIGHT, CABLE?
FOR NOW.
ALL RIGHT.
I GET IT.
BUT THAT DOESN'T MEAN... I CAN'T JUST LET YOU WALK OUT OF HERE.
EVEN IF YOU WEREN'T A FUGITIVE...
...EVEN IF THE WHOLE WORLD DIDN'T WANT YOUR HEAD...
...YOU'RE SICK. YOUR POWERS ARE OUT OF CONTROL.
YOU NEED HELP--
RRRUUUMBLE
WHAT NOW?
THAT HELP YOU MENTIONED? I THINK IT'S HERE.

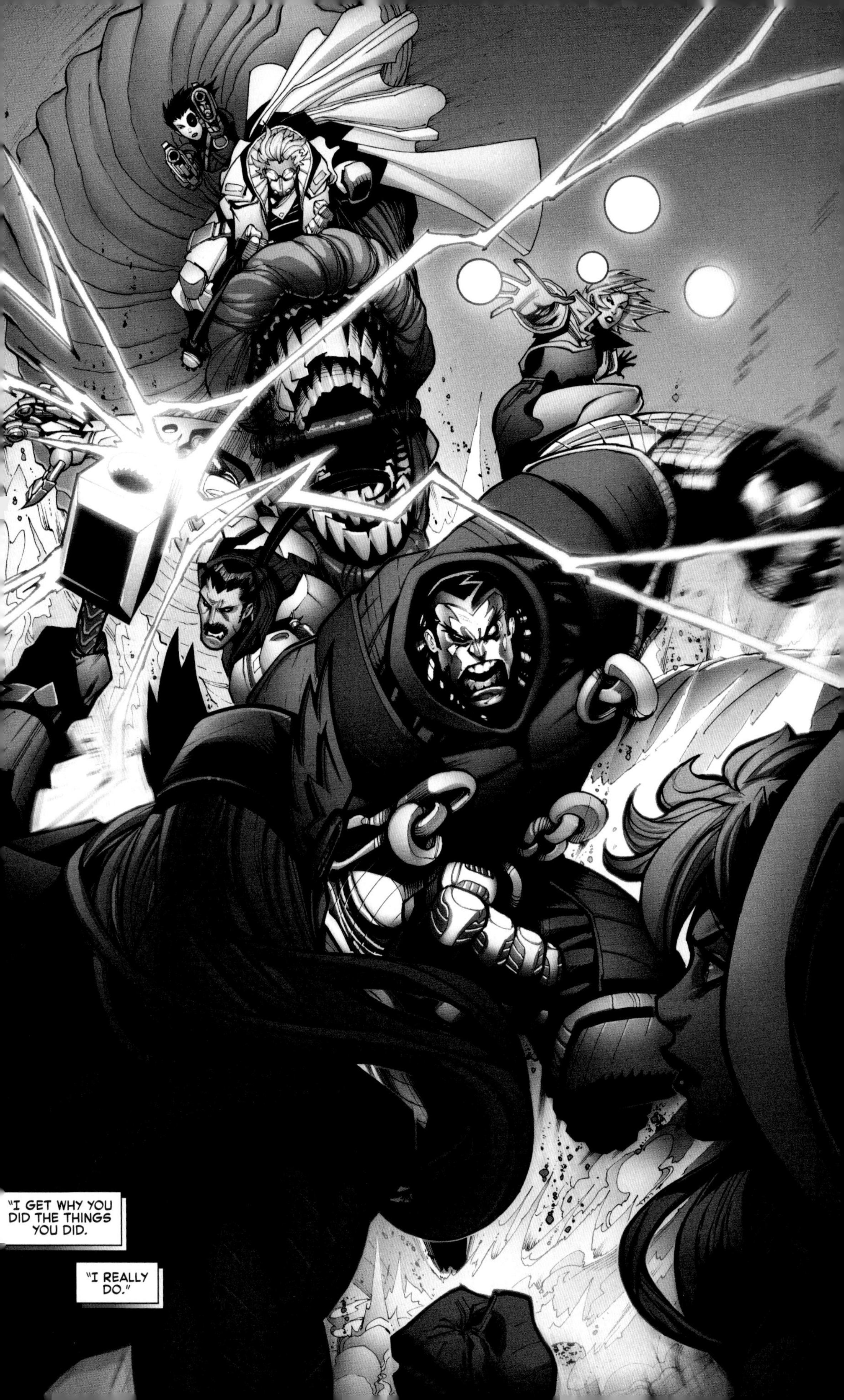
"I GET WHY YOU DID THE THINGS YOU DID.
"I REALLY DO."

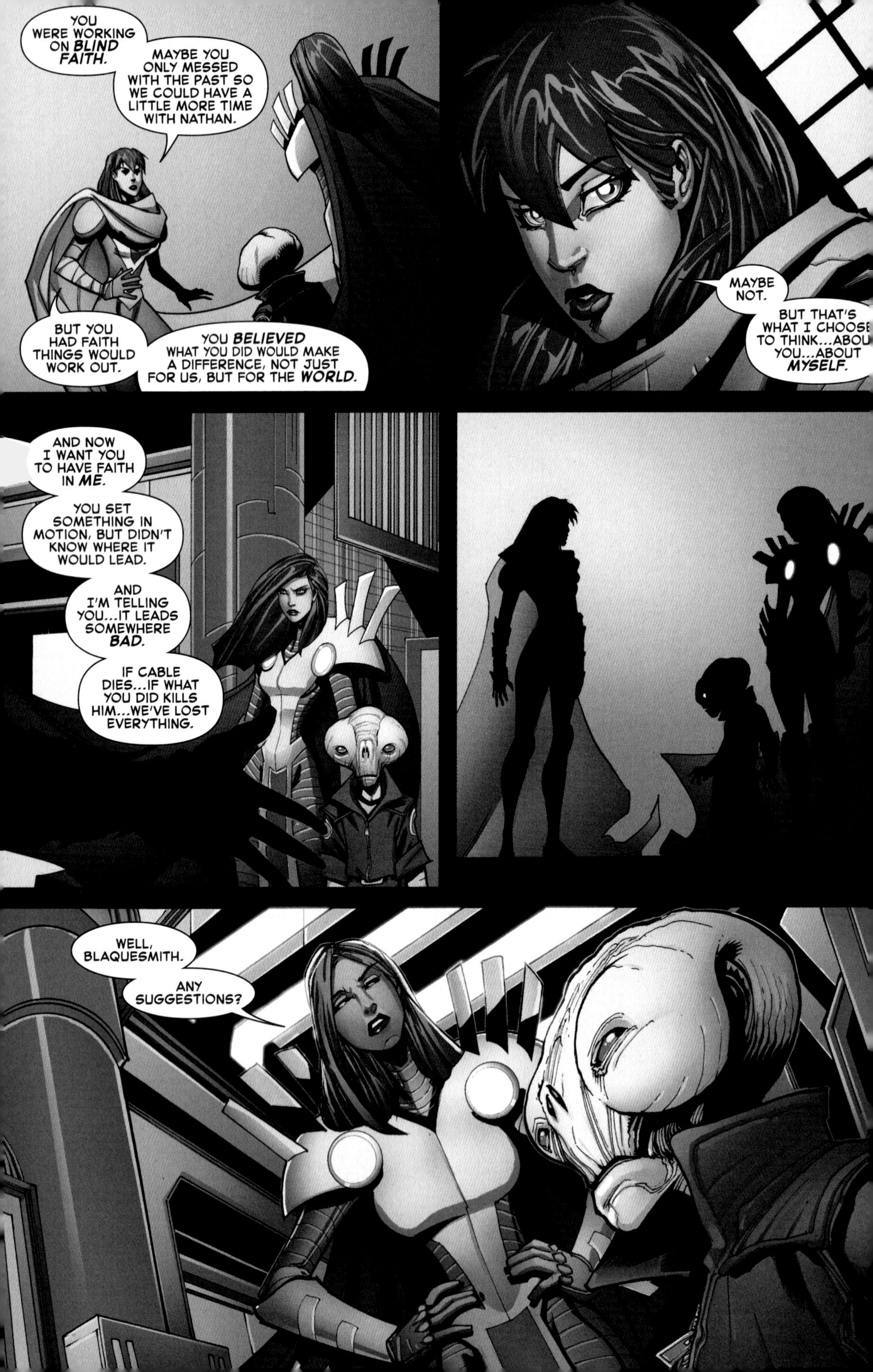

YOU WERE WORKING ON BLIND FAITH.
MAYBE YOU ONLY MESSED WITH THE PAST SO WE COULD HAVE A LITTLE MORE TIME WITH NATHAN.
BUT YOU HAD FAITH THINGS WOULD WORK OUT.
YOU BELIEVED WHAT YOU DID WOULD MAKE A DIFFERENCE, NOT JUST FOR US, BUT FOR THE WORLD.
MAYBE NOT.
BUT THAT'S WHAT I CHOOSE TO THINK...ABOUT YOU...ABOUT MYSELF.
AND NOW I WANT YOU TO HAVE FAITH IN ME.
YOU SET SOMETHING IN MOTION, BUT DIDN'T KNOW WHERE IT WOULD LEAD.
AND I'M TELLING YOU...IT LEADS SOMEWHERE BAD.
IF CABLE DIES...IF WHAT YOU DID KILLS HIM...WE'VE LOST EVERYTHING.
WELL, BLAQUESMITH.
ANY SUGGESTIONS?

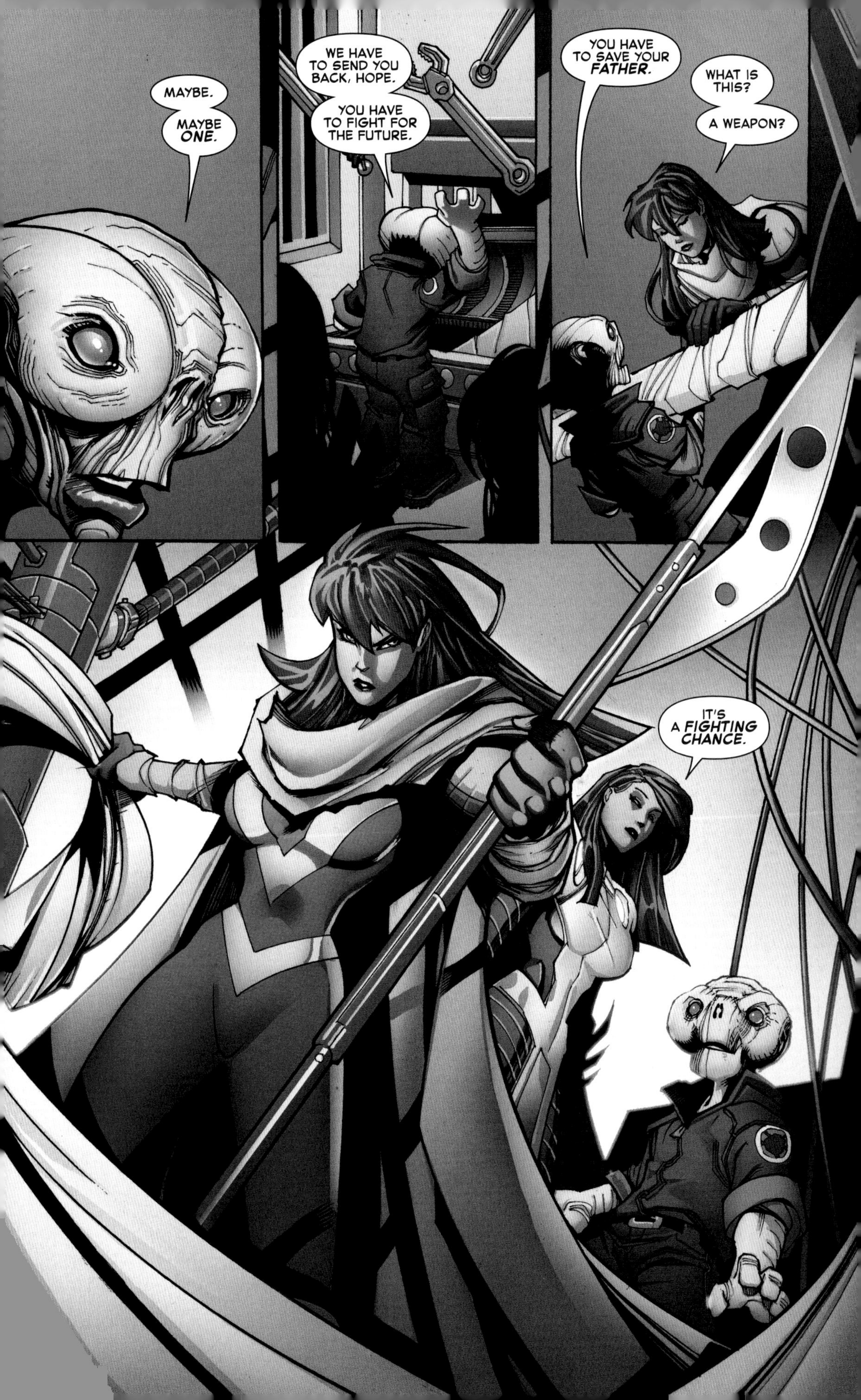
MAYBE.
MAYBE ONE.
WE HAVE TO SEND YOU BACK, HOPE.
YOU HAVE TO FIGHT FOR THE FUTURE.
YOU HAVE TO SAVE YOUR FATHER.
WHAT IS THIS?
A WEAPON?
IT'S A FIGHTING CHANCE.

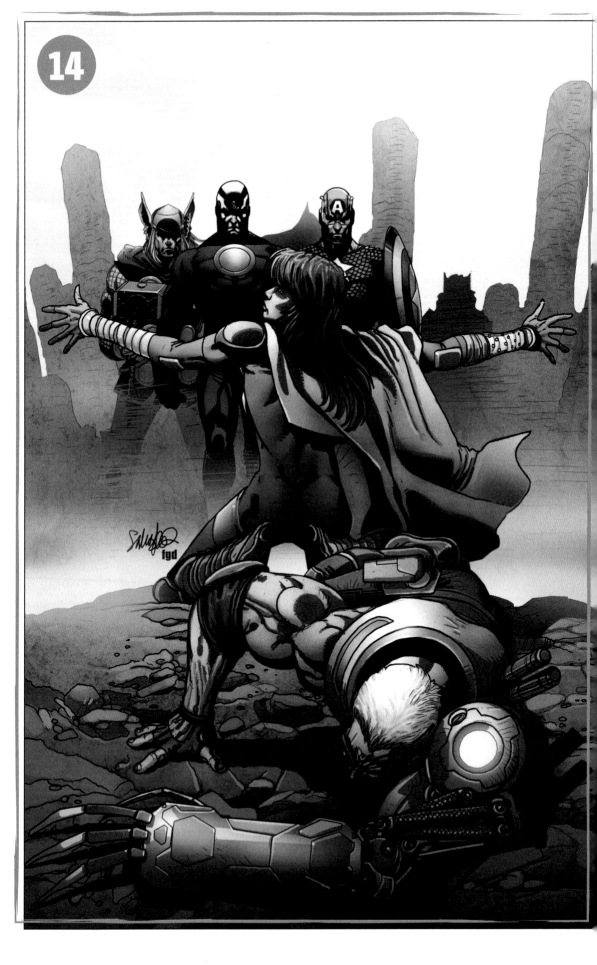

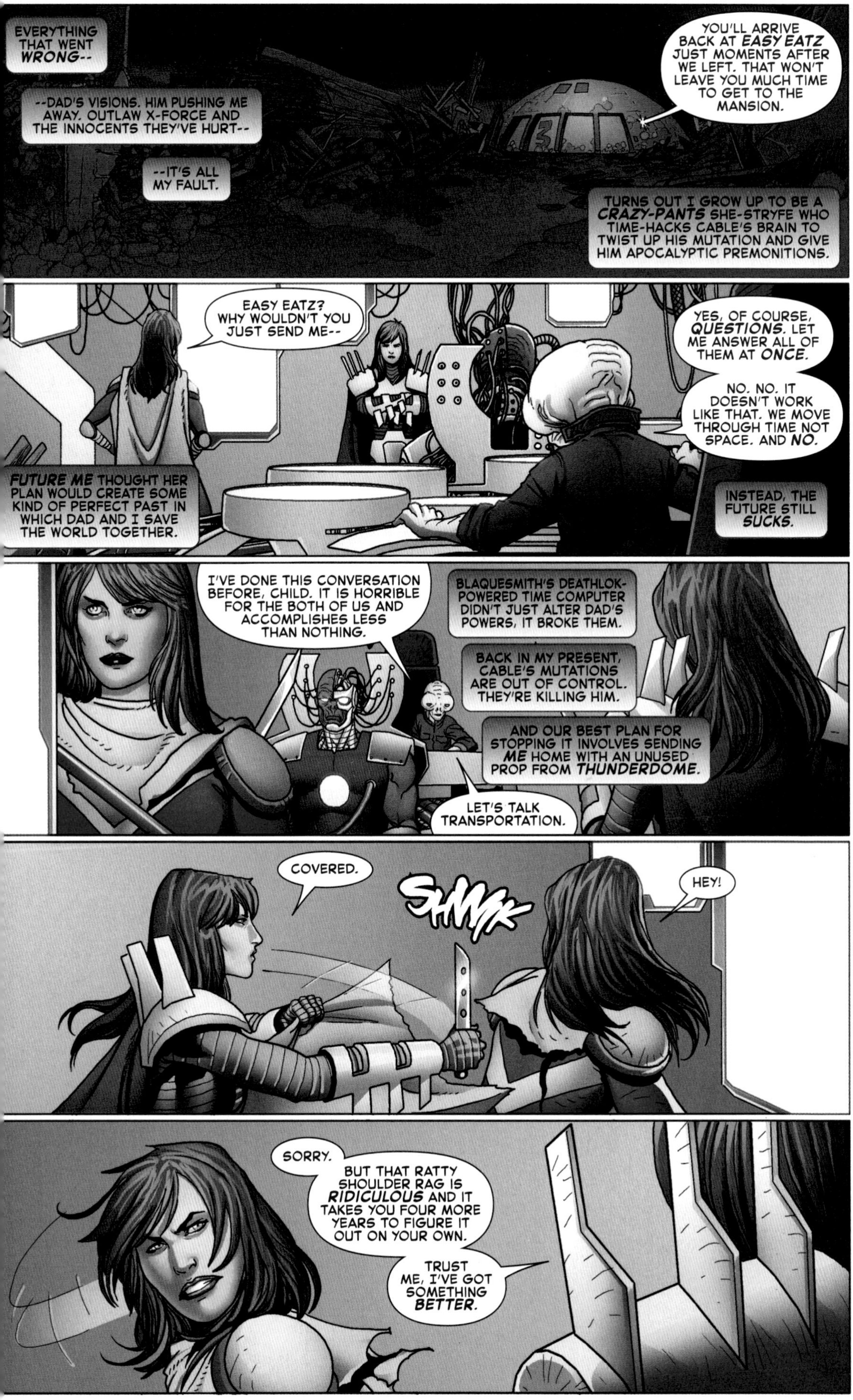
EVERYTHING THAT WENT WRONG--
--DAD'S VISIONS. HIM PUSHING ME AWAY. OUTLAW X-FORCE AND THE INNOCENTS THEY'VE HURT--
--IT'S ALL MY FAULT.
YOU'LL ARRIVE BACK AT EASY EATZ JUST MOMENTS AFTER WE LEFT. THAT WON'T LEAVE YOU MUCH TIME TO GET TO THE MANSION.
TURNS OUT I GROW UP TO BE A CRAZY-PANTS SHE-STRYFE WHO TIME-HACKS CABLE'S BRAIN TO TWIST UP HIS MUTATION AND GIVE HIM APOCALYPTIC PREMONITIONS.
EASY EATZ? WHY WOULDN'T YOU JUST SEND ME--
YES, OF COURSE, QUESTIONS. LET ME ANSWER ALL OF THEM AT ONCE.
NO. NO. IT DOESN'T WORK LIKE THAT. WE MOVE THROUGH TIME NOT SPACE. AND NO.
FUTURE ME THOUGHT HER PLAN WOULD CREATE SOME KIND OF PERFECT PAST IN WHICH DAD AND I SAVE THE WORLD TOGETHER.
INSTEAD, THE FUTURE STILL SUCKS.
I'VE DONE THIS CONVERSATION BEFORE, CHILD. IT IS HORRIBLE FOR THE BOTH OF US AND ACCOMPLISHES LESS THAN NOTHING.
BLAQUESMITH'S DEATHLOK-POWERED TIME COMPUTER DIDN'T JUST ALTER DAD'S POWERS, IT BROKE THEM.
BACK IN MY PRESENT, CABLE'S MUTATIONS ARE OUT OF CONTROL. THEY'RE KILLING HIM.
AND OUR BEST PLAN FOR STOPPING IT INVOLVES SENDING ME HOME WITH AN UNUSED PROP FROM THUNDERDOME.
LET'S TALK TRANSPORTATION.
COVERED.
SHNKK
HEY!
SORRY.
BUT THAT RATTY SHOULDER RAG IS RIDICULOUS AND IT TAKES YOU FOUR MORE YEARS TO FIGURE IT OUT ON YOUR OWN.
TRUST ME, I'VE GOT SOMETHING BETTER.

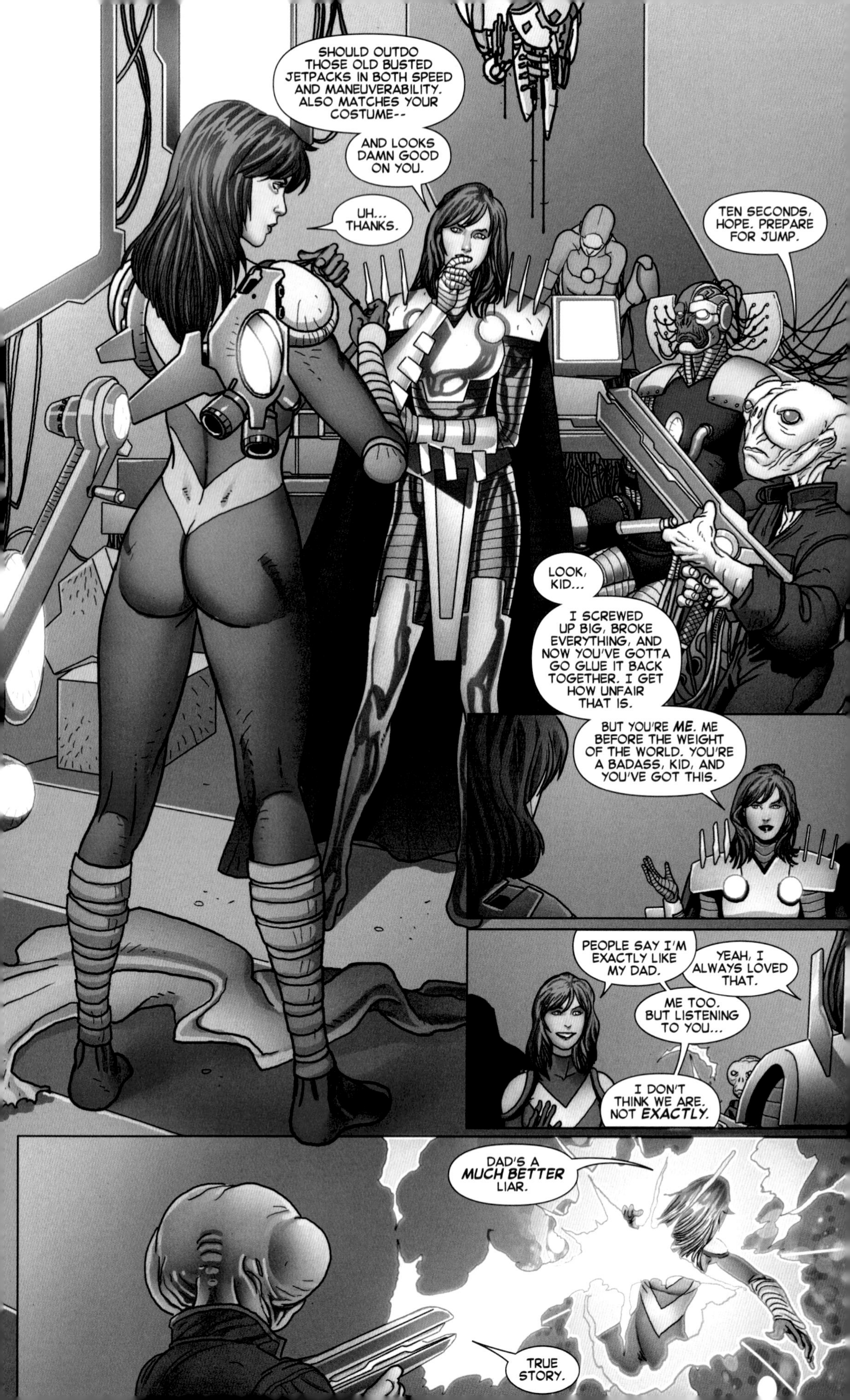
SHOULD OUTDO THOSE OLD BUSTED JETPACKS IN BOTH SPEED AND MANEUVERABILITY. ALSO MATCHES YOUR COSTUME--
AND LOOKS DAMN GOOD ON YOU.
UH... THANKS.
TEN SECONDS, HOPE. PREPARE FOR JUMP.
LOOK, KID...
I SCREWED UP BIG, BROKE EVERYTHING, AND NOW YOU'VE GOTTA GO GLUE IT BACK TOGETHER. I GET HOW UNFAIR THAT IS.
BUT YOU'RE ME. ME BEFORE THE WEIGHT OF THE WORLD. YOU'RE A BADASS, KID, AND YOU'VE GOT THIS.
PEOPLE SAY I'M EXACTLY LIKE MY DAD.
YEAH, I ALWAYS LOVED THAT.
ME TOO. BUT LISTENING TO YOU...
I DON'T THINK WE ARE. NOT EXACTLY.
DAD'S A MUCH BETTER LIAR.
TRUE STORY.

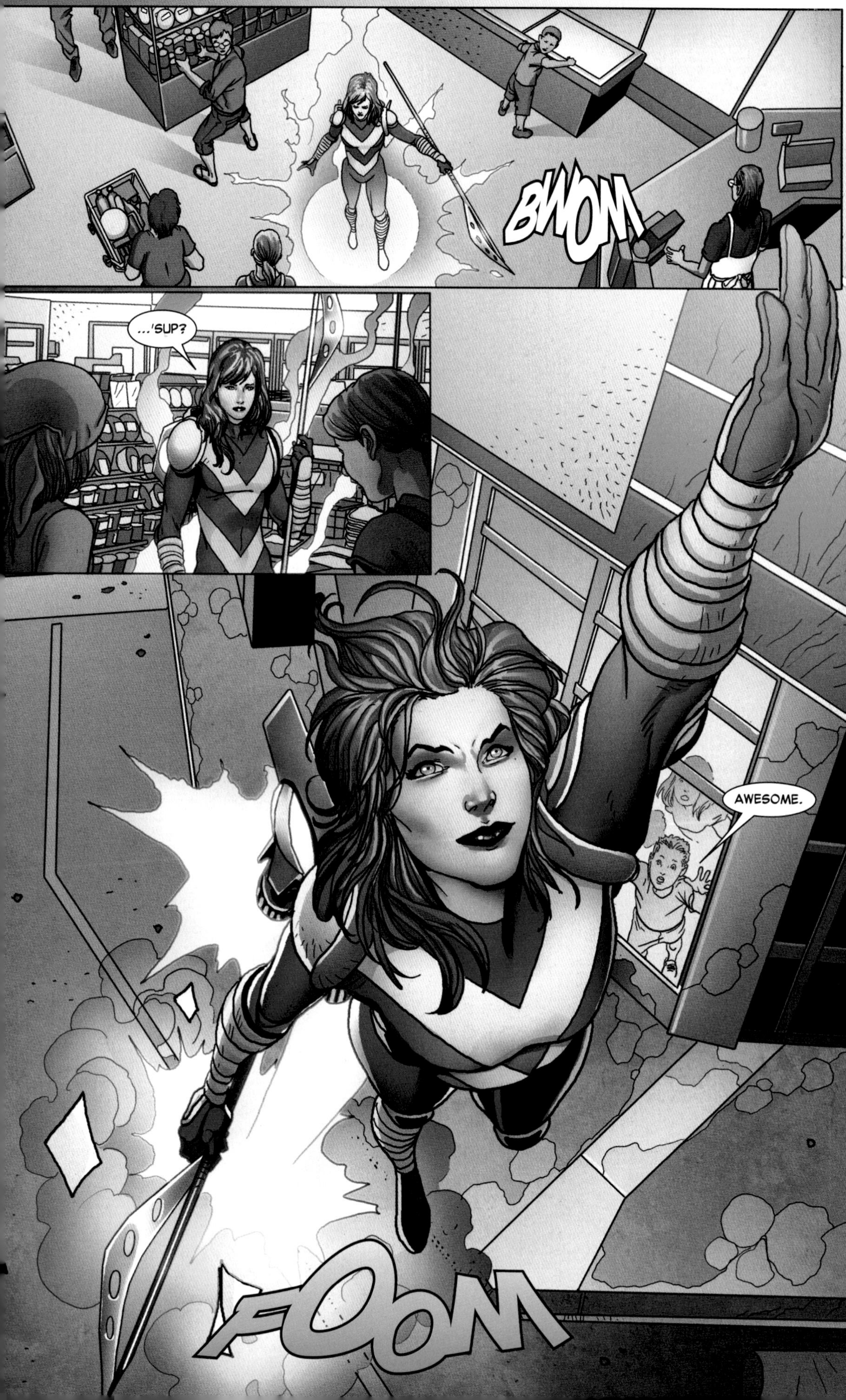
BWOM
...'SUP?
AWESOME.
FOOM

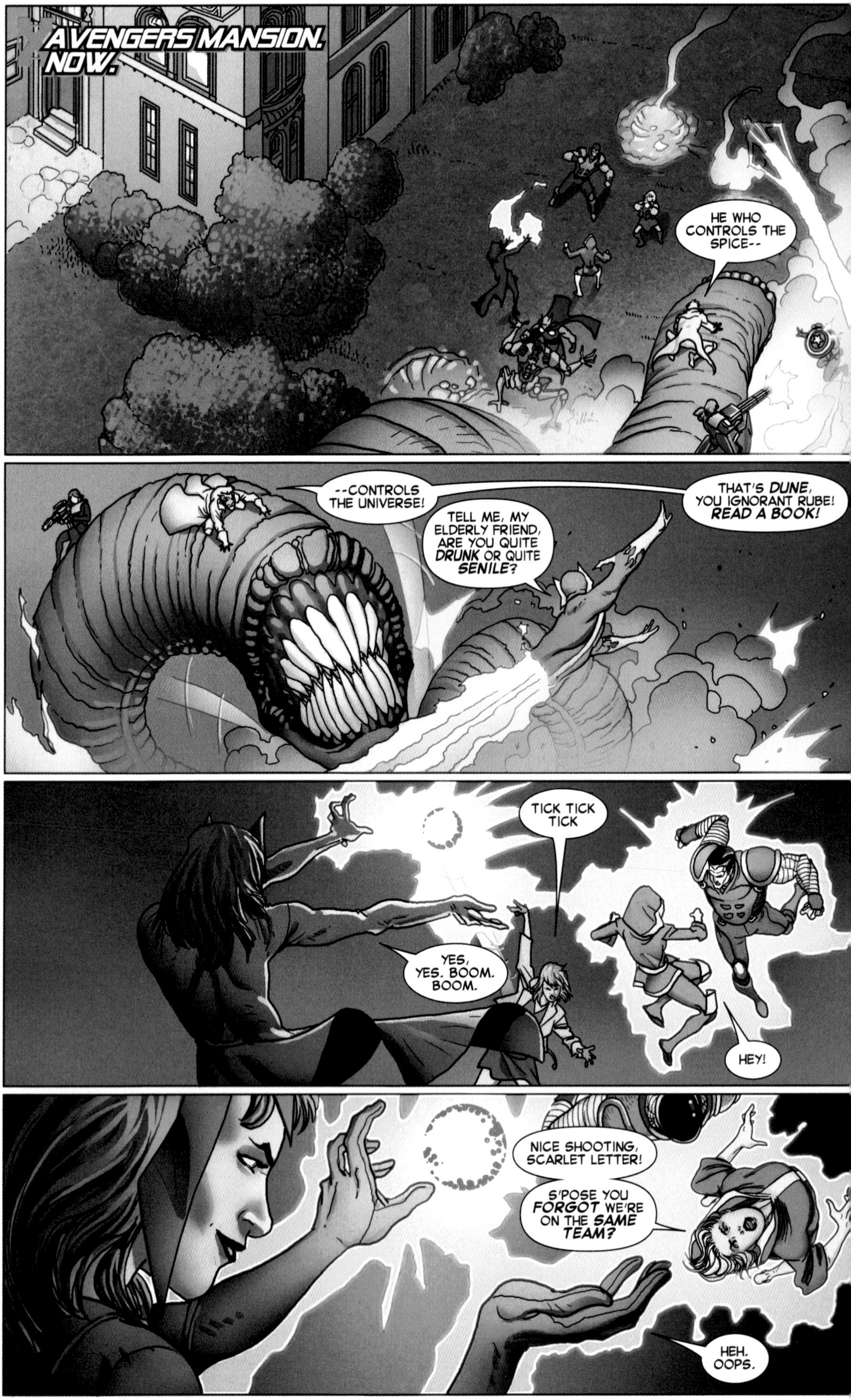
AVENGERS MANSION. NOW.
HE WHO CONTROLS THE SPICE--
--CONTROLS THE UNIVERSE!
THAT'S DUNE, YOU IGNORANT RUBE! READ A BOOK!
TELL ME, MY ELDERLY FRIEND, ARE YOU QUITE DRUNK OR QUITE SENILE?
TICK TICK TICK
YES, YES. BOOM. BOOM.
HEY!
NICE SHOOTING, SCARLET LETTER!
S'POSE YOU FORGOT WE'RE ON THE SAME TEAM?
HEH. OOPS.

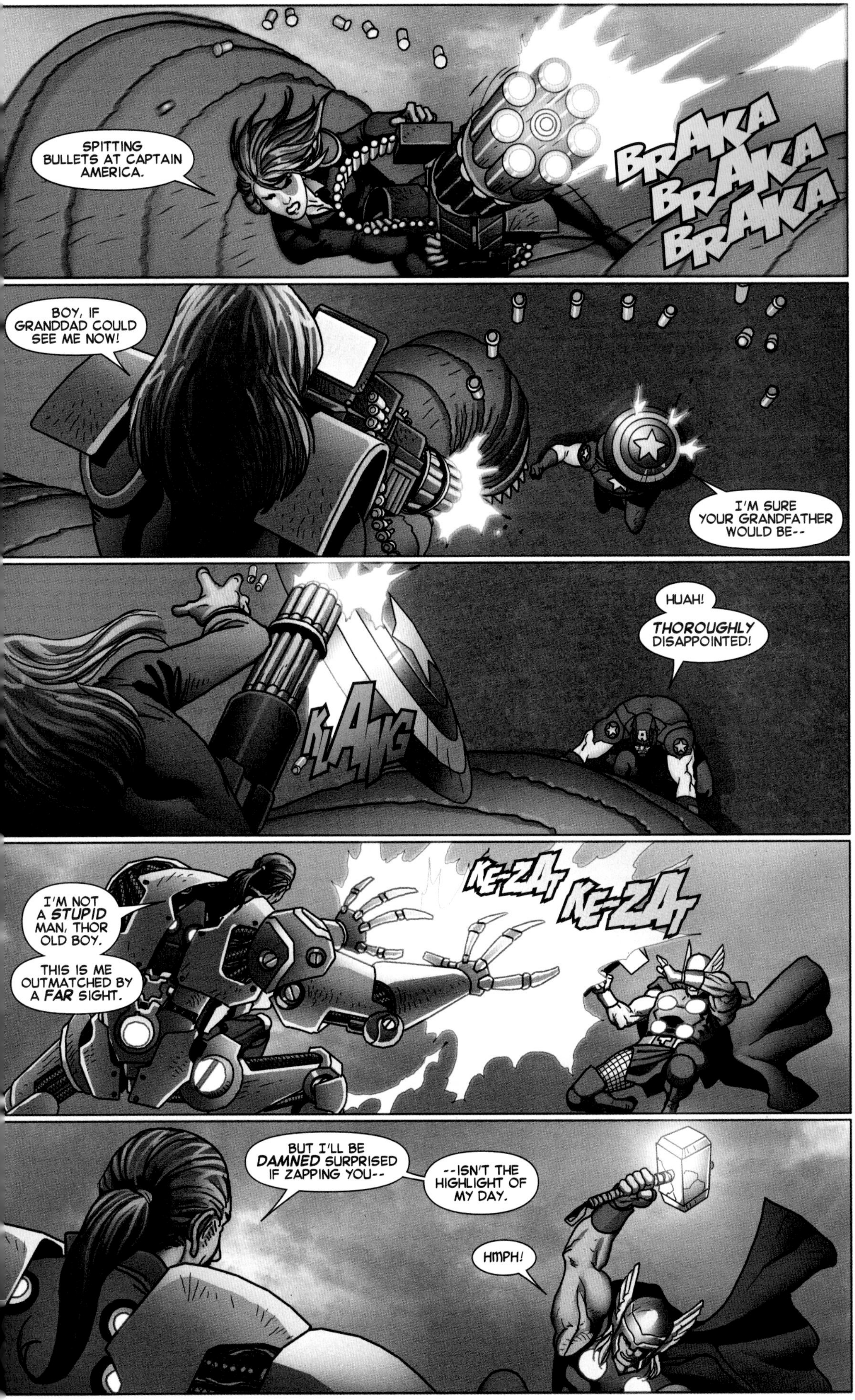
SPITTING BULLETS AT CAPTAIN AMERICA.
BRAKA BRAKA BRAKA
BOY, IF GRANDDAD COULD SEE ME NOW!
I'M SURE YOUR GRANDFATHER WOULD BE--
HUAH!
THOROUGHLY DISAPPOINTED!
KLANG
I'M NOT A STUPID MAN, THOR OLD BOY.
THIS IS ME OUTMATCHED BY A FAR SIGHT.
KE-ZAT KE-ZAT
BUT I'LL BE DAMNED SURPRISED IF ZAPPING YOU--
--ISN'T THE HIGHLIGHT OF MY DAY.
HMPH!

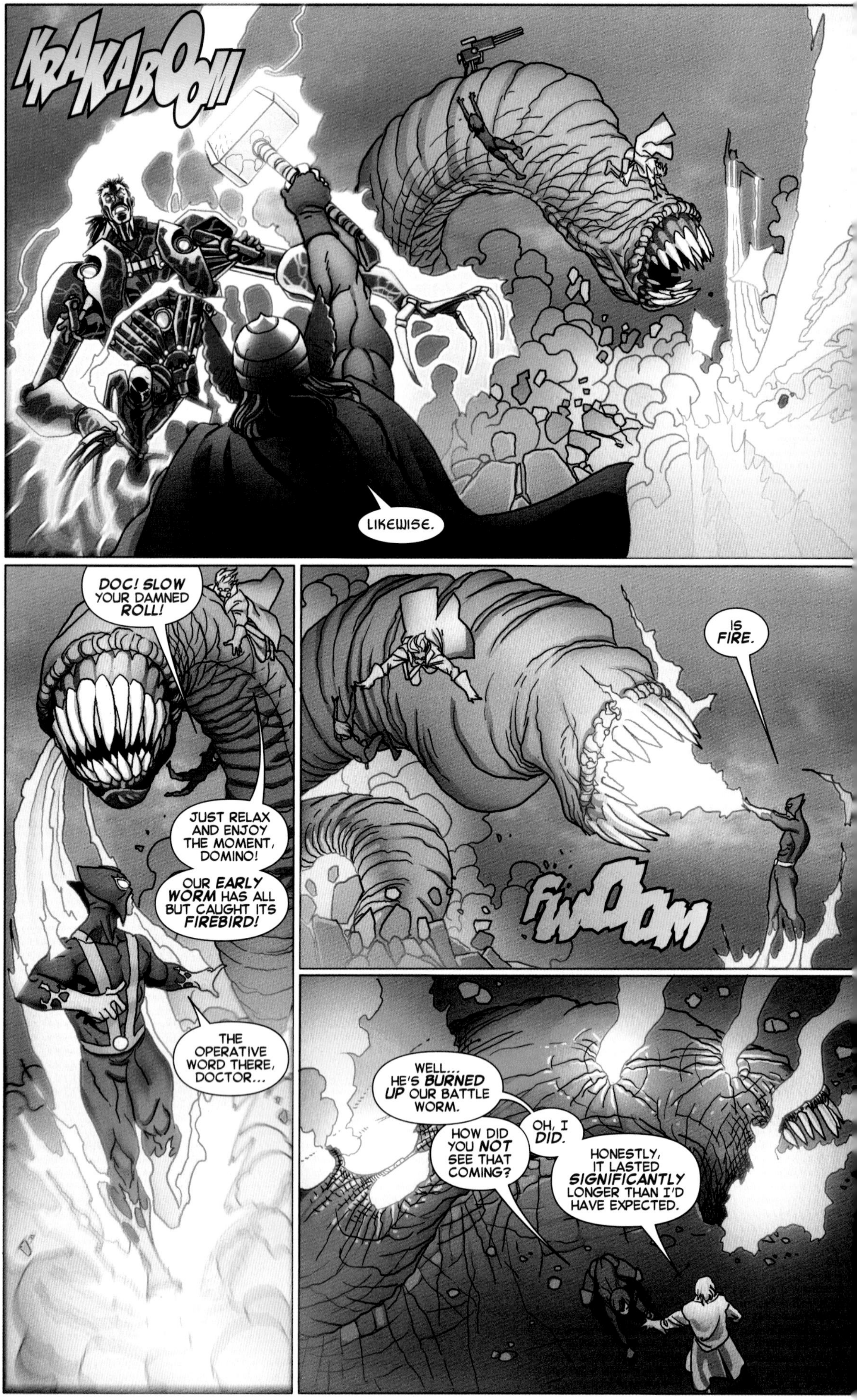
KRAKABOOM
LIKEWISE.
DOC! SLOW YOUR DAMNED ROLL!
JUST RELAX AND ENJOY THE MOMENT, DOMINO!
OUR EARLY WORM HAS ALL BUT CAUGHT ITS FIREBIRD!
THE OPERATIVE WORD THERE, DOCTOR...
IS FIRE.
FWOOM
WELL... HE'S BURNED UP OUR BATTLE WORM.
HOW DID YOU NOT SEE THAT COMING?
OH, I DID.
HONESTLY, IT LASTED SIGNIFICANTLY LONGER THAN I'D HAVE EXPECTED.

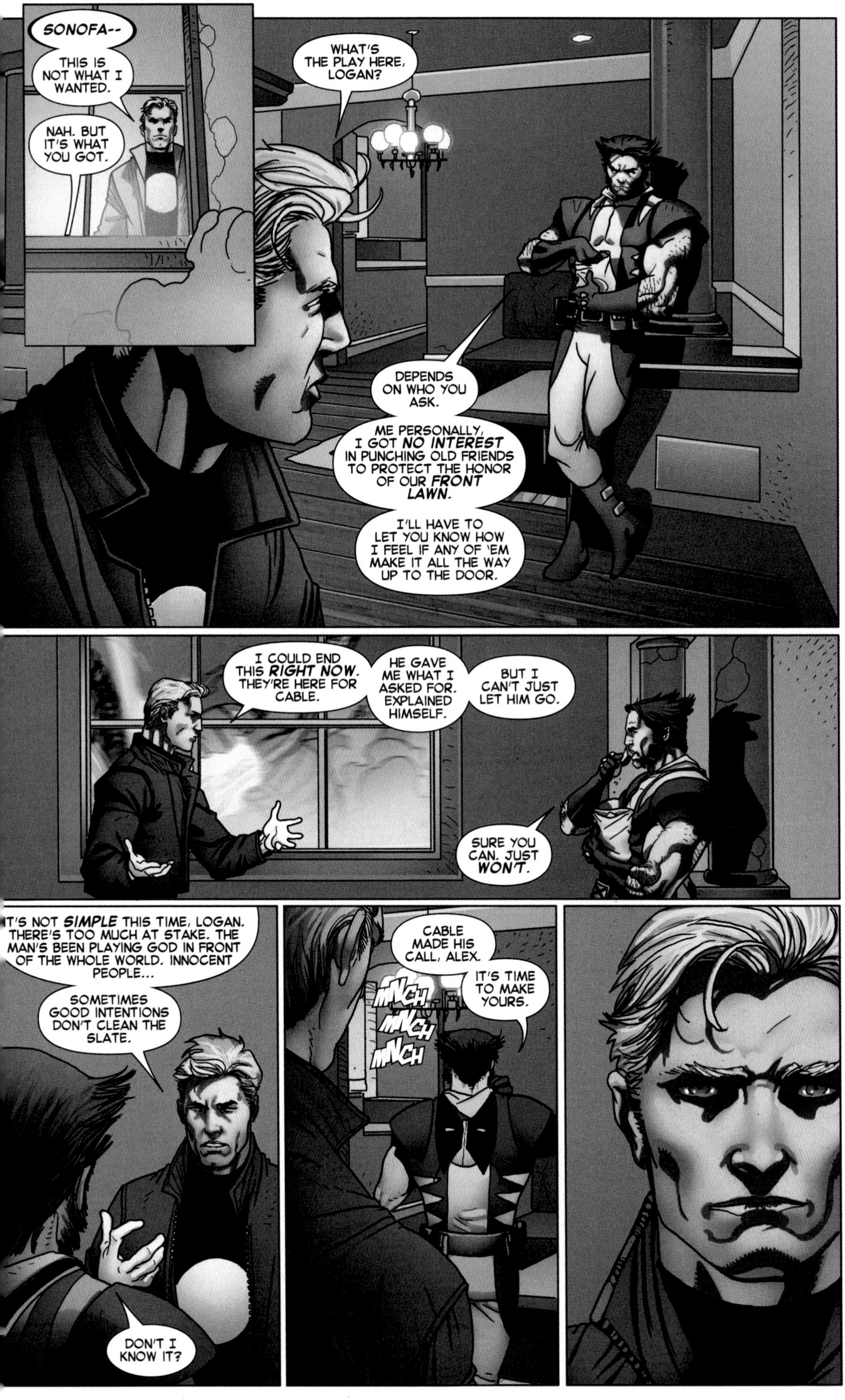
SONOFA--
THIS IS NOT WHAT I WANTED.
NAH. BUT IT'S WHAT YOU GOT.
WHAT'S THE PLAY HERE, LOGAN?
DEPENDS ON WHO YOU ASK.
ME PERSONALLY, I GOT NO INTEREST IN PUNCHING OLD FRIENDS TO PROTECT THE HONOR OF OUR FRONT LAWN.
I'LL HAVE TO LET YOU KNOW HOW I FEEL IF ANY OF 'EM MAKE IT ALL THE WAY UP TO THE DOOR.
I COULD END THIS RIGHT NOW. THEY'RE HERE FOR CABLE.
HE GAVE ME WHAT I ASKED FOR. EXPLAINED HIMSELF.
BUT I CAN'T JUST LET HIM GO.
SURE YOU CAN. JUST WON'T.
IT'S NOT SIMPLE THIS TIME, LOGAN. THERE'S TOO MUCH AT STAKE. THE MAN'S BEEN PLAYING GOD IN FRONT OF THE WHOLE WORLD. INNOCENT PEOPLE...
SOMETIMES GOOD INTENTIONS DON'T CLEAN THE SLATE.
DON'T I KNOW IT?
CABLE MADE HIS CALL, ALEX.
IT'S TIME TO MAKE YOURS.
MNCH
MNCH
MNCH

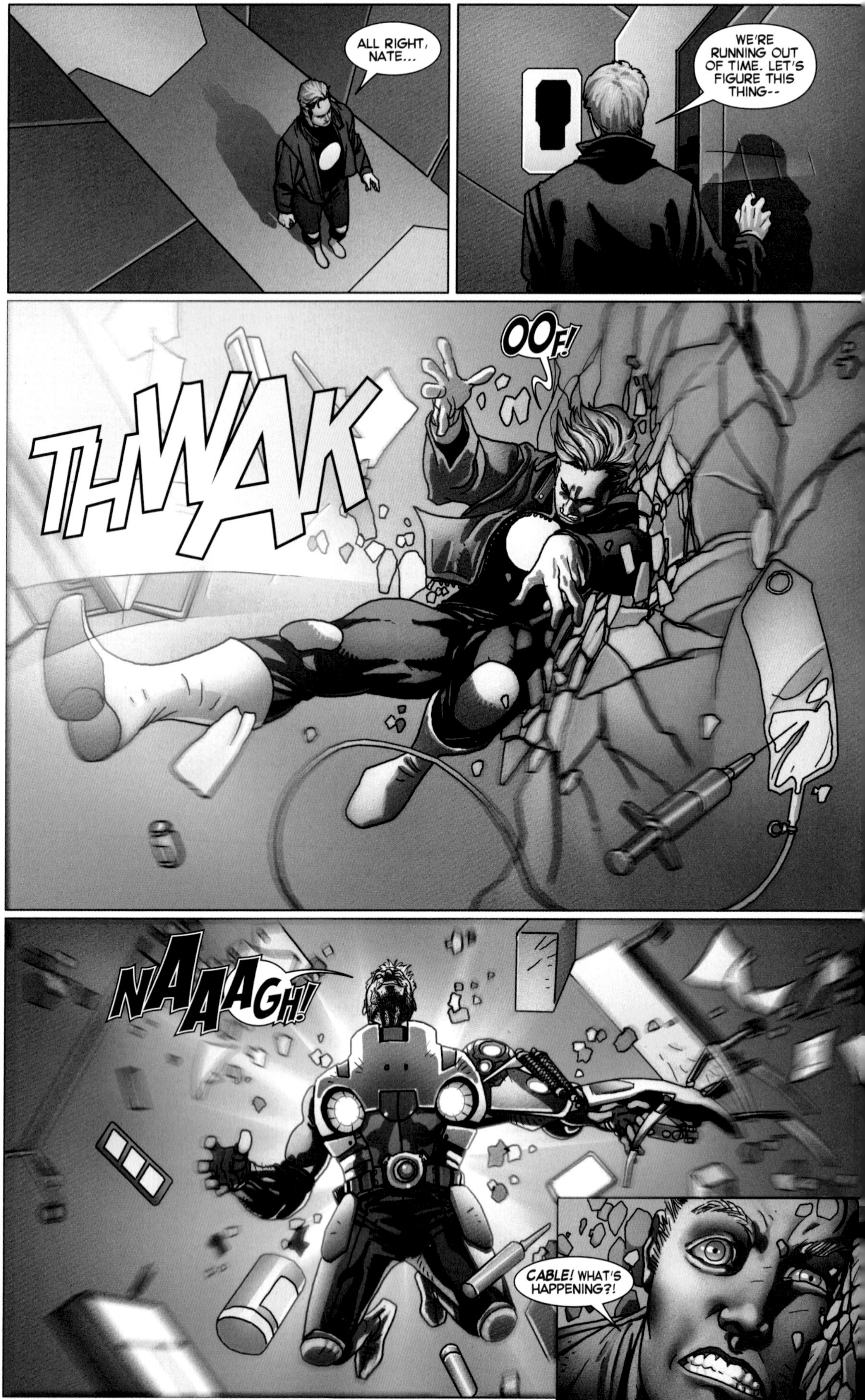
ALL RIGHT, NATE...
WE'RE RUNNING OUT OF TIME. LET'S FIGURE THIS THING--
THWAK
OOF!
NAAAGH!
CABLE! WHAT'S HAPPENING?!

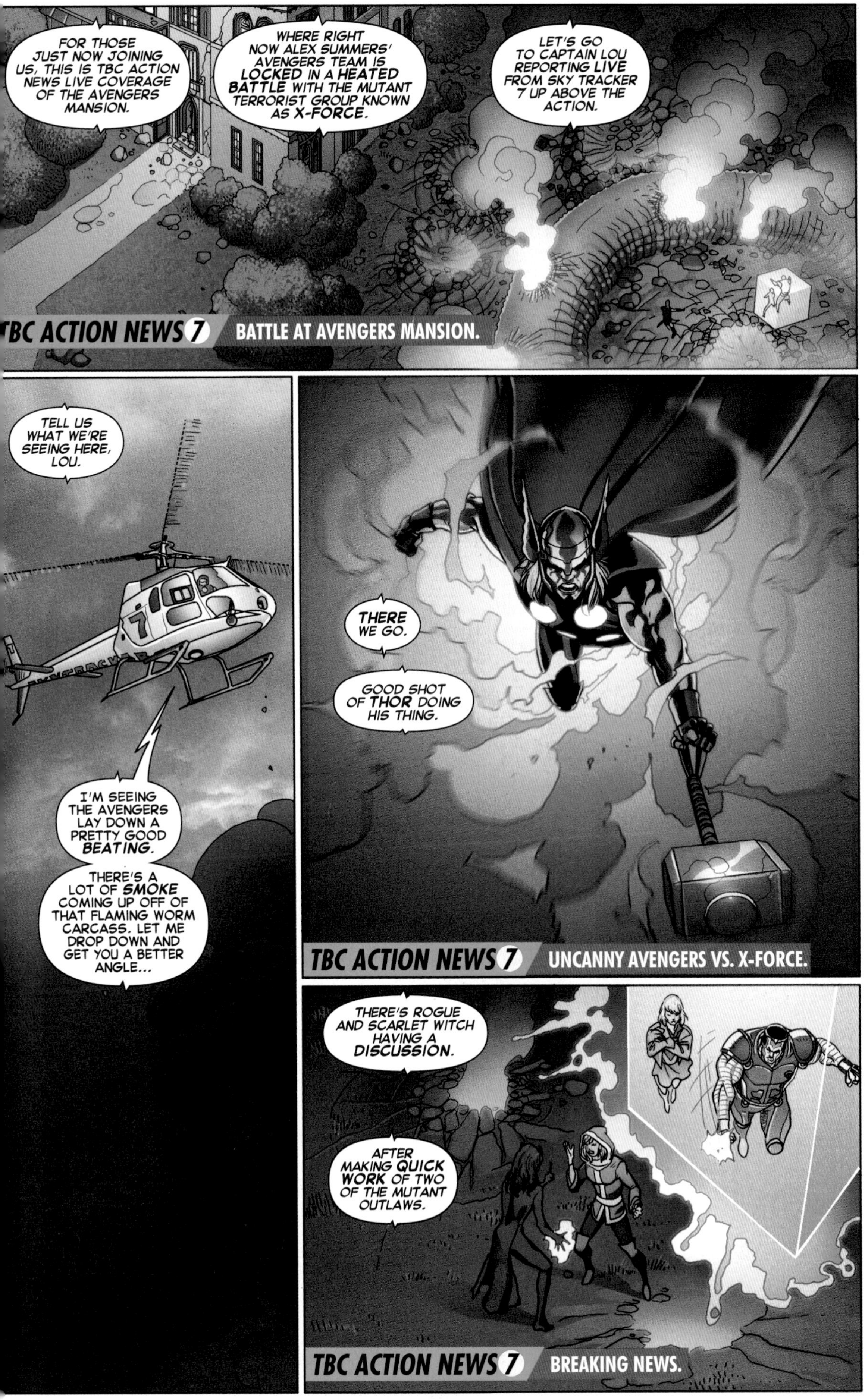
FOR THOSE JUST NOW JOINING US, THIS IS TBC ACTION NEWS LIVE COVERAGE OF THE AVENGERS MANSION.
WHERE RIGHT NOW ALEX SUMMERS' AVENGERS TEAM IS LOCKED IN A HEATED BATTLE WITH THE MUTANT TERRORIST GROUP KNOWN AS X-FORCE.
LET'S GO TO CAPTAIN LOU REPORTING LIVE FROM SKY TRACKER 7 UP ABOVE THE ACTION.
TBC ACTION NEWS 7
BATTLE AT AVENGERS MANSION.
TELL US WHAT WE'RE SEEING HERE, LOU.
I'M SEEING THE AVENGERS LAY DOWN A PRETTY GOOD BEATING.
THERE'S A LOT OF SMOKE COMING UP OFF OF THAT FLAMING WORM CARCASS. LET ME DROP DOWN AND GET YOU A BETTER ANGLE...
THERE WE GO.
GOOD SHOT OF THOR DOING HIS THING.
TBC ACTION NEWS 7
UNCANNY AVENGERS VS. X-FORCE.
THERE'S ROGUE AND SCARLET WITCH HAVING A DISCUSSION.
AFTER MAKING QUICK WORK OF TWO OF THE MUTANT OUTLAWS.
TBC ACTION NEWS 7
BREAKING NEWS.

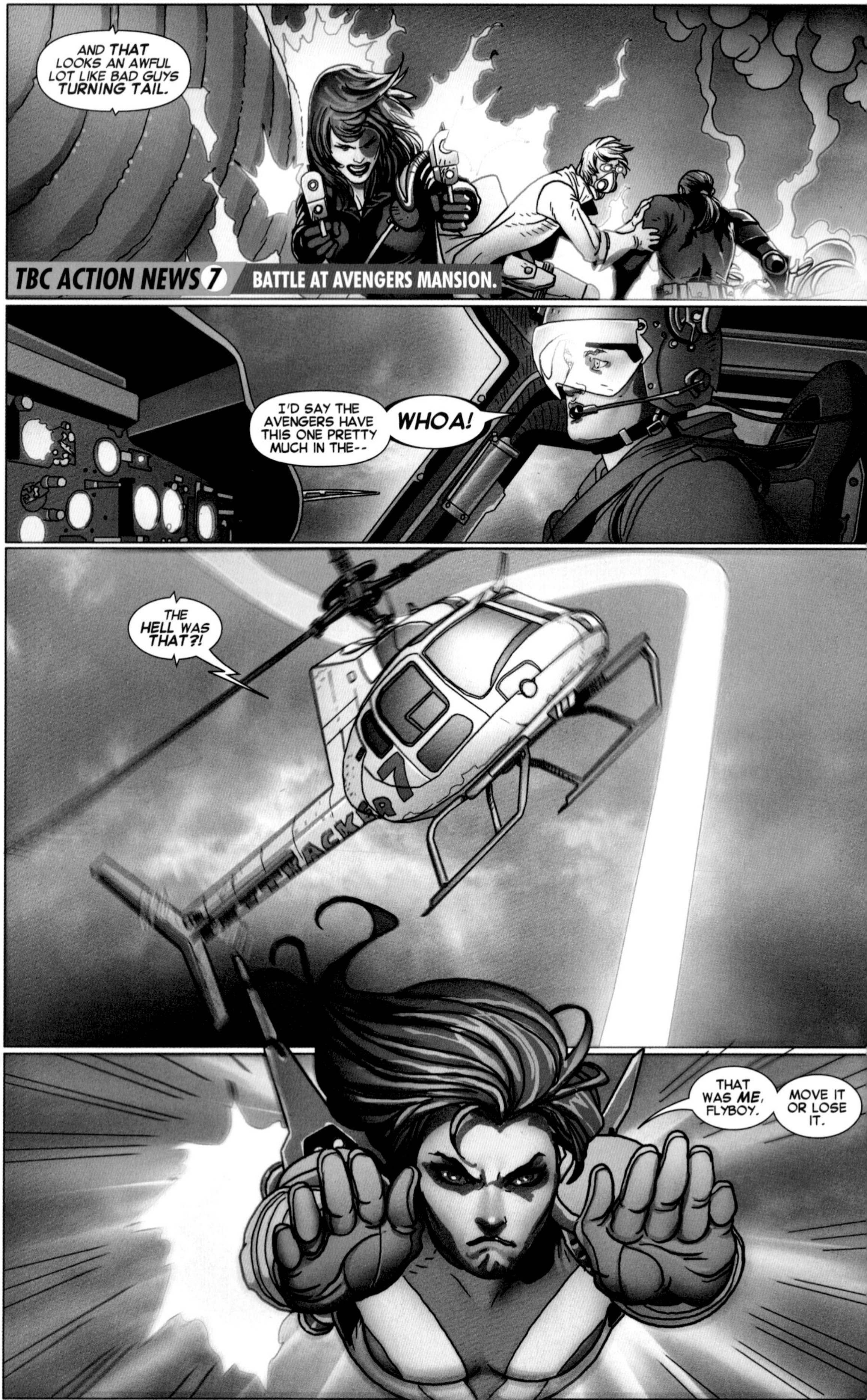
AND THAT LOOKS AN AWFUL LOT LIKE BAD GUYS TURNING TAIL.
TBC ACTION NEWS 7
BATTLE AT AVENGERS MANSION.
I'D SAY THE AVENGERS HAVE THIS ONE PRETTY MUCH IN THE--
WHOA!
THE HELL WAS THAT?!
THAT WAS ME, FLYBOY.
MOVE IT OR LOSE IT.

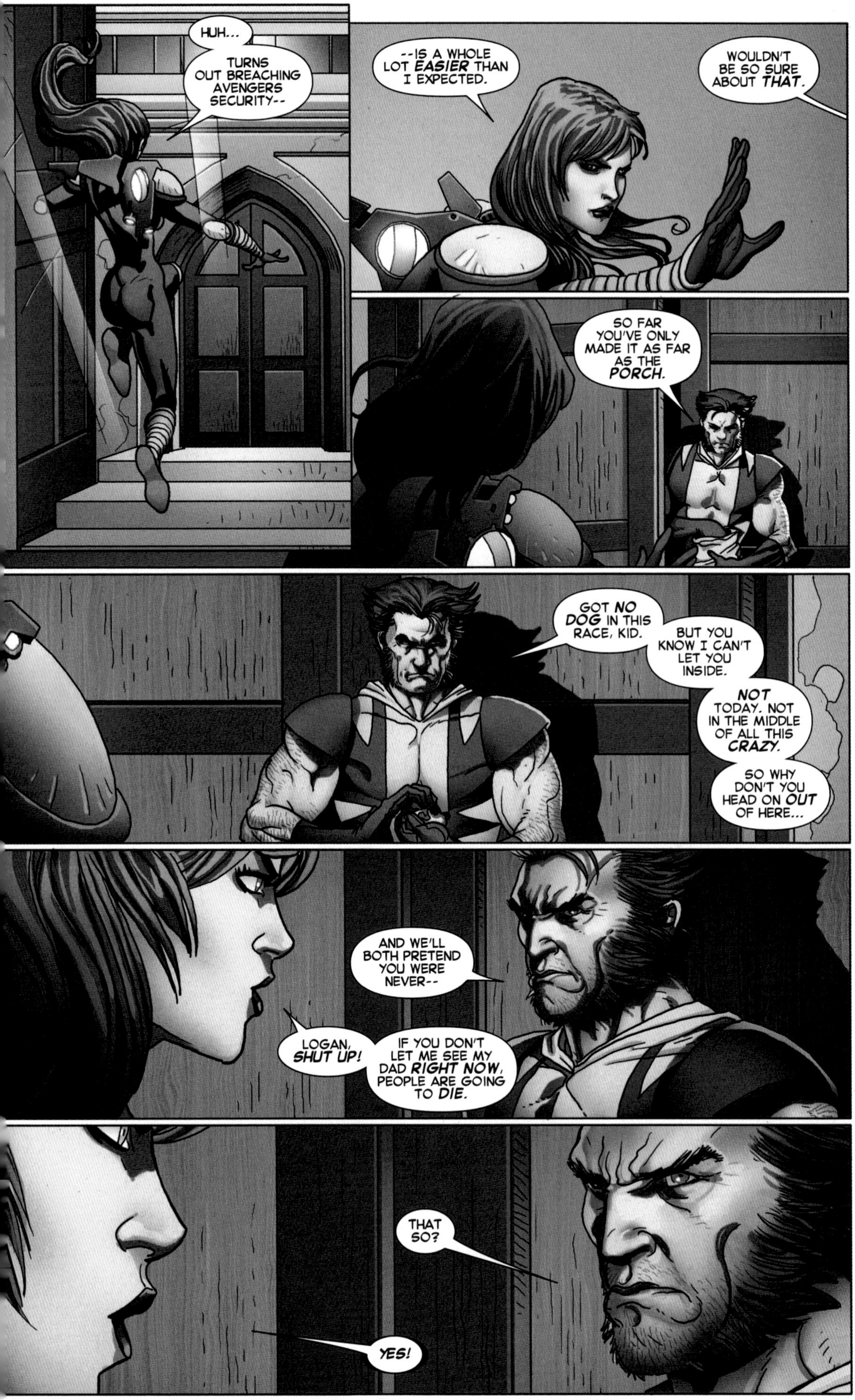
HUH...
TURNS OUT BREACHING AVENGERS SECURITY--
--IS A WHOLE LOT EASIER THAN I EXPECTED.
WOULDN'T BE SO SURE ABOUT THAT.
SO FAR YOU'VE ONLY MADE IT AS FAR AS THE PORCH.
GOT NO DOG IN THIS RACE, KID.
BUT YOU KNOW I CAN'T LET YOU INSIDE.
NOT TODAY. NOT IN THE MIDDLE OF ALL THIS CRAZY.
SO WHY DON'T YOU HEAD ON OUT OF HERE...
AND WE'LL BOTH PRETEND YOU WERE NEVER--
LOGAN, SHUT UP!
IF YOU DON'T LET ME SEE MY DAD RIGHT NOW, PEOPLE ARE GOING TO DIE.
THAT SO?
YES!

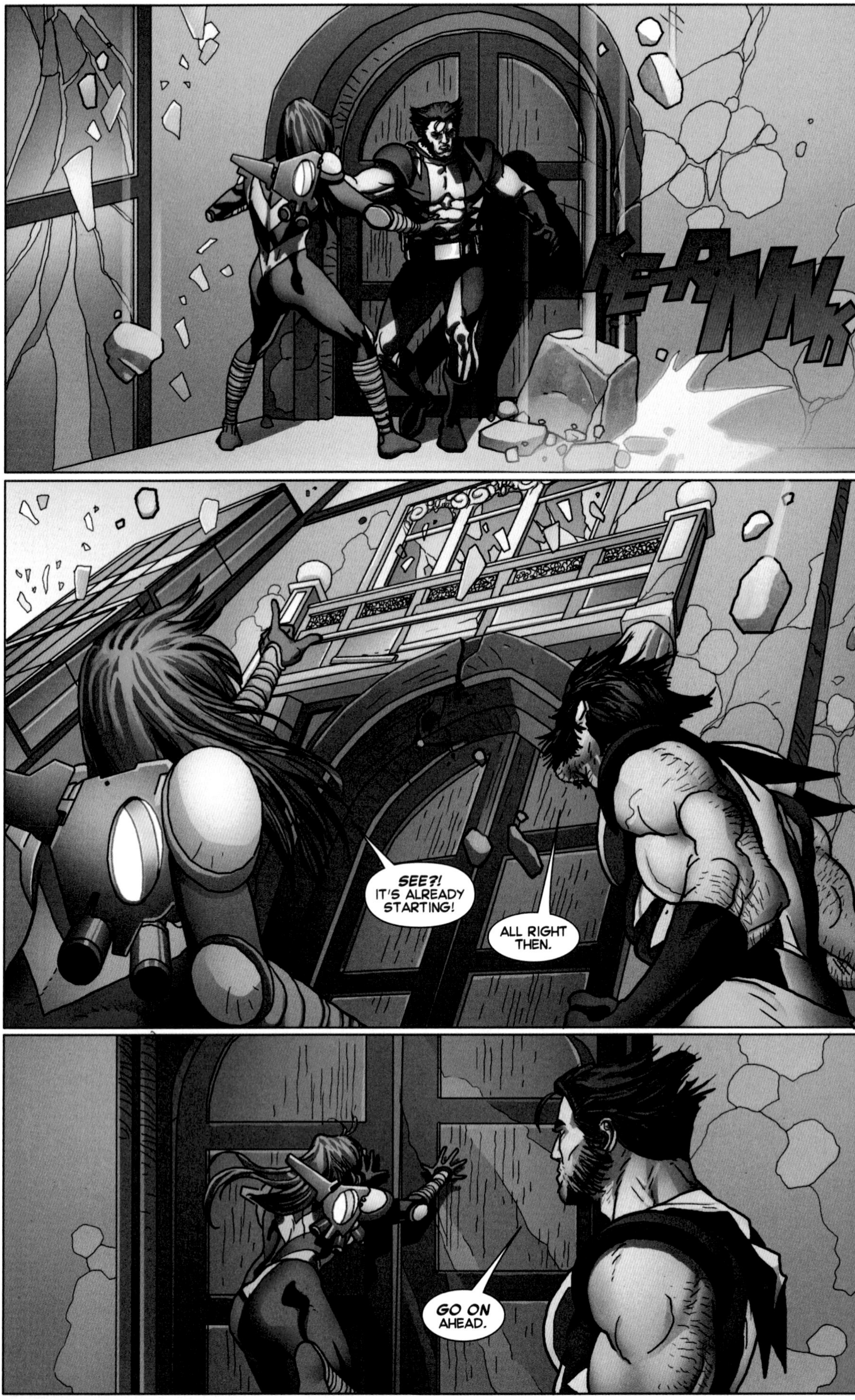
KE-RANNK
SEE?! IT'S ALREADY STARTING!
ALL RIGHT THEN.
GO ON AHEAD.

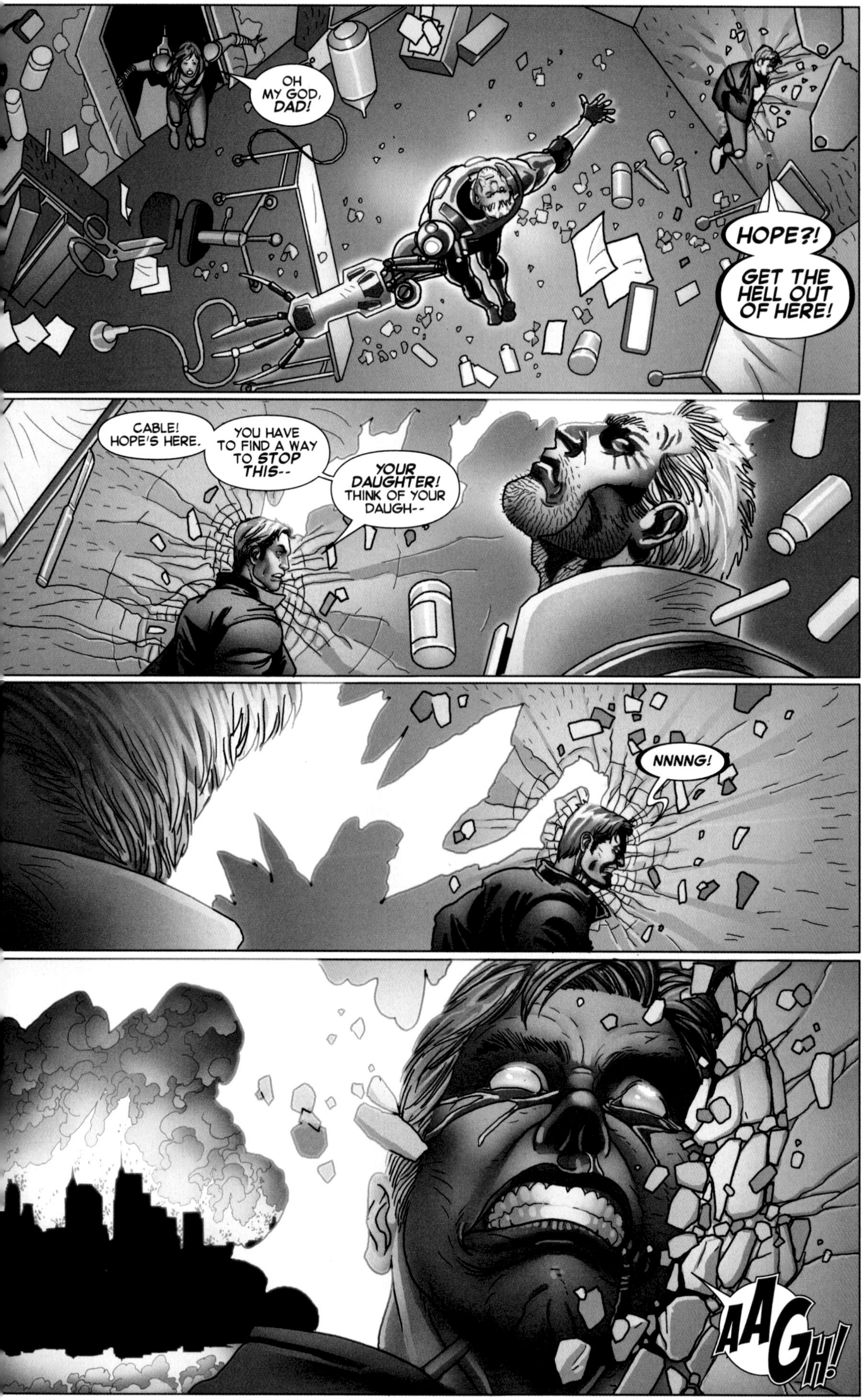
OH MY GOD, DAD!
HOPE?!
GET THE HELL OUT OF HERE!
CABLE! HOPE'S HERE.
YOU HAVE TO FIND A WAY TO STOP THIS--
YOUR DAUGHTER! THINK OF YOUR DAUGH--
NNNNG!
AAGH!

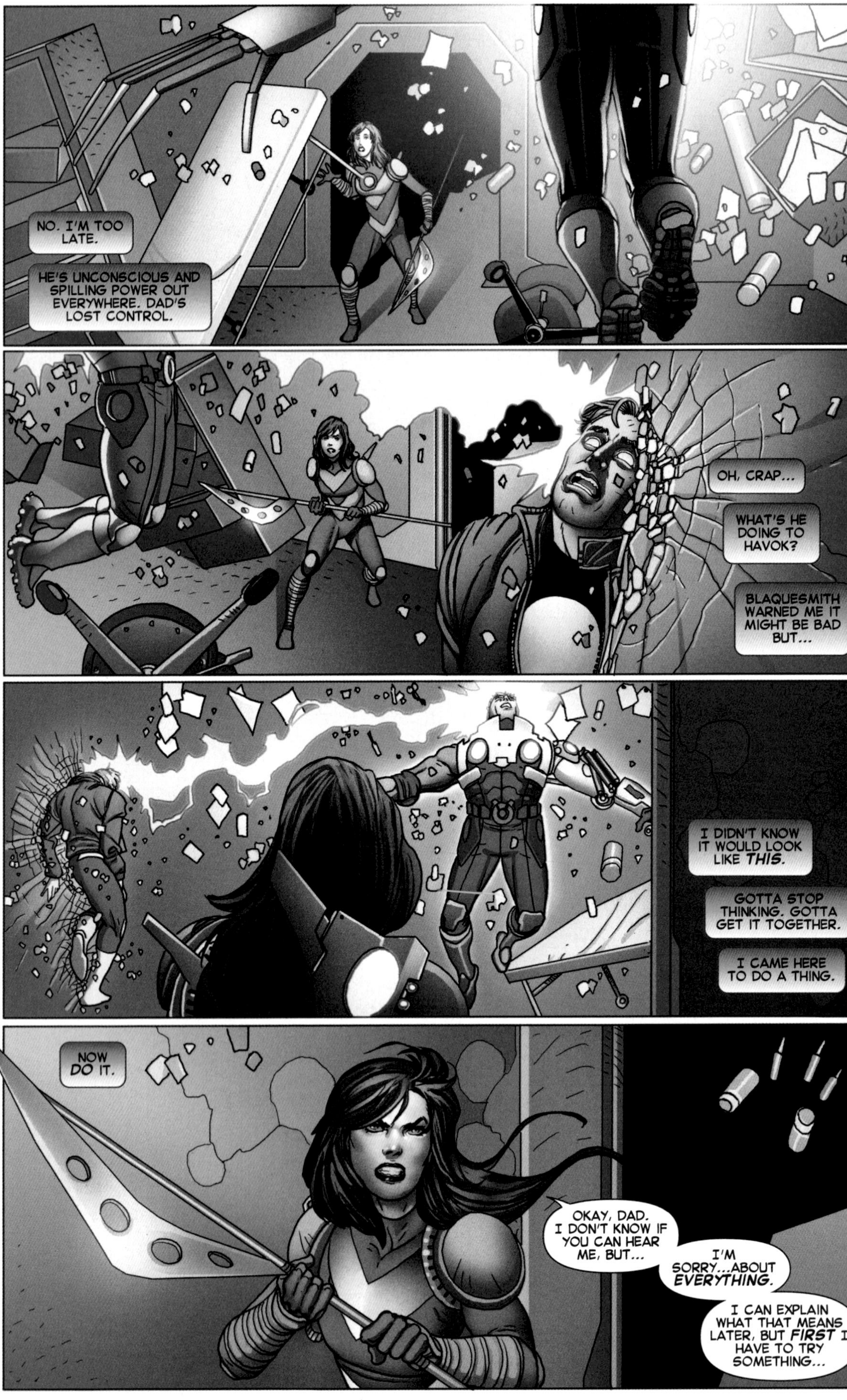
NO. I'M TOO LATE.
HE'S UNCONSCIOUS AND SPILLING POWER OUT EVERYWHERE. DAD'S LOST CONTROL.
OH, CRAP...
WHAT'S HE DOING TO HAVOK?
BLAQUESMITH WARNED ME IT MIGHT BE BAD BUT...
I DIDN'T KNOW IT WOULD LOOK LIKE *THIS*.
GOTTA STOP THINKING. GOTTA GET IT TOGETHER.
I CAME HERE TO DO A THING.
NOW *DO* IT.
OKAY, DAD. I DON'T KNOW IF YOU CAN HEAR ME, BUT...
I'M SORRY...ABOUT *EVERYTHING*.
I CAN EXPLAIN WHAT THAT MEANS LATER, BUT *FIRST* I HAVE TO TRY SOMETHING...

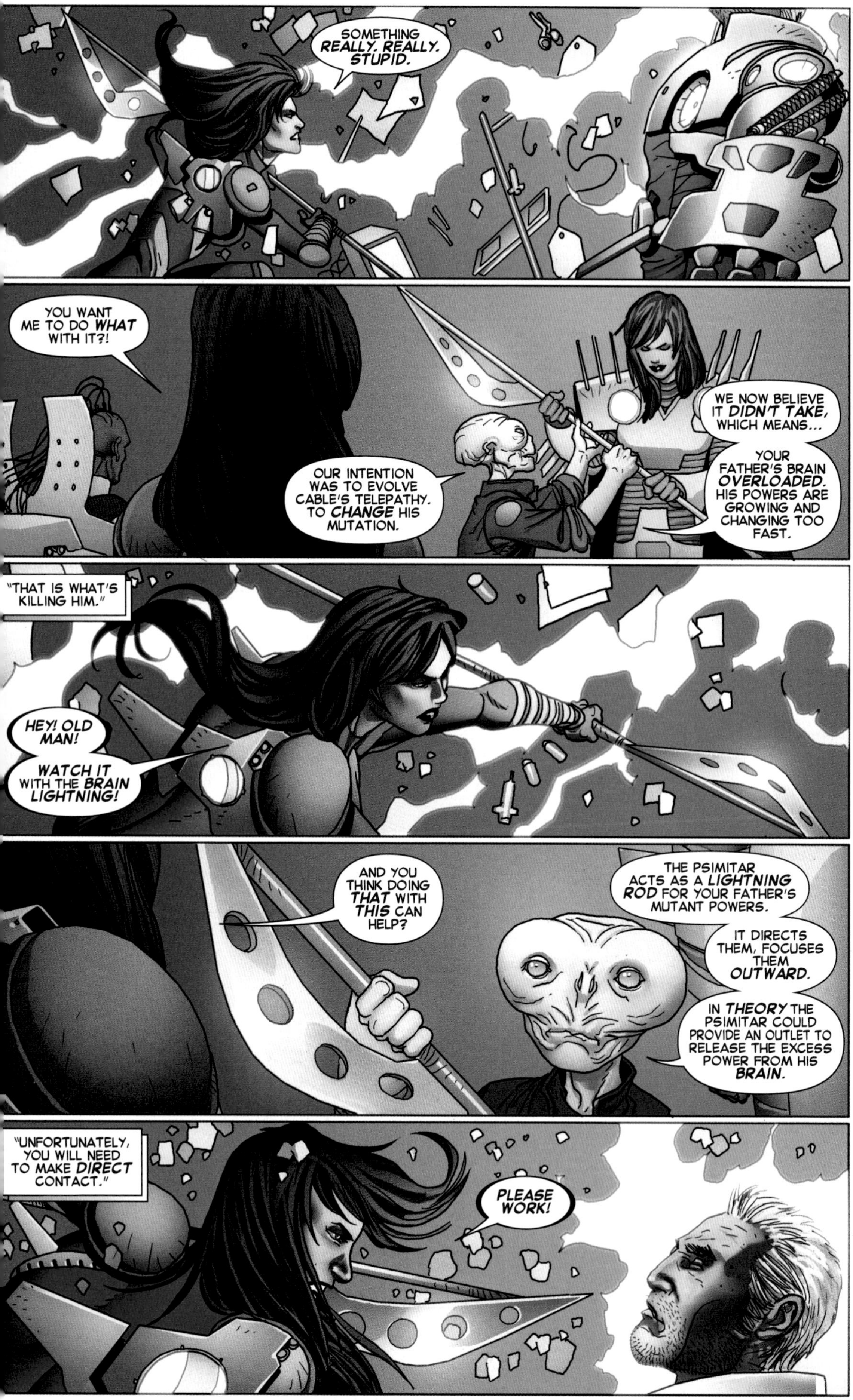
SOMETHING REALLY. REALLY. STUPID.
YOU WANT ME TO DO WHAT WITH IT?!
OUR INTENTION WAS TO EVOLVE CABLE'S TELEPATHY. TO CHANGE HIS MUTATION.
WE NOW BELIEVE IT DIDN'T TAKE, WHICH MEANS...
YOUR FATHER'S BRAIN OVERLOADED. HIS POWERS ARE GROWING AND CHANGING TOO FAST.
"THAT IS WHAT'S KILLING HIM."
HEY! OLD MAN!
WATCH IT WITH THE BRAIN LIGHTNING!
AND YOU THINK DOING THAT WITH THIS CAN HELP?
THE PSIMITAR ACTS AS A LIGHTNING ROD FOR YOUR FATHER'S MUTANT POWERS.
IT DIRECTS THEM, FOCUSES THEM OUTWARD.
IN THEORY THE PSIMITAR COULD PROVIDE AN OUTLET TO RELEASE THE EXCESS POWER FROM HIS BRAIN.
"UNFORTUNATELY, YOU WILL NEED TO MAKE DIRECT CONTACT."
PLEASE WORK!

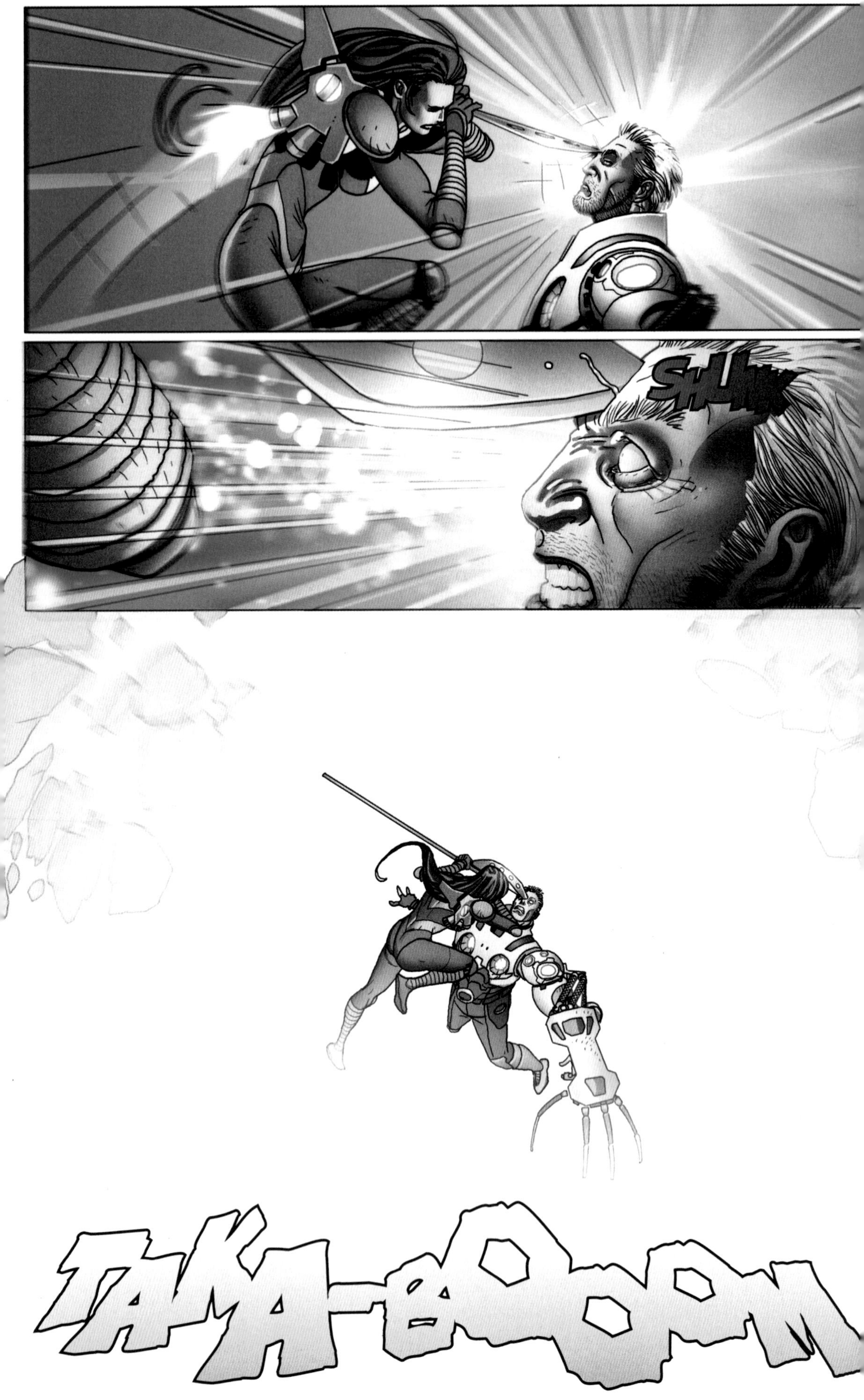
SHUNK
TAKA-BOOOOM

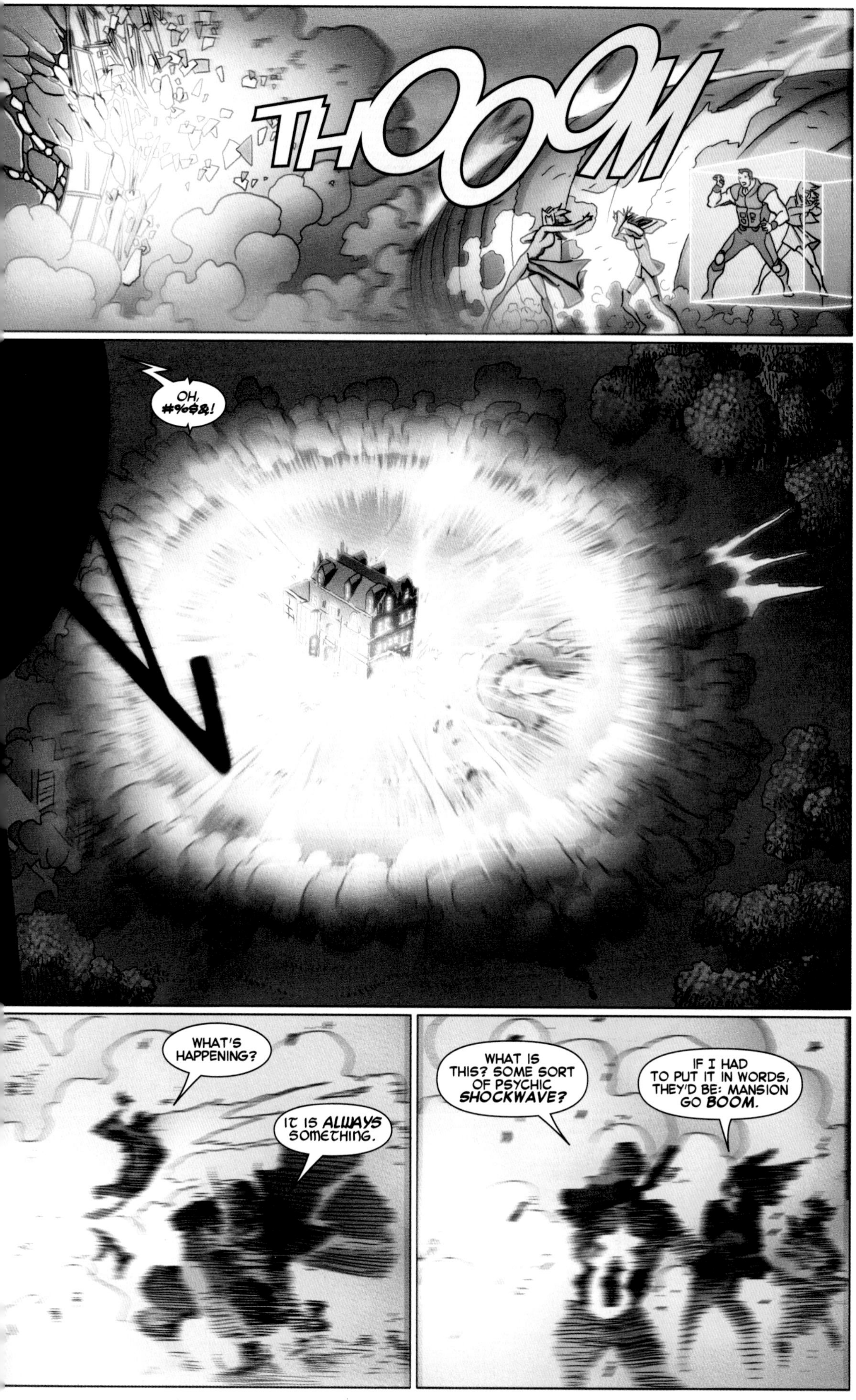
THOOOM
OH, #%$&!
WHAT'S HAPPENING?
IT IS ALWAYS SOMETHING.
WHAT IS THIS? SOME SORT OF PSYCHIC SHOCKWAVE?
IF I HAD TO PUT IT IN WORDS, THEY'D BE: MANSION GO BOOM.

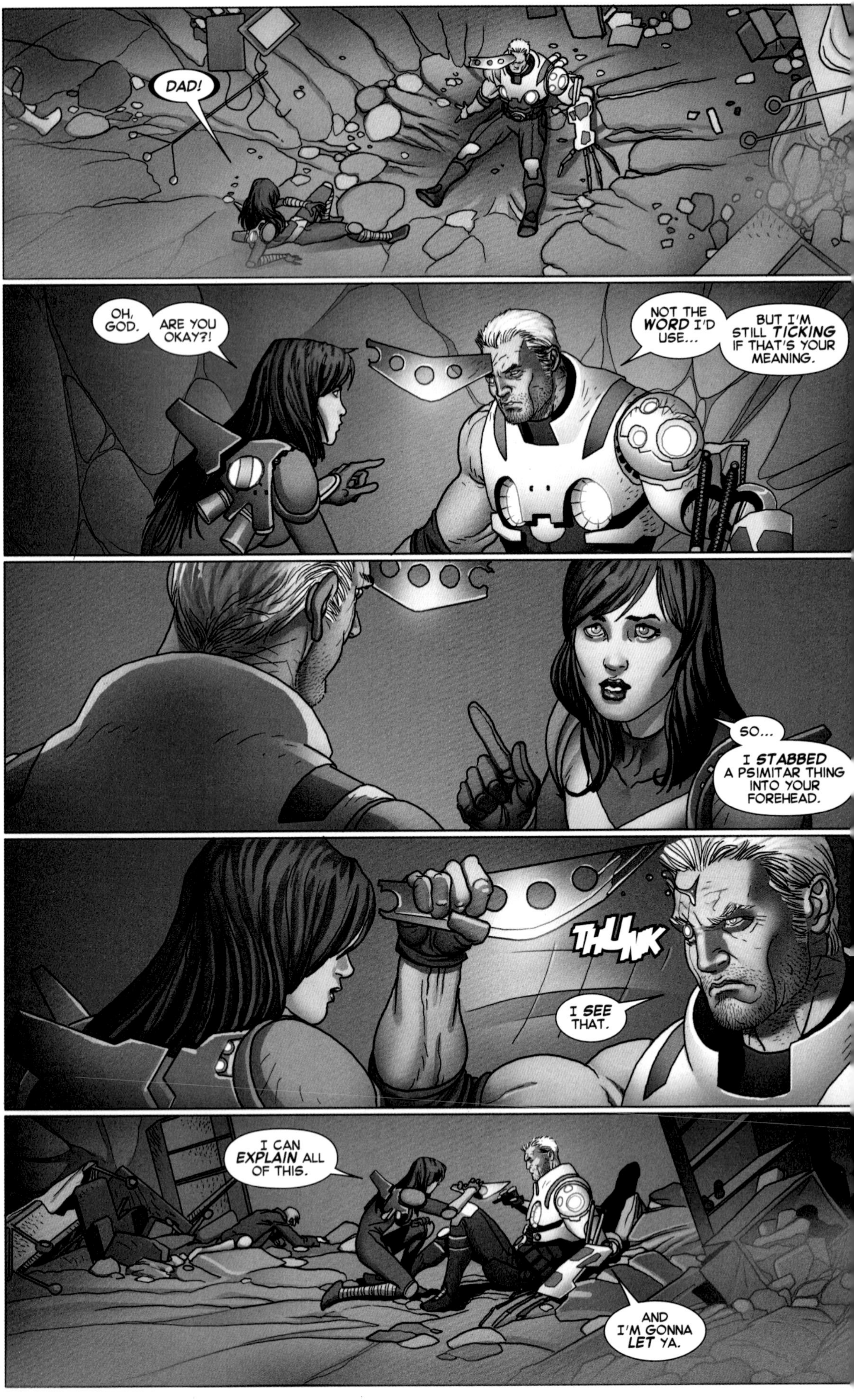
DAD!
OH, GOD.
ARE YOU OKAY?!
NOT THE WORD I'D USE...
BUT I'M STILL TICKING IF THAT'S YOUR MEANING.
SO...
I STABBED A PSIMITAR THING INTO YOUR FOREHEAD.
THUNK
I SEE THAT.
I CAN EXPLAIN ALL OF THIS.
AND I'M GONNA LET YA.

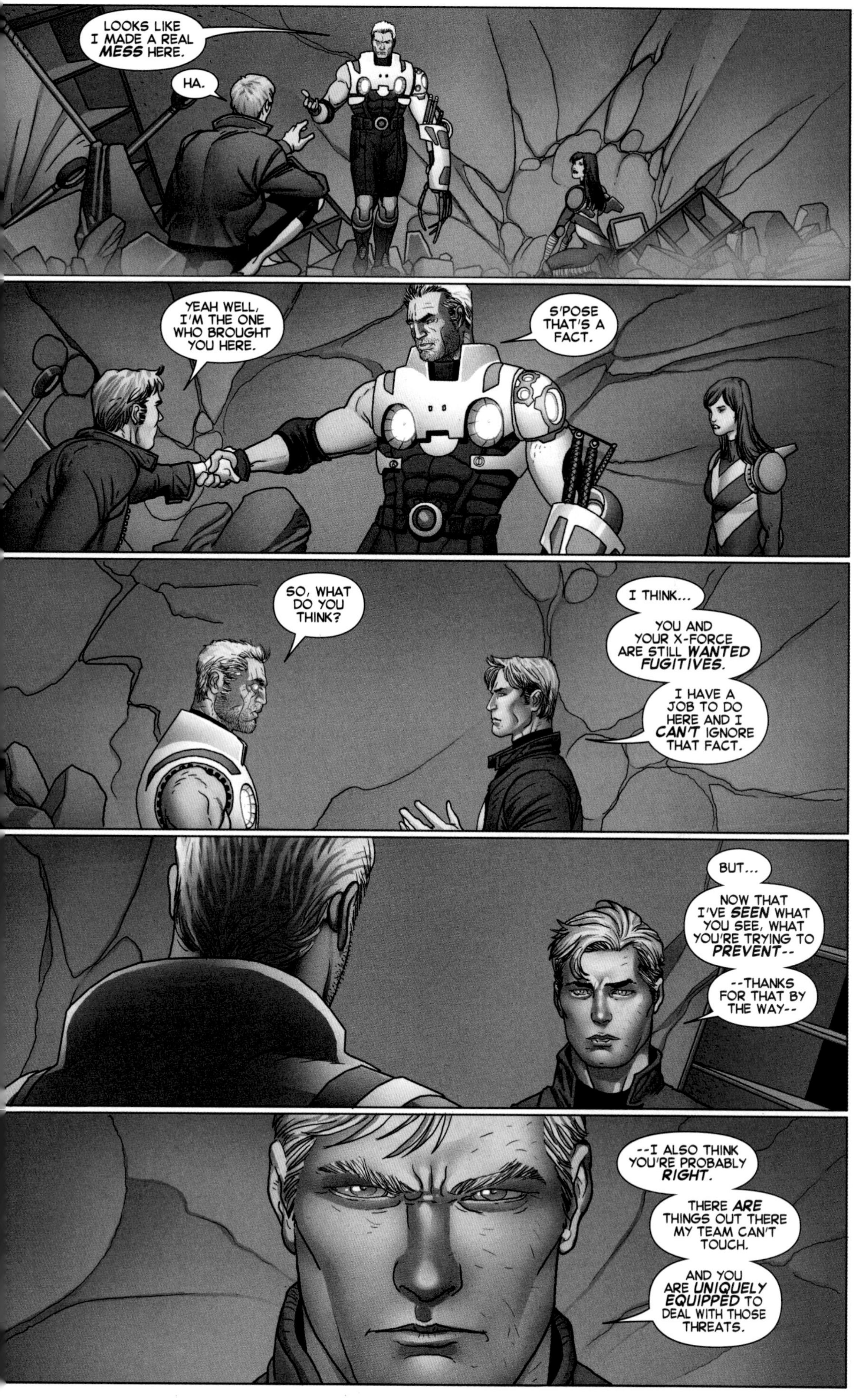
LOOKS LIKE I MADE A REAL MESS HERE.
HA.
YEAH WELL, I'M THE ONE WHO BROUGHT YOU HERE.
S'POSE THAT'S A FACT.
SO, WHAT DO YOU THINK?
I THINK...
YOU AND YOUR X-FORCE ARE STILL WANTED FUGITIVES.
I HAVE A JOB TO DO HERE AND I CAN'T IGNORE THAT FACT.
BUT...
NOW THAT I'VE SEEN WHAT YOU SEE, WHAT YOU'RE TRYING TO PREVENT--
--THANKS FOR THAT BY THE WAY--
--I ALSO THINK YOU'RE PROBABLY RIGHT.
THERE ARE THINGS OUT THERE MY TEAM CAN'T TOUCH.
AND YOU ARE UNIQUELY EQUIPPED TO DEAL WITH THOSE THREATS.

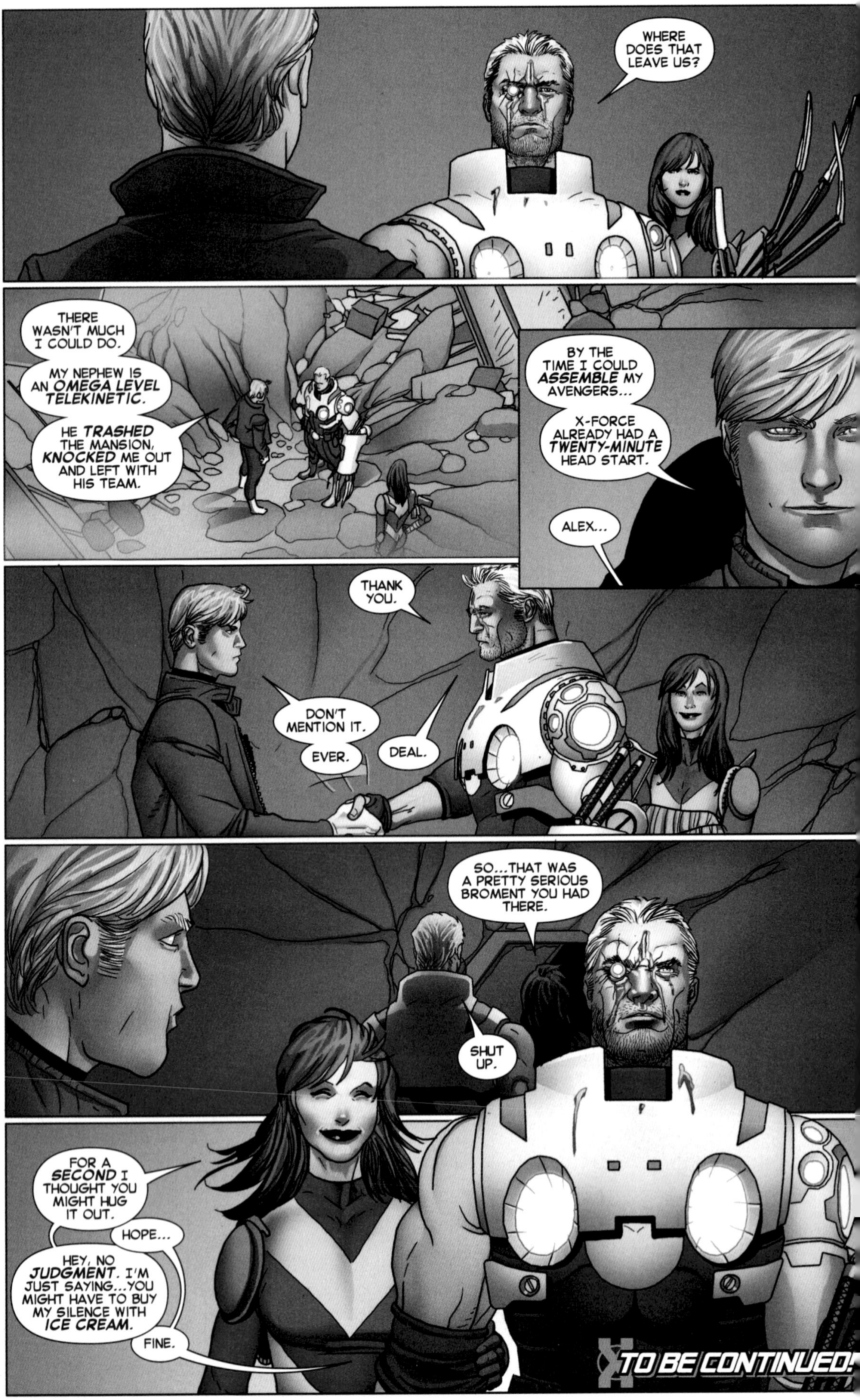
WHERE DOES THAT LEAVE US?
THERE WASN'T MUCH I COULD DO.
MY NEPHEW IS AN OMEGA LEVEL TELEKINETIC.
HE TRASHED THE MANSION, KNOCKED ME OUT AND LEFT WITH HIS TEAM.
BY THE TIME I COULD ASSEMBLE MY AVENGERS...
X-FORCE ALREADY HAD A TWENTY-MINUTE HEAD START.
ALEX...
THANK YOU.
DON'T MENTION IT.
EVER.
DEAL.
SO...THAT WAS A PRETTY SERIOUS BROMENT YOU HAD THERE.
SHUT UP.
FOR A SECOND I THOUGHT YOU MIGHT HUG IT OUT.
HOPE...
HEY, NO JUDGMENT. I'M JUST SAYING...YOU MIGHT HAVE TO BUY MY SILENCE WITH ICE CREAM.
FINE.
TO BE CONTINUED!

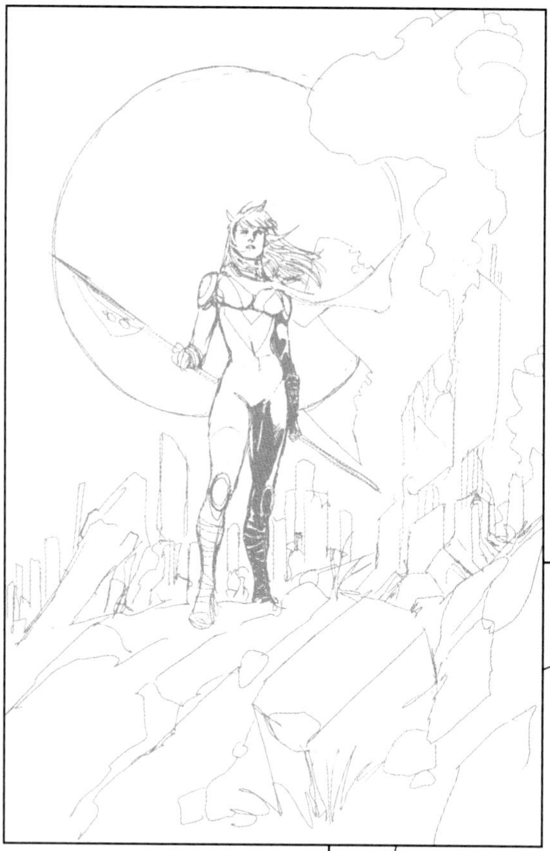

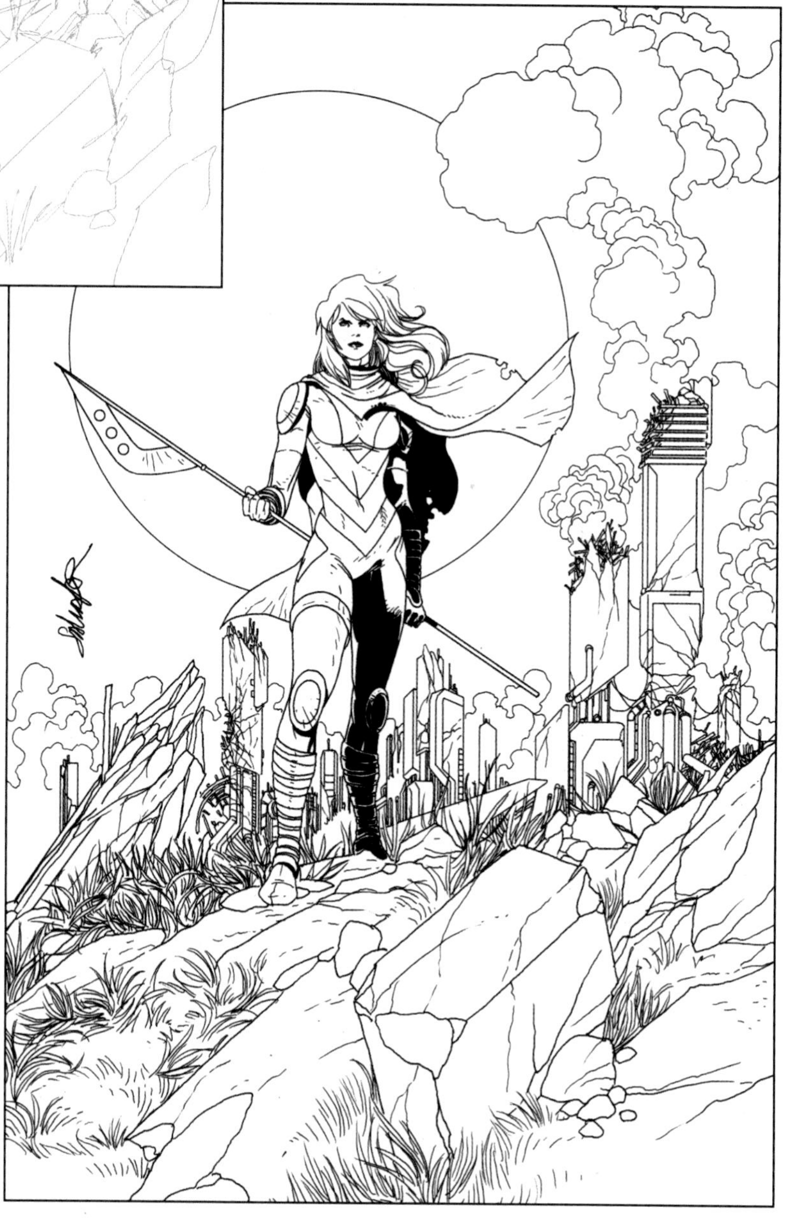

#13 COVER SKETCH AND ARTWORK BY SALVADOR LARROCA

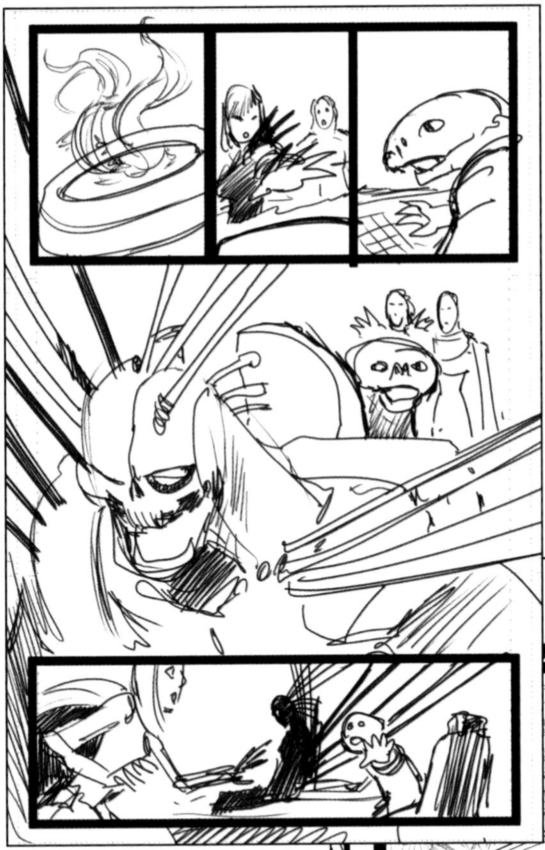

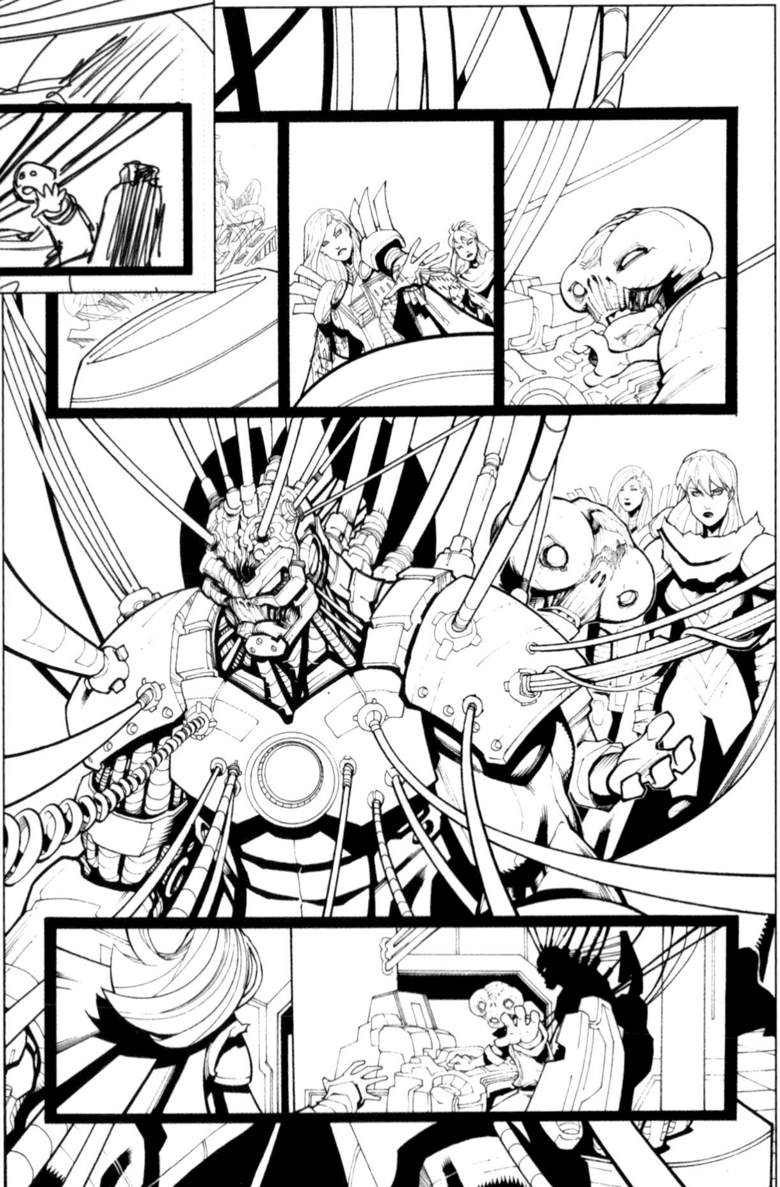

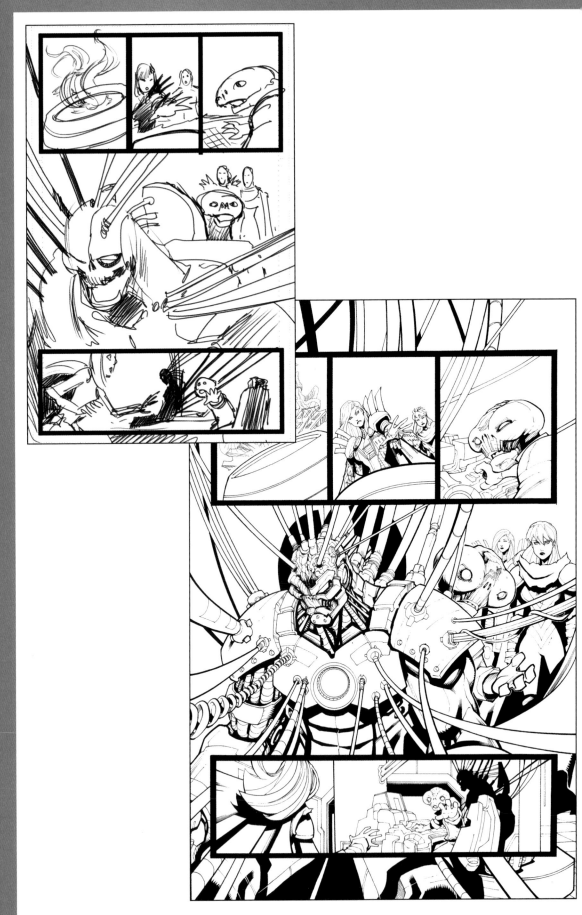

#13, PAGE 11 LAYOUT AND ARTWORK BY GERARDO SANDOVAL

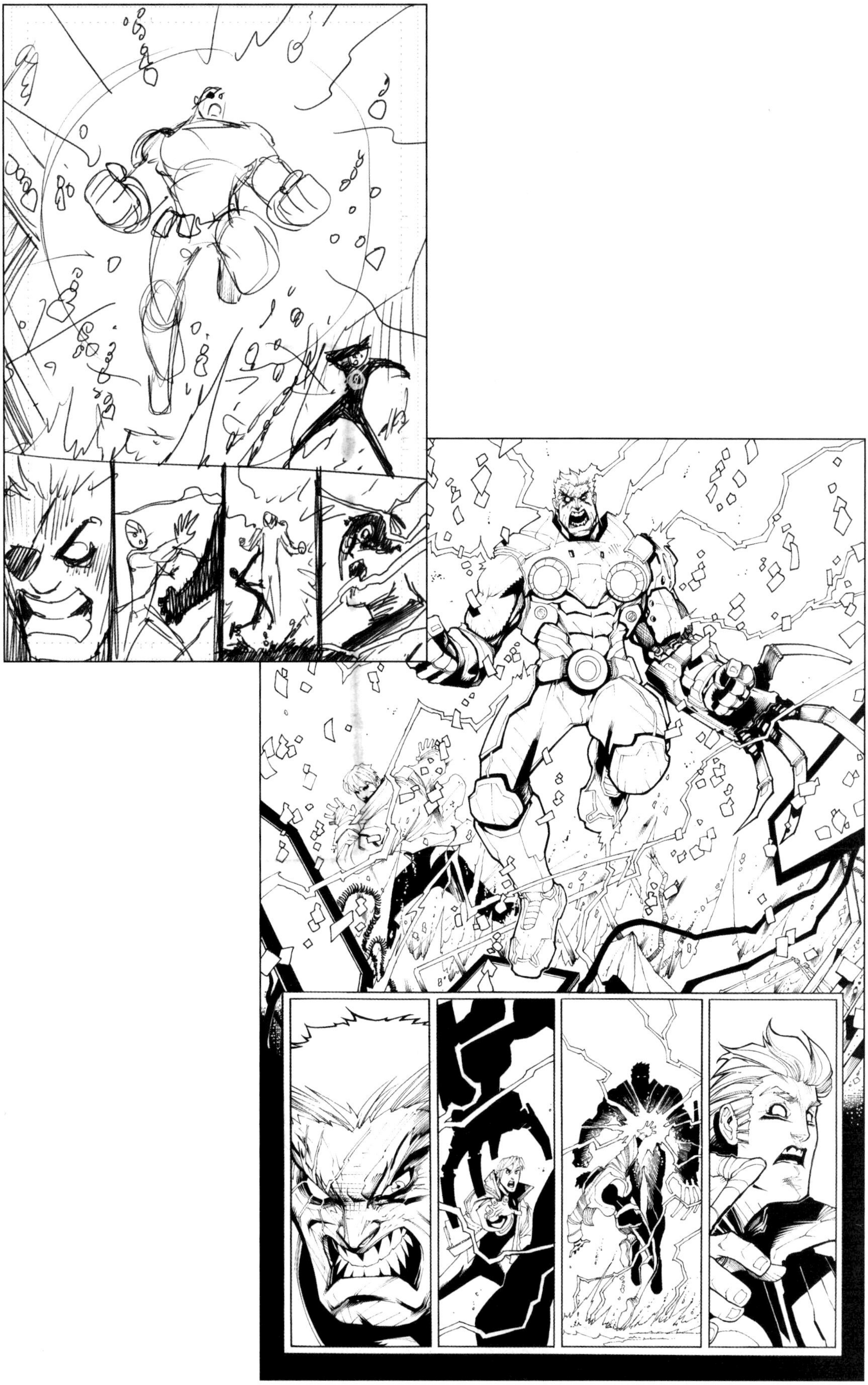

#13, PAGE 12 LAYOUT AND ARTWORK BY GERARDO SANDOVAL

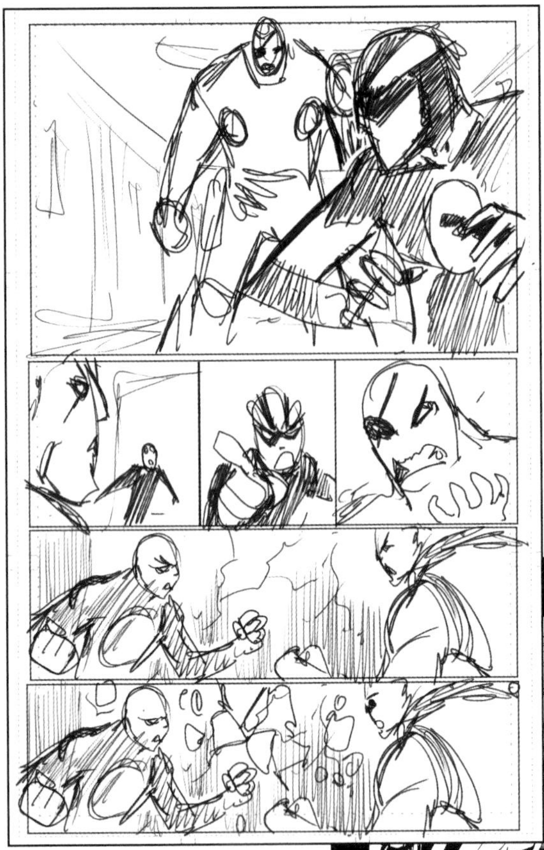
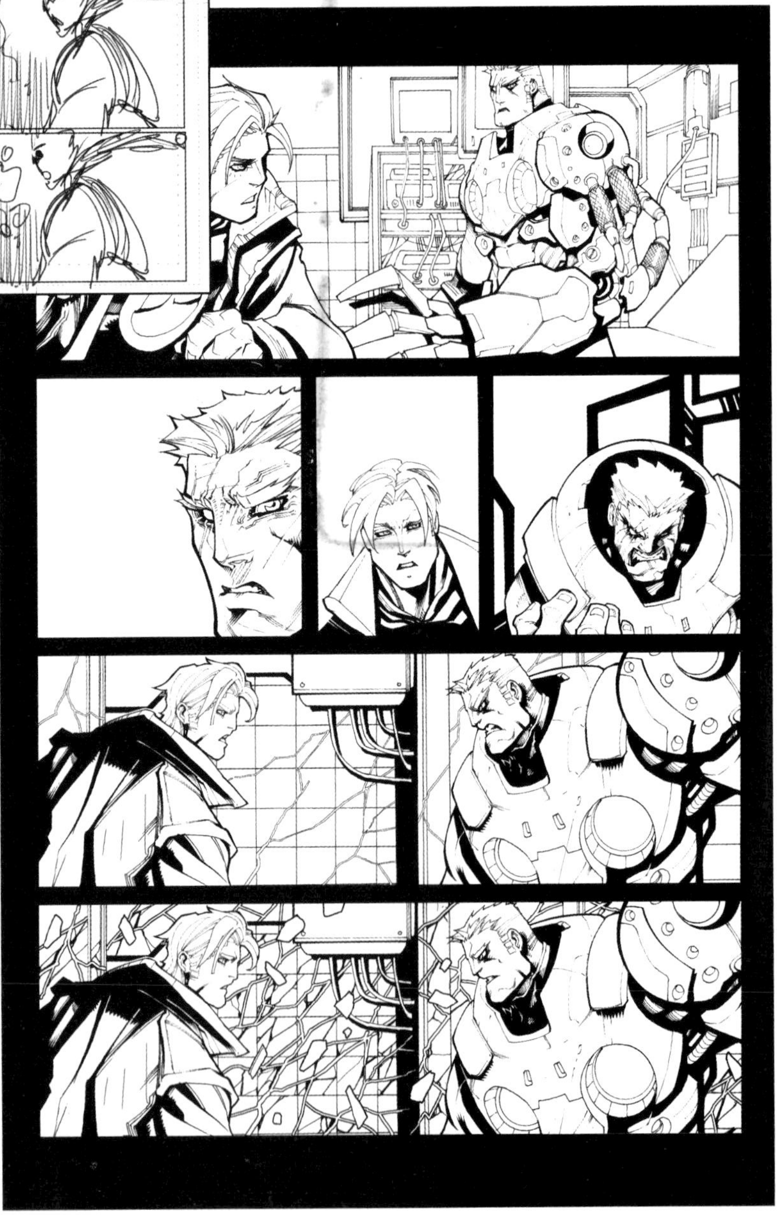

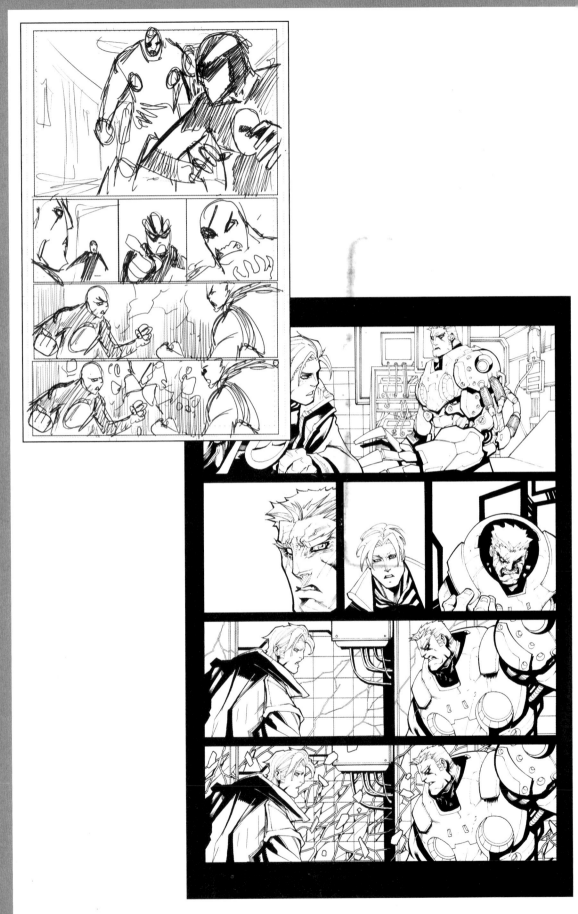

#13, PAGE 13 LAYOUT AND ARTWORK BY GERARDO SANDOVAL